D1715983

DANCING
With GOD

How to Connect with God
Every Time You Pray

By
Rabbi Mark Hillel Kunis

MENORAH
B O O K S

HONG KONG · JERUSALEM · LAS VEGAS

DANCING WITH GOD
How to Connect with God Every Time You Pray

Published by MENORAH BOOKS LIMITED

Copyright © 2016

COVER DESIGN: Gal Narunsky
COVER PHOTO: Alicia Kay Gelfond-Holtz

TYPOGRAPHY & LAYOUT: Gal Narunsky

EDITING: Phyllis Fraley, Gedaliah Fleer, Dr. Melvin Konner, Dr. David Blumenthal, Cheryl Tobin Kunis, Esther Cameron, Chaim Natan Firszt, Ashirah Yosefah

The Hebrew Siddur texts used in this book have been provided by Rabbi Avraham Sutton.

PRINTED IN ISRAEL

INFORMATION AND INQUIRIES: publisher@menorah-books.com,

ISBN: 978-1-940516-50-9

FOR ORDERS:
Internet: www.menorah-books.com
Email: orders@menorah-books.com

Table of Contents

In Memory

This book is dedicated to the memory
of my dear mother, Harriette Kunis,
Yita bat Zev Zelig,
who taught me that there is a God
in this world.

Who has not felt the yearning to seek God, to come closer
to Him[1], especially in times of crisis when we often find
there is nowhere else to turn? We desperately want and need to
connect to God, to know we are not alone—that there is something, some One beyond ourselves watching over us, Who cares.
This is what every soul hungers for. And prayer is the chief path
we have been given.

Truth be told, however, most people have a hard time creating a meaningful prayer experience. Perhaps this is because
prayer is not a function of the lips, nor even the mind—but of
the heart. Many wonder if their prayers really matter or if their
prayers are even heard because they cannot escape the feeling,
no matter how hard they might pray, that something is missing.
Some turn to the synagogue to find God. But we cannot expect
to just walk into *shul* (synagogue) and find God there, because to
find God in shul, we must first find Him in our hearts.

So how do we get there? How do we really connect with
God so that our prayers move from the head to the heart? In its
wisdom, Jewish tradition has created what can only be understood
as a dance that, if done properly, can lift the participant into an
intimate encounter with the Divine.

How is Jewish prayer a dance? One sits and stands, moves
one's hands, moves backward and forward, bows and rises up; one
chants and sings and embraces God. Each movement is pregnant
with meaning. Taken together Jewish prayer is nothing short of
a most intimate dance with the Creator.

The task of this book is to help the reader learn how to dance
in such a way that he will connect with God every time he prays.
Yes, every time!

This book has been written to help the beginner navigate
the sea of Jewish liturgy and immediately find meaning in his

prayer experience. It has also been written to help the seasoned *davener*, who may know most of the *Siddur* (Jewish prayer book) by heart, find the connection to God that has eluded him. I have included the texts of the prayers, and Biblical and Talmudic quotes to enhance its use in the classroom for adult education, high schools and universities. The liturgy that is explored in this book is mostly trans-denominational and can be found in prayer books of the Orthodox, Conservative, Reconstructionist and Reform movements.

If you frequently pray, think about your current prayer experience. How well is it working for you? If it is not working as well as you would like then read on. And if you do not pray often, know this book will speak to you.

It is my humble opinion that such a book is very much needed—for the beginner as well as for those fluent in Jewish prayer—because, after all, connecting with God is the primary function of prayer. What follows is a handbook for how to make the connection real.

I remember as a little boy in Talmud Torah, my teachers would drill us every day in the reading of the prayers. We even had contests with prizes for who could read the *Amidah* and the *Shema* (the two main prayers in the Jewish liturgy) the fastest. Yes, I developed a fluency with these prayers but I had little, if any, understanding of their significance or spiritual power.

It is told that the Kotzker Rebbe once asked a group of rabbis with whom he was meeting, "Where is God to be found?" His answer, after entertaining some of the responses, is as profound as it is instructive: "God can be found wherever you let him in." Judaism insists every human being can find a path to God—Jew or non-Jew, secular or religious. We were all created in the image of God. God gave each of us a holy eternal soul that yearns to cleave to Him.

But how? How do we let Him in? How do we dance with God?

I have spent my entire spiritual journey—my whole life—

searching for answers, and I believe I have rediscovered a path mostly ignored in our time—a path to help you give proper focus to your prayers and, at the same time, fill you with God's holy light. Some of the meditative exercises in this book may seem strange—especially for those who do not have much experience using meditative techniques in prayer. Please do not skip or ignore these. Give each exercise a serious trial of several tries even if you are not completely comfortable at first. The exercises will lead you to feel the connection, and you cannot fake feeling!

And so again I ask you to think about how you currently pray. How well is it working for you? Do you feel the presence of the *Shechina*, the indwelling Presence of God, when you pray? Have you given up on regular prayer?

The need to pray is woven into the spiritual DNA of the Jew. Isaac Leib Peretz, the great Yiddish writer, tells a touching story about Berel the tailor—a simple and pious Jew—and his son, who has just become a doctor.[2]

> The young man comes to visit Papa Berel in the *shtetl* and Berel asks him to come to *shul* (synagogue) on Shabbos morning. The young man refuses and asks, "Papa, if you knew that our neighbor, the widow, needed help, would you wait to give help until she came begging?"
>
> "Of course not," replies Berel. "I'd help the moment I knew her need."
>
> And the son says, "Well, God certainly knows when His creatures need help. He doesn't have to wait for us to come begging."
>
> "True," says Berel, "but asking for God's help is not the only reason we pray. We have to praise Him, too."
>
> "Papa," says the doctor, "how would you like it if someone were to keep praising you to your face all the time with 'Berel is a marvelous tailor. Berel is the only tailor. Berel is the greatest tailor!'"
>
> "It would make me sick," says Berel.

"You see," the doctor adds, "God is greater and wiser than we are. Do you think He needs or wants our constant praise?"

Berel nods thoughtfully, "You're right, absolutely right." And then he brightens, "But a Jew has to *daven*, doesn't he?"

A Jew has to *daven*, a Jew has to pray! This is in his *kishkes*, his guts. It is a hunger of the soul, an outpouring of longing for God, a yearning to connect with our Creator, to feel He is there listening and watching over us. The need to pray is, of course, universal. Human beings are not only thinking creatures but also praying creatures. The secularization of modern society may have suppressed this need, but it is still there—just under the surface. It is my humble prayer that this book will be a useful tool for the reader to connect and dance with God his Maker.

Why is prayer so hard? Again, it is because prayer is a function of the heart—not of the lips, nor the mind. To pray is to feel, and feelings cannot be mechanically manufactured by reading a script of prayers. And for this reason the *Talmud*[3] implores us: "Do not pray as if you were reading a letter."

Within the pages of this book you will find a path to not only come to a greater understanding and appreciation of Jewish liturgy, but a path within the script of the prayers to open your heart and find God. Come with me on an amazing life-changing journey as you begin your dance with God—a dance that can last a lifetime.

Cautionary note: Please take note the use of God's Names both in the Hebrew and English translations—as in the use of "God"—and transliterations in this book. This book, therefore, must be treated with the proper respect this engenders, like not taking it into inappropriate places, such as bathrooms. Also please note, for the sake of consistency throughout the book, except in gender-specific examples or stories, both male and female readers will be referred by the general use of the pronouns "he" and "his."

IN APPRECIATION

God has blessed me with significant teachers and mentors at different stages in my life, and I have been privileged to taste the holy waters of the well of their Torah—people like Rabbi Michael Katz, Rabbi Benjamin Blech, Rabbi Gedalia Fleer, Rabbi Mordecai Goldstein and Ilan Feldman. Much of what is contained in this book I have learned from them, and I am forever grateful. God has blessed me and enabled me to help others in their spiritual journeys by sharing with them some of what I have learned; and these students, as well as my generous teachers and mentors, in turn, have urged me to write this book. I pray that as you read and use the insights and suggestions that follow, new pathways to God may open for you as well.

The editing of this book has been a major challenge for several reasons, not the least is the use of English, Hebrew and Hebrew transliterations interspersed throughout. I am eternally indebted to the following who were crucial to the editing process: Phyllis Fraley, Gedalia Fleer, Dr. David Blumenthal, Dr. Melvin Konner, Cheryl Tobin Kunis, Chaim Natan Firszt, Ashirah Yosefah and Esther Cameron. I offer a special thanks to Rabbi Avraham Sutton for the Hebrew prayer texts. A special thank-you is to Alicia Kay Gelfond-Holtz for the cover picture. May Hashem bless all of you for your efforts.

CHAPTER 1

Getting Started

So often our prayer experience can become perfunctory or exceedingly frustrating, causing us to give up with the thought that perhaps God is unapproachable, or perhaps God does not care, or worse, perhaps there is no God! Living in this modern, technologically advanced world, we find it extremely difficult to deal with anything we cannot quantify or measure. So we either deny its existence or—and I suspect most of us fall into this category—push these questions aside to avoid thinking about them. And yet, as much as we may try to suppress it, our inner yearning for connecting with God never really goes away.

In Judaism, one of the prime vehicles for connecting with God is the Siddur, the Jewish prayer book, with its thrice daily prescribed liturgy. The problem for too many Jews is that this routine of prayer often becomes mechanical—mouthing the same prayers and singing the same melodies again and again without much thought given to their meaning.

Question: Does the *Siddur,* the prayer book—our prepared scripts of prayers—help or get in the way of connecting with God? Is there a point in sticking to a set scheduled *Amidah* text—which is our main prayer—three times a day? Why can't we just pray spontaneously when we feel like it?

The rift between structured prayer and the need for spontaneous prayer is one of the oldest controversies in Judaism. On one side, we have Maimonides,[4] who argues the commandment in Exodus[5], *Va-avad'tem et Hashem Elokeychem,* "And you shall serve the Lord your God," means it is incumbent on us to pray whether we are in the mood or not. For Maimonides, the act of praying itself helps put us into a sacred frame of mind and opens us up to the possibility of connection.

On the other side, Nachmanides[6] believes the commandment to pray is rooted in the verse from Numbers: "When you are at war in your own land against an aggressor who attacks you, you shall sound short blasts on the trumpets, that you may be remembered before the Lord your God and be delivered from your enemies." The sounds of trumpet blasts were to arouse the people to prayer and repentance and courage, reminding them God is with them. Authentic prayer is the voice that rises during times of crisis, crying out for help. For Nachmanides, prayer is, "I need you."

A colleague once suggested if you have trouble learning how to pray, have this kind of a conversation with your teenage child when he tells you:

> "Dad, I'm going out with the guys this Saturday night. Okay?"
>
> "Where are you going?"
>
> "Oh, we're going to a party in the next town."
>
> "How are you going to get there?"
>
> "Jack's father is loaning him the car."

Have a conversation like this with your teenager, and believe me, you will learn how to pray![7]

For Nachmonides, prayer is, "I need you." For Maimonides, prayer is "I serve you." Who is right? Our tradition says they are both right! Crisis can be a powerful incentive to pray, but you need not have a crisis in your life to find God. Shouldn't prayer be spontaneous? Of course! However, without a formalized prayer service and a set time to pray, we might never get around to praying. Nevertheless, we must guard that our prayers not become mechanical.[8]

What one's prayer experience can and should be is an intimate dance with God as one sings about the wonders of God, thanks Him for His blessings and asks for His help—all while sitting, standing and bowing before the Holy One Blessed be He.

There is a classic Chassidic story about an orphan shepherd boy who grew up in a small town in Poland knowing very little about being Jewish. One day, shortly before Yom Kippur, he met a group of people traveling to Mezibuj to spend the holiday with the Baal Shem Tov—the 17th century founder of Chassidut. The boy decided to join them, and soon he was standing with many people in the Baal Shem Tov's *shul* (synagogue).

But the boy didn't know how to pray. He did not even know the shape of the letter *alef*. He saw all the people praying earnestly from the depths of their hearts, and he also wanted to say something to God that came from deep inside. He didn't understand his feelings, but the turbulence inside his heart was about to explode. Suddenly his love for God flooded his heart and soul, and he could not hold his feelings in any longer. So he did the only thing he could do well. He drew a deep breath and let out the shrill whistle he would sound every evening when he gathered the sheep from the fields. Right in the middle of the prayer service, on the holiest day of the year, the shepherd boy whistled as loud as he could.

The people in the *shul* were shocked, especially because of the legend telling us that at the time of the destruction of the second Temple the Roman soldiers whistled as they destroyed it. Jews have since refrained from whistling in a synagogue. But the Baal Shem Tov calmed, them saying, "The celestial court was about to judge us and the world for the worse. A terrible decree was hanging over us, and the heavenly gates were closed to us. This shepherd boy's whistle pierced the heavens and erased the decree. His whistle saved us because it came from the very bottom of his heart, where he feels love for God even though he doesn't know or understand why."[9]

Most Jews today are raised in non-religious homes and, like the shepherd boy in the story, do not know where to begin. When they walk into a synagogue they expect to be inspired like those who go to the theater or a sports event expect to be entertained. But meaningful prayer is not to be passive but interactive. The problem is that for the most part, they may be competent with everything they do—work, sports and hobbies—but they feel incompetent, thus uncomfortable when they walk into a synagogue. The Hebrew may be too difficult to read fluently, let alone understand. The structure of the prayers, the melodies, the length of the service, all can be overwhelming to anyone who doesn't attend regularly. This can seem like an insurmountable wall in the path to God.

But if truth be told—and no criticism or disrespect is intended—you can go into the most orthodox of synagogues where the vast majority are so fluent in the ancient prayer service they know a good deal by rote, and yet few have developed more than a superficial path to God. Yes, they can recite the words; they may even know how to translate them, but have they found God in the words?

HOW TO READ THIS BOOK   This book is not just for casual reading. Do not be distracted by reading the endnote references, unless your curiosity is piqued. Then reread and study the various sections—The Three Pathways, The *Shema*, The *Amidah*, The Posture of Prayer, and so forth, and do the exercises, when indicated, one at a time. I suggest that each time, before you begin to pray, you spend a couple of minutes reading about one prayer in the service and, when you later reach that part of the service, lend a special focus to that prayer.

A WORD ABOUT THE REST OF THE *AMIDAH*   The key purpose of the first
18 chapters of this book is to give the reader an understanding
and appreciation of the time-tested method for connecting with
God with every prayer experience. The following seven chapters
will discuss the structure of Jewish prayer and attempt to answer
some fundamental questions concerning prayer and its efficacy.
The chapters on the rest of the *Amidah* were moved to the end
of the book as a supplement—not because it isn't important and
not because there are not major avenues of connection within
it—but because its length and many themes may distract the
reader from appreciating the thematic flow of the service. The
reader is urged not to forego studying these chapters. There are
crucial themes and opportunities for connection within them.
And so I recommend skipping the *Amidah* Supplement, along
with Chapter 8, "The Rest of the Shema," until you have achieved
a degree of comfort and mastery over the rest.

Here is the thing to remember about Jewish prayer: with
proper focus it will direct you into a state of connection. The exercises in this book were created to help you focus. Be patient by
giving yourself time. You probably will experience unexpectedly
quick moments of Divine inspiration and connection, but mostly it will take a while for your mind, heart and soul to adjust to
the newly found power in your prayers. As you seek to connect
with God, please remember God is waiting, even longing, for the
prayers of your heart.

FOR THE BEGINNER   If you can read Hebrew and follow the
prayer services well, you can skip to Chap-
ter 2. If you are not fluent with the prayers in the Siddur, if you
cannot read Hebrew well or at all, then the task of connecting
with God through Jewish prayer may seem overwhelming and
unreachable. I have found in my personal spiritual growth and in
my work teaching prayer that the first step in achieving a regular
connection with God is to develop a regular and meaningful

prayer routine you can live with—one you will actually do. If you have just completed learning the Hebrew alphabet, for example, and are therefore a slow reader, just reading the entire morning service can take hours. It is unrealistic to expect that this kind of commitment will be sustainable.

For this reason, I have created a "Beginner's Service" containing most of the important elements of Jewish prayer. This is a service with meaning and feeling that anyone, on any level, can realistically master. Once mastered, it lends itself to be expanded again and again until, after a while, you will have learned the entire service and regularly achieved a truly elevated spiritual prayer experience.

As we will learn in Chapter 14, "Avot," Judaism requires one to pray three times a day. If you are not yet ready for this kind of commitment, I suggest you find a block of time in your busy schedule—it can be as little as 15 to 20 minutes. The morning is preferable, if possible. But make a set time every day to be your holy time—your appointment with God.

Optimally, one should pray with a minyan—a quorum of at least ten—in the synagogue. The spiritual energy of those around you can help elevate your prayer experience. When you come to the synagogue for prayer, find a place to sit that feels comfortable for you and return to this place whenever you come there to pray.

If you find you cannot make it every day to the synagogue, then you should designate a set place at home for prayer. Once you have a meaningful prayer experience in a particular place, the next time you pray there the residual spiritual energy from your former encounter with God may propel you to greater heights in your coming prayer sessions. When I pray at home, for example, I like to pray by the dining room table where we have our Shabbat meals because this space is already invested with a special spiritual energy.

The next thing the beginner ought to do is to acquire a good Siddur—one with a good English translation and a readable Hebrew font. I would suggest *The Complete ArtScroll Siddur*,

The Koren Siddur or *The Daily Prayer Book* by Philip Birnbaum. There are several others that will work just as well. For those who are Conservative or Reform Jews in their orientation, the *Sim Shalom Siddur for Weekdays* contains all the basic prayers needed. ArtScroll also makes a *Transliterated Linear Siddur* in two editions—one for weekdays and one for Sabbath and festivals— that may be of help with the correct reading of the Hebrew. For simplicity's sake, I will refer to the page numbers for my Beginner's Service below from *The Complete ArtScroll Siddur* because I have found it is the most widely used. If you will be using another Siddur, just ask anyone familiar with Jewish liturgy to help you find the corresponding pages.

If you are a beginner, I urge you, before beginning your prayer routine, to read and study the first 18 chapters of this book and do the accompanying exercises a couple of times—especially the exercise in Chapter 18, "Dancing with God," which was formulated to form the foundation of your prayer routine—your dance with God. Then expand the "Dancing with God" exercise in Chapter 18 according to the time available to you following the Beginner's Service below.

BEGINNER'S PRAYER SERVICE   The service below is for praying at home, but can be easily expanded for personal use in the synagogue where one usually has more time. After the first few tries, it should take the beginner about 15 to 20 minutes. For the prayer sections of the *Shema* and the *Amidah*, one can follow the directions below or just go to Chapter 18, "Let's Start the Dance":

Page 2: THE *MODEH ANI* (I gratefully thank You) prayer is a good way to start any prayer session and also—as tradition has it—a good way to start the day. This acknowledges and thanks God for the miracle of life.

Page 19: The Morning Blessings, beginning with the second paragraph and recited in English through the middle paragraph of page 21, bless God for many of the special gifts He has given us.

Page 90: The *Shema* is recited with the six words of the first verse in Hebrew using the exercise and the "*Shema* Recitation Card" at the end of Chapter 7. Then recite the next verse in Hebrew, *Baruch Sheym*, as explained in the beginning of Chapter 8. Finally, recite the rest of the *Shema* in English from the top of page 93 until the middle of page 95.

Page 98: The *Amidah*: Praise. The *Amidah*, as we learn in the *Amidah* Supplement, Part 1, contains three major themes—praise, petition and thanks. As its name implies, it is recited while standing. First you take three steps back and then three steps forward, breaking through your personal barriers to prayer with each step as explained in the beginning of Chapter 13. Begin the *Amidah* with the first three words in Hebrew: *Baruch Ata Adonai*. My suggestion is to incorporate here the "exercise for the first three words," found towards in Chapter 14. Then recite the first paragraph of the *Amidah* in English. End the first blessing with the four words of increasing intimacy—*Melech, Ozeyr, uMoshia, uMageyn*—and the signature blessing as found at the end of Chapter 16.

The *Amidah*: Petition   In the exercise at the beginning of the *Amidah* Supplement, Part 2, I will ask you to prepare a list of all you might want to ask of God—not just one request, two or three, but as many as you want. Now is the time to recite this list to God—you can even read this if you cannot remember it all—asking Him for help. Then close your eyes and say aloud, "*Hashem*[10] help me!" Say this again, "Hashem help me!" Say it louder, "Hashem help me!" Say it with your heart, "Hashem help me!" And again from the deepest recesses of your soul, "Hashem help me!" Scream it out if you are in an appropriate place, "Hashem help me!"

THE *AMIDAH*: THANKS   Take a couple of minutes to thank God
for all the good He has blessed you
with in your life—health, family, home, friends, teachers, job,
synagogue and more. Abide for a moment in God's light, feeling
so grateful. When you are finished, take three steps back in humility before the Presence of God, feeling with confidence that
God has heard your prayers.

Page 159: THE *ALEYNU* prayer is used to conclude every major
prayer service. The first paragraph affirms our understanding
of God, and the second describes how wonderful the world will
be when the whole world will come to this understanding. It includes, as well, a reference to our task in this world: "to perfect the
world through the Kingdom of the Almighty," more commonly
referred to as *Tikun Olam,* "The Perfection of the World." I suggest
you read this in English from the middle of page 159 through the
middle of page 161. You might want to sing some of the *Aleynu*
prayer in Hebrew if you have learned this in the synagogue. There
are several transliterations that can be found online.

Page 476: *EYN KEYLOHEYNU* is a beautiful declaration of faith. I
conclude my morning prayers with *Eyn KEyloheynu* every day. Its
popular melodies are addictive. I urge you to learn to sing this in
Hebrew. When you go to the synagogue, this will be sung at the
end of every Sabbath and Festival service. Again, several transliterations and recordings can be found online. Do not be surprised
if you find yourself singing this in your head throughout your day.

EXPANDING YOUR PRAYER ROUTINE   After a while—and it
may take several weeks
or longer—you will be able to recite the Beginner's Service and
still have time left over from the time you have allotted for prayer.
I suggest you first recite more and more of the *Amidah* in English
as time allows—incorporating the learning found in the *Amidah*
Supplement. You can simply add another of the 19 blessings of

the *Amidah* after first reading about the blessing in these chapters. You will want to remember to include in your prayers the three major themes of the *Amidah: praise, petition and thanks.*

Once you are able to recite the full *Amidah*, begin to add more Hebrew to your prayers. Begin with the recitation in Hebrew of the rest of the first paragraph of the *Shema*—the *V'ahavta*; then the entire first blessing of the *Amidah*; and finally add the signature blessing at the end of each of the blessings of the *Amidah* in Hebrew. Take your time, one at a time.

For the next step I recommend the recitation of the blessings of the *Shema*—before and after—as described in Chapters 19 through 21—with the *Shema* in between.

When you are ready for more, I would advise adding portions of the *Pesuke d'Zimra*, Psalms of Praise, preliminary section of the morning service before the blessings of the *Shema*—first in English and later add the Hebrew when you can. King David's psalms are very powerful spiritual prayers. These are written according to precise spiritual formulas and the very recitation can bring one to spiritual heights. Begin with the opening blessing, *Baruch Sheh-amar* found on page 59 through the top of page 61. I would then go to Psalm 100, a psalm of thanksgiving in the middle of page 65. Continue with *Y'hi Ch'vod* and *Ashrei*, Psalm 145, through page 69. Then add Psalms 146, 148 and 150 through the middle of page 75. Finally the *Pesuke d'Zimra* ends with a concluding blessing, *Yishtabach*, at the top of page 83. When you are ready, you can include more of the psalms and prayers you have skipped.

CAUTION   This is your prayer routine. This is your appointment with God. What I have suggested is just that—a suggestion! Our tradition prescribes the recitation of the *Shema* with its blessings and the *Amidah*. Other than this, adjust your routine to make it meaningful for you. As you do, you will find your ability to gain meaning in all the prayers of the Siddur will grow.

Why Am I Here?

Everyone's spiritual journey eventually must come to the basic question that we all ask, but so little has been written about: Why am I here? Why did God create me with my talents and deficiencies, born to my parents in the time and place I was born? Why did He create some people with brilliant minds and others with developmental disabilities? Why are some musically talented and others artistically talented? Why are some people rich and others poor? You can easily ask a dozen more "whys." Who hasn't asked, at some time or another, "Why am I here?" The answer is very deep and profound, and knowing it should make a profound difference in how you live your life.

According to Kabbalah,[11] when God created the world, He also created all the souls that will ever be. One by one He places a particular soul into a particular body. Why?

God put your soul into your body, with all its talents and deficiencies, born to your parents in the time and place you were born, because these were the optimum conditions necessary for the development or growth of your soul or as Kabbalah puts it, *tikun hanefesh* (repair of the soul).[12] The purpose of life, therefore, is not to be happy—although this is what most parents want for their children. The purpose of life is to develop and perfect your soul![13]

And perfecting your soul is virtually impossible in the world of the souls. You cannot be compassionate in the world of the souls, for no one there needs your help. You cannot resist temptation in the world of the souls, for there is no temptation. It is only here in this world, when our lives seem to be falling apart all around us, that we can demonstrate the growth and development of our souls by reaching out and helping someone else with their pain, with their suffering.

About 38 years ago, Dr. Raymond Moody Jr. published his groundbreaking work, *Life After Life*.[14] There were similar works published around the same time, but his became an underground best seller introducing the world to what became known as the "near death experience." Since then we have been inundated with books, movies, television shows, magazine articles, etc. all describing this experience which has been documented some ten thousand times. In almost every case, a person who is clinically dead—without breath or heartbeat—separates from and hovers over his own body. He may see others trying to revive him. He goes through a long dark tunnel toward an amazing light. When he reaches the light he sees a group of familiar people, who have previously died, coming to greet him. He then sees a panorama of his life unfold before him like a movie. He is overwhelmed by intense feelings of joy, love and peace and wants to stay, but he is told that it is not his time and he must go back.[15]

When Moody[16] interviewed people who had these experiences, he asked if they had any regrets about how they had lived when they saw the panorama of their lives unfolding before them. All of them responded that they mostly regretted not sufficiently understanding "the importance of two things in life: learning to love other people and acquiring knowledge." In fact, many of them subsequently changed their lives to pursue more learning and acts of love towards their fellow human beings. Why are these pursuits so crucial? Because these are essential ingredients of soul growth and development, which is the main purpose of life!

If God then created each of us to develop and perfect our souls, then let us ask an even bigger question: Why did God create the world? I will answer this question in Kabbalistic terms and its answer may surprise you.

God created the world because He "willed" to have an opportunity to display His goodness.[17] It makes no sense to speak of God "needing" anything, for God has no needs. In order to display His goodness it was necessary to create a being as much like Him as possible. God's display of His goodness would then be revealed in the subsequent relationship with that being.

The sages of the Talmud[18] compare it to a calf and its mother: "More than the calf wants to suckle, the cow wants to provide it with milk." God wants, more than anything, to shower His love upon us. What it all adds up to is that God wants a relationship with us so that He can be good to us! Remarkable!

Scientists tell us the universe was created with a "Big Bang." At first, everything was energy and then there was this Big Bang and from a spot no larger than the period at the end of this sentence that energy flowed out into the world and all the solar systems and stars then emanated from it. This all leads to a very religious idea: that there was a beginning to our world. And this beautifully coincides with the Kabbalistic point of view that everything was created from God's loving energy.[19] As the Psalmist teaches,[20] *Ki amarti, olam chesed yibaneh* (I have said the world is built of love).

Kabbalah teaches that in order to create the world, God had to do a *tzimtzum*. *Tzimtzum* is a Hebrew word meaning "contraction." Is it a coincidence that human beings are born with contractions as well? Hardly.

Kabbalah teaches that before creation there was no room for the world because God's Light filled everything.[21] God had to contract himself in order to make room for the world. Rabbi Joseph Soleveichik[22] makes the exquisite point that this creation story is a model for our relationships. If we are so full of ourselves that there is no room for anyone else in our lives, how can we possibly have a relationship with anyone? As Rabbi David Aaron expresses it in his book *Endless Light*:[23] "In order to love, you need to withdraw yourself from the center and create a space for an *other*. Love starts only when you do that—move your self out of the way to make room for another person in your life." All relationships require a *tzimtzum* to be meaningful.

What God expects from us, beyond all else, is a relationship. Wow! Keeping the laws of the Torah and our traditions, isn't this what God expects of us? Yes, that is true, but only because God's laws are an expression of His love for us. The Torah is God's guide for a better life. It is, as my friend the scholar Rabbi Yaakov Fogelman z"l describes, "God's factory-authorized manual" for how to be in this relationship. And our traditions are an expression of our love for God. By embellishing the Law's requirements, our traditions demonstrate our love. The minutiae of Jewish law and tradition are also, if understood in this context, a dance of love that we do with our Creator.

The Three Pathways

A*l sh'losha d'varim ha-olam omeyd: al haTora, v'al ha-avoda, v'al g'milut chasadim.* (The world stands upon three things: upon Torah, upon worship, and upon acts of *chesed*, loving kindness.) This is the formula, according to the Talmud,[24] upon which the continued existence of the world depends. These three foundations are so important, that if for one moment no one was studying Torah, or praying or doing acts of *chesed*, God would withdraw His support and the world might then fall apart. The main point of the Talmud is that the continued existence of mankind, created in the image of God, would be severely threatened if we allowed the world to deteriorate to the point where these three fundamental pathways to God, and thereby God Himself, were ignored. What a blessing it is that God—Who cannot be seen, heard or felt—has given us a formula to connect with Him. And not just coincidentally, it also happens to be a formula for spiritual health and balance. Kabbalah teaches that the *neshama*, the human soul, is a microcosm of the world. And so by extension, if the study of Torah, worship and acts of *chesed* are fundamental to the existence of the world, these, too, are critical to the existence and health of the soul. If there is a sense of emptiness in your life, if despite all the material things you have acquired there is a gnawing feeling in your gut that something is missing, then you need to get your soul into a state of spiritual balance, and that balance can only be achieved by making these three pathways a major focus of your life. You can achieve a state of enlightenment and connection with God through any one of those paths. But spiritual balance can only be achieved when sufficient attention is given to all three.

The greatest degree of intimacy with God usually comes through worship, and therefore, worship is the major focus of this book.[25] But let me leave you with a word about the other two—the study of Torah and acts of *chesed*.

AL HA TORAH (UPON TORAH):   Why is Torah study so essential? In the ancient pagan world—before the Torah was given—the texts that were holy to them were kept secret by priestly clans. If one wanted to know what the gods expected of him, he would ask the priest who would consult the sacred writings and tell him. As you might guess, this led to much confusion, corruption and even abuse.

The Torah, on the other hand, was made available to all. In fact, it was a sacred obligation for everyone to study Torah so that each person would learn for himself what God expects of him and how he could make proper moral judgments.

You might ask: Can atheists not be good and moral people? I once asked an atheist who claims to have a high moral standard, why he doesn't steal. He responded that it is for the good of society that people refrain from stealing. Then I asked him, if he were very hungry would he then feel it was proper to steal some food? "Yes," he said, "that is different because I would need to eat." But put the same questions to a religious Jew, Moslem or Christian, and the response would be that scripture teaches us, "Thou shalt not steal!" Unless one's life is in danger, one does not steal. Why? Because this is what God expects from us. One cannot justify immoral behavior merely to relieve one's own discomfort.

Ethical relativism—the idea that there are no moral absolutes, no moral rights and wrongs—is very popular today in defending criminal behavior. It has no place in a truly moral world. It reminds me of the story of the shopkeeper who remarked to his friend that he faced a moral dilemma. He told his friend that someone had come into the store to purchase something and had mistakenly given him a hundred dollar bill instead of a ten. He did not notice the error until some time later. "I see," said the friend, "your dilemma is whether or not to return the hundred dollars to the customer."

"Oh no," said the shopkeeper, "of course I'll keep the money. My moral dilemma is whether or not to tell my partner about it!"

The ongoing study of Torah is essential in order to constantly be aware of what God expects from us. But this pathway to God goes much deeper—to the very core of our souls. I often ask students who study Torah to notice how they feel after a Torah study session. It may seem like a strange question to ask, but try it. Notice how you feel after a good session of Torah study. "Good, elevated, inspired," are among the many responses I have received. Some even report a noticeable physical difference. Why? It is because the truths of Torah resonate to the very core of one's soul, and in fact, animate our souls. And when our souls—that image of God in each of us—become animated, we feel a profound connection with our Creator.

The Torah is the word of God, and when we study it, we hear the voice of God speaking to us! In a discussion with Rabbi Shimon Greene of Yeshiva Birkas HaTorah in Jerusalem about the benefits of studying Talmud, the Oral Torah, he took this a step further: "Studying Talmud—with its development of life's core issues and the weighing of the different facets of the Torah's response—is like entering into the mind of God." It is amazing! When we study Torah, we have the capacity, on some mystical level, to enter into the mind of God. This can be a profound connection! That is why the study of Torah is a major pathway to God.

G'MILUT CHASADIM (ACTS OF CHESED, LOVING KINDNESS).

Chesed is the Hebrew word for "love." But *chesed* is not really romantic love, although romantic love to endure needs *chesed* at its core. Romantic love is better served by the Hebrew word *ahava*. *Chesed* is an altruistic love, a love that comes from a sense of overwhelming kindness. It is a love for your fellow human being, given without a thought of being repaid or being loved in kind. A relationship based on *chesed* is a relationship that can be sustained, unlike a relationship based on self-interest.

Abraham is the archetype of *chesed* in Jewish tradition and the paradigm story in the Torah of *chesed* is the story of Abraham and the three angels.[26] Abraham is sitting in his tent recuperating from his circumcision when God pays him a visit.[27] *Vayeyra Eylav Hashem* (God appeared to Abraham.) He is in the presence of God—a state most spiritual masters would say is the highest spiritual level a human being can possibly achieve. Suddenly he sees off in the distance three strangers approaching. *Vayaratz likratam* (and he ran to greet them), saying in effect to God, "Sorry God. I don't mean to be rude, but I have more important things to do right now. I have to take care of these men. Don't go away; I'll see you later."

What a *Chutzpa!* If the President of the United States or the Prime Minister of Israel called you, would you put either of them on hold while you took care of other errands? Is that not what Abraham does with God in this story? What could be more important than communing with God, especially when He comes to visit? But for Abraham, despite the pain of his recuperation, extending himself to help a fellow human being in need takes precedence even over his very intimate encounter with God. From this the sages comment, *Gedolat hachnasat orchim mikabalat p'ney haShechina* (Greater is hospitality to wayfarers than receiving the Shechina, the Divine Presence).[28]

In other words, when we reach out to help our fellow human beings in need, despite all the personal problems we face, despite the fact that we may be hurting as well, we become an extension of God on earth. It is almost a merging with God, which can be a very powerful pathway to Him. It also helps us achieve a powerful sense of self-worth because when we engage in acts of *chesed*, we know that our lives have not been wasted, that we have made a difference in the world.

This pathway is part of what Kabbalah refers to as *Tikun Olam* (repair of the world). Our acts of kindness and charity can help heal the world just as the study of Torah and prayer are acts of *Tikun Hanefesh* (repairing the soul) that we mentioned earlier. These two expressions of *tikun* (repair) are deeply connected because when one works to better the world, this invariably helps perfect one's soul. And when one works on perfecting one's soul, it will inevitably lead to acts of bettering the world.

Do you want a quick, easy recipe for adding spiritual balance to your life through acts of chesed? I was inspired once by something a colleague said. "Very simple, three times a week, do a special *mitzvah*; go out of your way to help someone. That is all it takes. Writing a check does not count. You really have to do it." It could be for someone you know, or a worthy organization or even becoming an activist for a worthy cause. At least three times a week, go out of your way, become God's hands and make a difference in this world. Don't make excuses and tell yourself that you are very busy. We are all busy! You find time to eat three times a day; you find time to watch your favorite television program; you find time to get to the gym. This will make you feel good faster and better than going to the gym, as you open this essential pathway and your soul merges with God. As an added incentive, King Solomon teaches us, *Tzedaka tatzil mimavet* (Charity can save one from death.)[29]

The study of Torah and acts of chesed—both time-honored pathways to God—are critical to the health of the soul. But true intimacy with God can only be achieved through *avoda*, worship—deep prayer and meditation. The following chapters are meant as a guide, both for the novice and for one who prays regularly, for how to find intimacy with God through Jewish prayer.

CHAPTER 4

Avoda: Becoming Intimate with God

It is told of the Sanzer Rebbe that he once was asked, "What do you do before you pray?" The Rebbe replied, "I pray that I may be able to pray!"[30]

Did you ever feel you were doing God a favor when you went to the synagogue or when you prayed one of the prescribed prayer services at home? If so, you have got to change your thinking. It is the other way around. God is doing us a favor by providing us with the optimal setting for an intimate encounter with Him. If you have rarely, if ever, had this experience in your prayers, then pay close attention.

The Talmud[31] tells us our earliest sages would extensively prepare for an intimate prayer experience: *Chasidim harishonim hayu sho-im sha-a achat lifney hat'fila* (The first pious ones would wait one hour and pray.) Just as an athlete must warm up before a game in order to be at his best, we also need to warm up—especially after a night's sleep—in order to be at our best before God. What would these "first pious ones" do during that hour? Whatever it was, it was meant to prepare body, mind and soul to receive the *Shechina*, the Presence of God in prayer.

I remember once walking along the streets of Jerusalem after three o'clock in the morning, returning home from a wedding celebration. I saw here and there men walking in the quiet streets, each carrying what looked to me like a volume of the Talmud under one arm, and a *tallit* and *tefilin* bag under the other. At first I thought it was some special occasion I was unfamiliar with, so I asked one of them. He told me he rises early every day to study Torah for two hours before he prays. It makes sense. If the study of Torah can animate the soul, what better way to prepare for prayer?

What was it that the "first pious ones," the Sanzer Rebbe and those early morning walkers along the streets of Jerusalem were trying to achieve with their elaborate preparations? They were trying to ensure that when they finally recited the prayer service, it would be a true encounter with God and not just a perfunctory ritual. You see, even for the great spiritual masters, encountering God in prayer was no simple feat and certainly not to be taken for granted.

But, you might ask, if encountering God is such an arduous task for the most pious, would it not be an almost impossible task for the rest of us? Let me caution you not to become overwhelmed, not to think too little of your own spiritual potential. Remember, every one of us is a holy soul, and with some direction, effort and focus, every one of us can regularly encounter God in the most intimate way through our own *avoda*—our own deep prayer and meditation. And so the Talmud[32] teaches: "God appears far, but no one is closer than Him. He is high above His universe, but a person can enter a synagogue, stand near the pulpit, and pray in a whisper—and God hears his prayer."

How about starting by withdrawing for just a few minutes each day from the rat-race routine we are so caught up in to set aside a specific time to be with yourself and God? I know this is not so easy because the whole pace of our times is against it. So open your appointment calendar and schedule a daily appointment with yourself. You can get up a few minutes earlier or take the time before bed. We are so connected today with our smart phones, IPads, laptops, email, social networks, Twitter and texting that it is difficult to be alone. So shut it all down for that special time to just be with yourself and God.

If someone called me on the phone and my secretary said,

"The rabbi is busy now, he is talking to someone," they would understand. But if she were to say, "The rabbi is busy now, he is talking to himself," or "he is listening to himself..." they might wonder about the rabbi's sanity. And yet, just as we set aside fixed times to talk with others, should we not have fixed times to talk to ourselves too? If we never allow a moment for ourselves to catch our breath and think or feel or pray or just do nothing, then what kind of lives are we living?

Isaiah[33] says it best: "In sitting still and rest shall you be saved; in quietness and serenity shall be your strength." In a world in which there is so much pressure upon us to be doing things all the time...in a world where everyone says to us, "Don't just stand there, do something," we need to say to ourselves, "Don't just do something, stand there," at least long enough for our souls to catch up with ourselves.[34] And in that private time with yourself, find a moment to pour out your heart to God. First thank Him for all the blessings in your life and then ask Him for help in the areas of your life that need help. (See exercise below.)

WHO AM I?   Don't hesitate to pray by asking yourself, "Who am I that God should be listening to my prayers? I'm just a sinner and have not done as much as I should have to help my fellow man." Nevertheless, the sages learn from the Torah that God longs for our prayers.

In the second chapter of the Torah,[35] God tells us that before He created man, He had not brought rain upon the earth because there was no one to work the soil. The Talmud[36] elaborates and tells us this was because there was no one to recognize the goodness of God and His gift of rain and pray for it. This, the Talmud says, teaches us God longs for our prayers.

V'asu li mikdash v'shachanti b'tocham (And make Me a sanctuary that I may dwell among them) commands the Torah.[37] Why doesn't God say, "Make me a sanctuary that I may dwell in it—in the sanctuary?" The sages comment that God resides not within the sanctuary so much, but within the heart of every person, unless, of course, we dispossess Him! But I don't think this is a problem for most of us. Most of us have not dispossessed God from our hearts. Most of us are desperately seeking God. It is important to know as well that, as our tradition teaches, God longs for our prayers.

After a lengthy description of the sanctuary and the *Mishkan*—the Tabernacle, the portable Temple the Jewish people built while traveling from Egypt to the Promised Land—the Torah[38] then tells us the purpose of a house of God: "That they shall know that I am the Lord their God, Who took them out of the land of Egypt to dwell in them, I am the Lord their God." It seems this verse is saying that God is freeing the Jews from Egypt and then commanding them to build a sanctuary was to fulfill a divine need,[39] which is to dwell in them.

In other words, God wills to have a relationship with us.[40] But can God really be said to have a need or a desire? Accordingly, Nachmanides on this verse tells us this is a "great secret!"

YOUR SACRED SPACE: A WORD ABOUT CHOOSING A HOLY PLACE:

It is important to create a holy place—a sacred space—for yourself where your prayers will be more effective over time. Choose a place at home—the (dining room) table is my favorite. If it is possible, choose a place—a specific seat—in your shul and return there every time you come. You may have a favorite place by a stream or a lake. When you pray again and again at the same place, it becomes easier to get into an effective prayer state because some of the spiritual energy you released there in the past still lingers. As the Talmud[41] teaches, "When one has a fixed place of prayer, the God of Abraham helps him."

What is deep prayer and how is it distinguished from other types of prayer? Deep prayer is that prayer that wells up from the deepest recesses of our hearts. It can only occur when one is truly focused on a prayer—putting everything else out of mind. If one is in a hurry and grabs an apple and, before he eats it, blesses

God who created the fruit of the trees, he has recited a prayer that has meaning, but it hardly qualifies as deep prayer. On the other hand, if a loved one is having serious surgery, and if in a quiet place with tears in your eyes you then beg God to be merciful and bring about a full recovery, that can be a form of deep prayer. The prophet Jeremiah[42] tells us God says, "You will call out to Me… you will pray to Me and I will listen to you. You will seek Me and you will find Me if you search for Me with all of your heart."

But you need not have a crisis in your life to pray deeply and connect with God. The emotional release and spiritual uplift that can accompany such an experience can be felt regularly by each of us. How? Let me illustrate with a simple exercise of guided imagery.

EXERCISE: Find a quiet place where you will not be interrupted or distracted. I recommend that you go to www. DancingWithG-d.com to find an easy-to-use recorded version of this exercise. Alternatively, you can record the following instructions very slowly and play them back as you do the exercise or, if needed, have someone read it to you. Most smart phones and tablets have a recording app, so this should be relatively easy. Do this for all the exercises in this book. Try not to feel squeamish or uncomfortable if this is something new and different for you. Approach this with anticipation and excitement, for it can be a helpful key in opening new pathways to God. Do not be discouraged if the gates of heaven do not open the first time you attempt this. Try it once a day for two weeks and each time notice afterwards how you feel physically, emotionally and spiritually. Notice also any subtle changes in your life—your attitude, the attitude of others toward you and, in general, how life treats you. I suspect you will find your newfound connection to God has made a profound difference. Please note that I often use the term *Hashem* (The Name) to refer to God in the exercises because I feel it has a special spiritual power. But you can substitute "God" if you like. Here's the exercise.

Sit in a comfortable chair, close your eyes and relax. Take a series of slow, deep breaths. There are four types of breaths: in the nose and out the mouth; in the nose and out the nose; in the mouth and out the mouth; in the nose and out the mouth. In order to achieve a very relaxed state, ten of each is recommended. Change the order each time until you find the order that works best for you. When you breathe in, imagine yourself breathing in the light of God; and when you breathe out, breathe out your troubles and cares—the list of things you worry about every day. Breathe in God's light and out with your troubles.

Go to www.DancingWithG-d.com to find an easy-to-use recorded version of this exercise. Alternatively, you can record the exercise yourself and play it back, or have someone read the following to you after you have done the breathing exercises:

> Imagine you are walking in a beautiful green field. Feel the warmth of the sun on your back. Smell the aromatic fragrance of the trees and the wild flowers. Hear the beautiful songs of the birds. You feel so calm and relaxed. With every step feel more and more relaxed…. Now see in front of you a beam of light six to eight feet in diameter descending from heaven. It has always been there, but you have never noticed. It is a light unlike anything you have ever seen—intense, yet neither burning nor threatening. The light beckons. Step into the light. Feel its warmth and embrace, like God is hugging you with His light. Abide for a moment in the Divine embrace. You now feel lighter and calmer, more at peace with yourself than you have ever felt before. Abide in the light for a few moments. Pause...
>
> Now breathe in the light and let it go to every fiber of your body with its healing powers…
>
> Take a couple of minutes to thank God for all the good He has blessed you with in your life—health, family, home, friends, teachers, job, synagogue, etc. Abide for a moment in the light feeling so grateful. Pause...

Now think of some of the challenges you face in life and ask God for help. Pause... Say out loud with me, "Hashem help me!" Say it again, "Hashem help me!" Say it louder, "Hashem help me!" Say it with your heart, "Hashem help me!" Say it again from the deepest recesses of your soul, "Hashem help me!" Scream it out (if you are in an appropriate place), "Hashem help me!" Once more, "Hashem help me!"

Abide in the light for another moment or two, enjoying the embrace of God's light, knowing your prayers have been heard. Notice how you feel physically, emotionally and spiritually. When you open your eyes, you will feel better and more aware than you have all day. Pause...Open your eyes.

How did you feel? Many feel physically relaxed and refreshed with a feeling of emotional release and spiritual connectedness. Again, do not be discouraged if you did not feel much different nor have an overwhelming spiritual experience. Try it every day for two weeks and you will notice a significant difference. In fact, do it every day for the rest of your life and not only will your blood pressure go down, but you will feel as though you are always walking in the presence of God. Not everyone has the discipline to do this every day unless this becomes a part of a daily prayer routine. You will later see how to incorporate this exercise in your *Amidah* prayer experience. Done regularly, this will have a profound impact.

Once you have been able to connect with God through meditation, you can draw upon that meditative experience to help you pray more deeply with every prayer opportunity, whether it is a formal service, a blessing over food or the spontaneous outpourings of your heart and soul. You need not make every prayer a ten or twenty-minute meditation but, for a moment you should be able to call upon that state of connectedness with God you achieved in your most powerful meditations and use this sacred memory to create a similar connection in the prayer you are reciting. And if you make the effort to understand each word and the concept it represents as you recite, the experience of any prayer can be even more powerful.

For those of us who are not fluent in reading Hebrew, let alone in understanding it, can we make a divine connection in the prayer service? Absolutely! Every time! Even if you are not fluent in the whole service, you can become fluent in part of it, even if only by memorizing a few words and learning the meaning and concepts. The first verse of the *Shema* has only six words, and yet it is our most important and potent prayer. Most of the service can and should be said in a language you can understand[43]— English for those who are unfamiliar with the Hebrew. But the Hebrew should not be abandoned. It is a holy language and there is a special *kedusha* (holiness) in the prayers written in Hebrew. Every word, every letter is infused with *kedusha* and with great spiritual power—like a mantra. So for the prayers that become especially meaningful to you, learn the Hebrew, even if you have to memorize, even if you have to learn from a transliteration.[44] This will heighten your prayer experience.

The Baal Shem Tov (early 18th century), founder of Chassidut taught: "Our main link to God is through words—words of Torah and prayer. Every single letter in these words has an inner spiritual essence. You must attach your thoughts and innermost being to this essence…When you draw out a word and do not want to let it go, you are in a state of attachment to God![45]"

For each of us—the novice and the experienced *davener* alike—there will be certain prayers we become attached to more than others. Rabbi Gedalia Fleer of Jerusalem once suggested to me that when we find particular meaning in a prayer or even in a verse from a prayer, we should become friends with it. Read a commentary or two about it. Learn everything you can about its words, structure and deeper meaning. You might even create your own melody for it. Make it special; cherish it; make it your own. You will then find yourself eagerly anticipating the approach of this prayer in the service when you pray. You literally will feel that you cannot wait to get to it. And once you have achieved a heightened spiritual experience with a verse, every time you return to it you can draw upon some of the spiritual energy you had released to recreate that heightened spiritual state.

In the next chapter we will learn how your soul can soar to the highest heights while saying the first six words of the *Shema Yisrael*.

Shema:
Let Your Soul Soar

The *Shema* consists of three passages from the Torah: Deuteronomy 6:4–9; Deuteronomy 11:13–21; and Numbers 15:37–41.[46] Since its origin is from the Torah—and therefore from God—the *Shema* is especially holy and can resonate with a power unlike any other prayer. Actually it is not a prayer at all in the usual sense. Most prayers are either prayers of petition—asking God for what we want or what we think we need—prayers of thanksgiving, or prayers of praise. In fact the English word "prayer" comes from the Latin *precaria*, meaning, "petition." But the *Shema* does not contain a word of petition, praise or even thanksgiving. It is, therefore, not a prayer in the ordinary context.

The *Shema* is a declaration of faith and much more.

The most important part of the *Shema* is its opening verse. Citing Rabbi Meir, the Talmud[47] teaches that if you can only concentrate intensely on one verse of the *Shema*, it should be this verse. In fact, this verse is the most potent in all of Jewish prayer. It is the first prayer taught to a child and the last words recited before death. Jewish martyrs bravely died for the sanctification of God's Holy Name with the words of the *Shema* on their lips. It is just six words:

שְׁמַע יִשְׂרָאֵל יְ-ה-ו-ה אֱלֹהֵינוּ יְ-ה-ו-ה אֶחָד:

Shema Yisrael, Hashem Eloheynu, Hashem Echad
Listen Israel, Hashem is our God, Hashem is One

Let us analyze the meaning and the spiritual power in each word.[48]

שְׁמַע/SHEMA (LISTEN)   What does it mean to really listen? What are we supposed to hear? Part of the skill of deep prayer is listening—really paying attention to the words of our prayers and what emerges from our inner self as we recite these words. But listening involves much more. It means blocking out all thoughts of pressure and anxiety, the things that worry us, the long list of things we need to do, the fears that cripple us, everything that overtakes our consciousness and prevents us from focusing within, from listening to that inner voice. But this kind of listening is not easy. In fact, most of us are uncomfortable being alone with ourselves.

It sounds strange, but this is true. When you walk into your home and no one is there, what do you do? If you are like most people, you will immediately turn on the stereo or the television. In our cars it is the radio, the CD, the mp3 player or the Bluetooth from our cell phones. We cannot even get into an elevator without hearing Muzak (elevator music). Today our cell phones come equipped with multi-media formats enabling us to walk around with earbuds in our ears, oblivious to the world around us. We cannot even take a walk and be alone with ourselves. Why? Could it be that we are afraid to be alone with ourselves? But we must spend time with ourselves if we ever want to spend time with God. We need alone time to be able to hear our inner voice and, perhaps if we are worthy, to feel the Presence of God as well.

Seeing usually is connected to logic. When one has trouble grasping a concept another may say to him, "Look at it this way." And when one understands the logic of an argument one says, "I see!" But when one is looking for guidance that goes beyond logic we say, "Listen to your heart!" When God says "Listen Israel" in the *Shema*, He is summoning us to a deeper place, a place we can only access by listening. If you do not take the time to just be with yourself and hear your own inner voice, then you may never be able to receive the Presence of God.

Let us go even deeper. While the common usage of the word *shema* (listen) is "to hear with the ear," the literal meaning of *shema* is actually, "to construct oneness out of pieces."[49] For example, the Bible[50] tells us about King Saul's response to the threat of the wicked people of Amalek: וַיְשַׁמַּע/*va-y'SHAMA Shaul et ha-am* (Saul gathered the people together) to form an army. It does not follow the context of this verse to think that *va-y'SHAMA* means that Saul "listened" to the people. Obviously it means that he "put them together." When we "hear," it is really a process of assembling bits of information we perceive to be put together so that they can be understood and heard.

If this is the case, then how do we understand the meaning of *Shema Yisrael*? Most prayer books and Bibles translate it something like, "Hear O Israel." This is a poor translation that does not begin to convey the meaning or the power of the words. Translating *Shema Yisrael* as, "Hear O Israel" would mean, "listen Israel" or "pay attention Israel" because what the Torah is telling you is very important—i.e., so in case you are not listening, listen! But that is absurd! The Torah does not speak to those who are not listening. The problem is we have an English ear. "Hear O Israel," is rhetorical; it is dramatic. It does not have to mean anything. It just sounds good. But the Torah does not use an expression just because it sounds good. In the Torah, every word is essential.

So what does *Shema Yisrael* mean? For King Saul, the word *va-y'shama* meant to gather his people; for us the *Shema Yisrael* means, "You, *Yisrael*, you the Jew, listen from a deep place within, listen for your *sh'lichut* -- for your mission -- which is *Shema* -- to assemble the broken pieces, to make oneness out of a broken world." Hashem is *Echad* (One) as we say at the end of this verse. Take the brokenness of this world, the broken pieces, and bring these pieces together to become one with God.

You are to go out into this confused world which teaches the opposite of truth, and where everything looks like it is in shambles, because it is one cobbled piece after another and so little makes sense… and you *shema*, you put this together to make a perfect oneness. You, go out and hear what is true. *Shema*, once you have heard the message you must become a vessel to spread the word to all of Israel, and then to the entire world.[51] The unfolding of the rest of the verse makes the message of the word *shema* even stronger.

There is a fantastic insight into this first verse of the *Shema* in the Jerusalem Talmud[52] which demonstrates that this verse is not only an expression of "what" we believe, but also of "why" we believe. What did the Jewish people hear at Mt. Sinai when they received the Ten Commandments? They only actually heard the first two commandments.[53] They became frightened from their very intense encounter with God and begged Moses to go and get the other commandments for them from God. And he did.

What is the first Commandment? *Anochi Hashem Elohecha* (I am the Lord your God). This is found in this first verse of the *Shema* in the words *Hashem Eloheynu* (Hashem is our God). The second commandment is, *Lo yih'yeh l'cha elohim acheyrim al panai* (You shall not have any other gods before Me). This we find restated in the affirmative at the end of the *Shema* verse with the words *Hashem Echad* (Hashem is One). The *Shema Yisrael* is then a condensation of the first two of the Ten Commandments. What makes these first two commandments different and special? *Shema*—we actually heard them.

EXERCISE   Let's summarize what we have learned so far in an exercise of preparation before saying the *Shema*. When you next pray the morning or evening service and recite the *Shema*, incorporate what you have learned here to heighten your *Shema* experience. Go to www.DancingWithG-d.com to find an easy-to-use recorded version of this exercise. Alternatively, you can record the exercise yourself, speaking very slowly, and then play it back as you do the exercise:

> Sit in a comfortable chair; place your hands in your lap and your feet on the ground. Close your eyes and place your

right hand over them to help you focus. Take several deep breaths. With each breath become more and more relaxed. Pause… In your relaxed state you can now see the light of God right in front of you. Enter into the light. Notice how wonderful this is to be in God's light. It is like God is hugging you! Breathe in the light with its holy essence and let it go to every fiber of your being. Breathe out all your cares and troubles and everything toxic within you. Breathe in and out—in and out.

Now that you are in the light, you are ready to say the *Shema*, to dedicate yourself to gathering the broken pieces of this world, to see the Oneness and the Truth, to become a vessel of sorts to spread the word of God that you will receive, to be intimate with God as you listen deeply with your whole being to the crucial message of God's Oneness that follows. For that message is so incredibly powerful that, even though it is recited twice daily, one never gets tired of listening to it. Now, very slowly, say the six words of the *Shema: Shema…Yisrael…Hashem…Eloheynu…Hashem… Echad*, "Listen Israel (You, Yisrael, you the Jew, listen from a deep place within, listen for your *sh'lichut*—for your mission—which is Shema—to assemble the broken pieces, to make oneness out of a broken world), Hashem is our God, Hashem is One."

יִשְׂרָאֵל: The next word is יִשְׂרָאֵל/*Yisrael* (Israel), and there are at least five ways to understand the message of the name *Yisrael*.[54] Each is terribly profound and meaningful. When God calls Jacob "Israel," He calls upon him to rise to his higher self, his soul self. You can use these five meanings as a ladder to rise to the *Yisrael*, the higher self, within you—your soul self. Let us unpack these one by one and you will see what I mean:

1. *Yisrael* is more than the name of the Jewish people and their land. It is the special name given to Jacob in the Bible. Jacob

was returning home after an absence of 22 years. He had fled from his home because his brother Esav[55] had threatened to kill him. Now Esav was coming to greet him along with four hundred soldiers. Terrified of the upcoming confrontation, Jacob divides his family into two camps, strategizing that if one is attacked, perhaps the other will be able to escape. He cannot sleep knowing his brother will be arriving in the morning, and so he wanders off into the wilderness where he is mugged by an unknown attacker. He struggles with him all night until his attacker demands to be let go. Jacob insists on a blessing from his assailant before he will release him and the assailant agrees declaring: "No longer will it be said that your name is Jacob, but Israel, for you have wrestled with God and with man and have prevailed."[56]

Yisrael (Israel) literally means יִשָׂר/*yisra* (wrestle) and אֵל/*Eyl*, (God). The first understanding of *Yisrael* is "he who wrestles with God." The commentaries differ as to exactly who was this attacker of father Jacob. But whether his attacker was the spiritual emissary of Esav, or another spiritual entity, or just an inner struggle within Jacob himself, we can say with certainty that Jacob was in the midst of a deep spiritual struggle.

One can imagine some of the questions that might have passed through his mind: "Why is this happening to me? God promised to protect me in that dream I had when I left home, the one with angels ascending and descending a ladder to heaven. But my brother is coming with a mighty force to kill me. Could it be that God was not truthful with me, that God does not keep all His promises? Could it be that God cannot keep all His promises? Maybe that dream where God first spoke to me and promised to protect me, was only just a dream? Is God real?" Jacob was struggling with the whole concept of God, but he prevailed, and in the end, his faith was much stronger for the struggle. And so when Jacob is called "Israel" in the Torah, it is because he has risen to his higher self.

Because "Israel" literally means "one who wrestles with God," when we wrestle with God and prevail, our faith becomes stronger. Do we not all seem to struggle with God from time to time? Do we not all ask, at one time or another, "Why is this happening to me? Is God real?" As we recite the word *Yisrael*, we should first try to feel some of the pain of our own struggles with God and—as we do—we begin the ascent to the Israel within us—to our higher selves.

2.   What really happened to Jacob on that night? According to the Midrash,[57] his mysterious attacker was the *saro shel Esav* (the "spiritual emissary of Esav") trying to prevent Jacob from assuming the leadership of God's people. If that was the case, then Jacob was not just fighting for his life, but for the future of God's people. In this sense, the name Israel—יִשְׂרָ/*yisra* (wrestle) and אֵל/*Eyl*, (God)—can also properly be translated as, "one who wrestles FOR God." We, the descendants of Jacob, the People of Israel—God's people—have been attacked again and again by enemies determined to eliminate us and prevent us from bringing the message of God's Torah to the world. But God, in His mercy, has never allowed our attackers to destroy us because of the promises made to our forefathers,[58] and because we have considered it a privilege to wage the holy fight for God—even to the extent of *Kiddush Hashem*, martyrdom, if necessary.

So Israel—יִשְׂרָ-אֵל/*Yisra Eyl*—can mean either, "one who wrestles WITH God," or "one who wrestles FOR—on behalf of—God." After you recite the word *Yisrael* and recall your struggles with God, reach down for that extra bit of faith that tells you perhaps there is a purpose to your struggles, and resolve to work on behalf of God in this world with acts of *chesed* (kindness) and *rachamim* (compassion). As you do, you will rise to the next level despite your struggles.

3.   Another approach to the meaning of *Yisrael* comes from the Ralbag,[59] who teaches that יִשְׂרָאֵל/*Yisrael*, is a contraction of שַׂר-אֵל (*sar Eyl*,) which means, "a prince or champion of God." When one has come through a personal struggle with God to

then struggle on behalf of God in helping to perfect the world, one can become a "champion of God"—not in the sense of being the strongest or the most pious—but in the sense of utilizing the challenges that life throws at us…to champion God in the world, to face our trials in a Godly, *mentchlichkeit* way that inspires others to see God. So be a champion of God. It is your destiny and part of your true essence—your higher self.

4.   Still another approach comes from the *Kli Yakar*,[60] who divides the letters of יִשְׂרָאֵל/*Yisrael*, into the words: יָשָׁר-אֵל/ *yashar Eyl*. *Yashar* means, "straight," and *Eyl* is "God." *Yashar Eyl* can mean either "straight with God" or "straight to God." Perhaps this is a progression stemming from the other rungs of meaning on the ladder. After struggling with God, if you then struggle on His behalf, you can become a prince and champion of God. In the process, you should begin to see God's goodness in the world, dissipating your struggle thus allowing you to become, *yashar Eyl* (straight with God).

The message then, as we recite the word *Yisrael*—thinking about our struggles with Him and then struggling on His behalf, becoming His champion—is to become straight with God. For once we begin to see and understand that God has His reasons for doing what He does, once we begin to get over the struggle, we can allow our souls to really soar as we become the Israel within us and ascend higher towards God as we move onto the final rung.

5.   The Midrash[61] understands the Hebrew letters of יִשְׂרָאֵל/ *Yisrael* to be a contraction of the words: אִישׁ-רוֹאֶה-אֵל/*ish ro-eh Eyl* or שֶׁרוֹאֶה-אֵל/*sheh-ro-eh Eyl* (one who sees God). This is not at all surprising because the Hebrew word שׁוּר (not commonly used) means "to see,"[62] and *Yisrael* might then come from שׁוּר-אֵל which means, "see God." The *Kli Yakar* above relates the word *yashar* to the act of seeing, bringing proof verses from the Bible. Jacob was called Israel because, through his incredible spiritual journey, he elevated himself to such an extent that he

could see God. It is not that he could physically see God. It is that he found evidence of God everywhere he went—in every place and in everything. This is, perhaps, the highest level anyone can strive to achieve.

The deepest spiritual truth is that there is no such thing as real evil or negativity in the world. It is only an illusion. Negativity only has the power we give it! The first blessing we recite before the *Shema* paraphrases a master verse from the Book of Isaiah[63] that teaches this truth: "I, God, am the One Who forms light and creates darkness; Who makes peace and creates evil. I am God, Maker of all these." (See Chapter 20, "The Biggest Blessing," for an explanation of this first blessing before the *Shema*.) It is God that creates the possibility of evil in the world in order to further the development of our souls by giving us moral choices. But behind the evil, behind the negativity is God!

When hardships confront us, it is hard to see God. But, as we shall see in the next chapter when we unpack the meaning of the two names of God in the *Shema*, when bad things happen to us, they are usually a form of good-not-yet-understood. So, if we stay on a proper path trying to figure out our *shlichut*, our mission, in life, if we make a strong effort to come close to God, we can elevate ourselves so that we too can see God in every place and in every situation—even in hardship.

We, the children of Jacob who was called Israel, have had amazing spiritual experiences where we—as a people—have had the opportunity to see God manifest in the world. When we crossed the Red Sea, the Torah[64] tells us: "Israel saw the great hand that God had inflicted upon the Egyptians, and the people revered God, and they had faith in God and in His servant Moses." The heightened sense of spiritual awareness in actually seeing God's hand in action was truly awesome and elevated their awareness of God in the world.

Each of us has had experiences in our own lives in which we could see the hand of God in action—the birth of a child, a *simcha* (personal joyous occasion), surviving an accident or an illness. The modern State of Israel is a miracle in itself with hundreds of millions of Arabs against a few million Jews and we have witnessed miracle after miracle in its struggle for survival. When Saddam Hussein sent his deadly scud missiles into Israel during the first Gulf War (1991), not a single person was killed. While sadly we cannot say the same in regard to Hezbollah and Hamas' thousands of rockets, the small amount of casualties is still amazingly miraculous. Similarly, in Operation Cast Lead, the 2009 war in Gaza, an astonishingly low number, ten Israeli soldiers, lost their lives—and some of those from friendly fire.

The problem for many of us, however, is that we do not acknowledge the presence of God in our lives and attribute such miraculous moments to mere coincidence or freak occurrence. When we were children, it was easy for us to see God in the world. As the children's song goes, "Hashem is here. Hashem is there. Hashem is truly everywhere!" Children are more open and aware. When we get older and skepticism sets in, it becomes harder and harder to acknowledge the presence of God right in front of our eyes. The Midrash's understanding of *Yisrael* as "one who sees God" presents a challenge to us to find the sparks of God in every encounter in life's journey.

Which understanding of the name Israel is correct? All are! All are deeper and deeper layers of this holy name given by God to His people—five layers of increasing intimacy with God. So let us find the Israel in you—your higher self—as we climb its spiritual ladder from 1) one who struggles with God, to 2) one who struggles on behalf of God, to 3) one who becomes a champion of God, to 4) one who becomes straight with God, and finally to 5) one who sees God everywhere in everything. *Shema Yisrael.* Hello, the Israel in you, are you listening? Let us try to find it with this brief exercise.

EXERCISE   This exercise is best done in a sitting position with your feet on the floor and your hands on your knees. Review the exercise at the end of chapter 4 with more details for best using your breath in these exercises. As in the previous exercises, go to www.DancingWithG-d.com to find an easy-to-use recorded version of this exercise. Alternatively, you can record yourself speaking very slowly and then play back:

> Close your eyes and take a series of slow, deep breaths. With each breath you become more relaxed. Imagine yourself bathed in light, because as a holy soul, you always are. Feel your left arm becoming very heavy. Now feel your right arm as it becomes very heavy. Feel your left leg becoming very heavy and now feel your right leg as it becomes very heavy. Breathe in the light and let it go to every fiber of your body with its healing powers. Breathe out everything toxic within you. Breathe in and out—in and out.
>
> As we prepare to recite this first verse of the Shema, place your right hand over your eyes to help focus on the words, as is customary when reciting the Shema. Your eyes closed with a hand over your eyes constitute a double hiding, but your demonstration of that exposes your deep desire to go inside and find God despite the barriers—despite how hidden He may seem.

1. Now find the Israel within you struggling with God because life is sometimes too hard. Think of how you struggle with God at times. Remember a difficult struggle from the past. Do you feel the struggle? Good! Pause…

2. Now, with the struggle still strong in your heart, resolve with that part of you that believes in God to be "Israel"—the Israel inside of you that struggles on behalf of God. Do this without letting your personal struggle prevent you from doing acts of *chesed* (kindness): to help Israel, help your synagogue, help bring healing, help your neighbor, the poor, the oppressed, to increase the observance and learning of God's Torah in this world. Pause…

3. As you rise on your spiritual ladder doing God's work in this world, embrace becoming the Israel inside you that is a *sar, a* prince/princess—a champion of God. Feel the power, the energy of God filling you as you become God's champion. Pause…

4. Now let go of your doubts and become the Israel inside you that is straight with God—understanding that God has His reasons for doing what He does, that in the end, it is all for the good. Set aside your struggles with God and as you do, you will ascend even higher—straight toward God. Pause…

5. And finally, as you now have this heightened awareness, you will begin to see God everywhere and in everything. Your struggle with God will become more and more just a memory. In its place you will allow your true self, the real Israel in you to do what it has always wanted to do: to cleave to God and become one with Him. Take a few moments and feel one with God as you become one who sees God everywhere and in everything.

6. Open your eyes.

God's Name

The next two words of the *Shema* are יְ-ה-ו-ה אֱלֹהֵינוּ/*Hashem (Adonai) Eloheinu* (*Hashem* is our God). *Eloheinu*, a common usage for God literally means, "our אֱלֹהִים, *Elohim*," or "our God." This is amazing in itself if we think about it. God is the *Eyn Sof*, the Infinite, the Source of our being, and He asks us to call him ours! This, according to Rabbi Aryeh Kaplan, z"l,[65] "is the greatest possible gift." It tells us that what God wants from us is an intimate relationship. We are His people and He is *our* God.

Let us examine these two words: *Hashem Eloheynu*. These are the two major names of God.[66] Isn't it strange that God Who is One has two primary names: *Hashem* and *Elohim*? Why is it necessary to mention both names in the *Shema*? If the intent of the *Shema* is merely to express our belief in monotheism—i.e., that God is One—then it should be shortened to, *Shema Yisrael Hashem Echad* (Listen Israel. God is One).

So what is contributed by the use of both names, *Hashem Eloheynu* in the middle of the *Shema*?

Rabbi Benjamin Blech[67] teaches that each name of God refers to a different way in which He relates to us. Each of us has different names, depending upon how we relate. I am Mark or Meyer or Rabbi or, as my grandchildren call me, "Sabba."

When we think of God, we usually relate to Him in two ways. When we think about how much God has given us, we think of Him as loving and kind and merciful. When life is not so kind to us and we are suffering, we wonder what we did to deserve such a fate? God, in this sense, is the Great Judge. Our sages describe these two attributes of God as *midat harachamim* (the attribute of mercy) and *midat hadin* (the attribute of justice).

ה-ו-ה-י *Hashem*, or the four-letter name of God, is written with the Hebrew letters *yud* (י), *hey* (ה), *vav* (ו) and *hey* (ה). It is "The Name", and it is filled with mystery—so much so that no one knows how to pronounce it. This is why it is so often referred to as *Hashem*, literally "The Name." There is a secret pronunciation that was only recited by the high priest in the days of the Holy Temple on Yom Kippur. The sages[68] have decreed that because this Holy Name cannot and must not be pronounced as we pray, we should substitute אֲדֹנָי/*Adonai* (my Lord) in our prayers in its place. The sages[69] teach that The Name is a contraction of Hebrew words *haya, hoveh, y'hiyeh*, "was, is, will be," indicating Hashem was, is, and always will be. He is the source of everything. He is merciful and can even supersede the laws of nature He created in order to be merciful.

We first encounter this name of God in the second chapter of the Torah. Here we read of God who sees that Adam is alone, has compassion upon him and makes a helpmate—Eve—to be with him. This name denotes *midat harachamim*—the "attribute of mercy."[70] This four-letter name of God is almost always the name used in the Torah when God speaks to human beings, because it is not natural for God to speak to a person—it is supernatural! This is only done because God, in His great mercy, has an important message to transmit to the person He speaks to.

אֱלֹהִים Why is God called *Elohim*? In order to properly answer this question we must use the tools of grammar and *gematria* (numerology)[71]—the adding of the numerical value of the letters—in order to unpack the deeper meanings. Do not be intimidated by the technical nature of *gematria*. It contains profound and deep secrets.

Most words in Hebrew have a three-letter root, but sometimes there is a shorter two-letter root and for this name of God there are both. What is the three letter root of *Elohim*? אֵלֶּה/ *Eyleh*—*alef, lamed, hey*—and it means "these." These what? Let us then look at the two-letter root, אֵל/*Eyl*—*alef, lamed*—which means "God," but also means "power," as Laban tells Jacob, *Yeysh l'eyl yadi laasot imachem ra* (It is in my power to do evil to you).[72] When we combine the two-letter and three-letter roots, what emerges is that *Elohim* means, "These Powers."[73] This is one reason, perhaps, why *Elohim* is in the plural form while denoting one God.[74]

Elohim is the name of God that we find creating the world as we read in the first chapter of the Torah. *Elohim*, therefore, is the Creator, and so *Elohim* refers to the way God reveals Himself in nature. It is fascinating and certainly not a coincidence that the *gematria*, the numerology of *Elohim* is eighty-six (*alef* + *lamed* + *hey* + *yud* + *mem*: 1 + 30 + 5 + 10 + 40 = 86), which is also the *gematria* for הַטֶּבַע /*haTeva*/nature, (*hey* + *tet* + *vet* + *ayin*: 5 + 9 + 2 + 70 = 86). In Kabbalah, when two words have the same numerical value, they share a similarity in essence. God in nature, therefore, is *Elohim*. Natural law is *Elohim*. All the forces of nature proceed from *Elohim*.

Elohim, "These Powers," is also the name of God that denotes the attribute of strict justice. In fact, the Torah uses *Elohim* to refer to judges[75] because the Torah's judges have "powers," based on God's law, to decide the fate of those who appear before them. The attribute of strict justice to which *Elohim* refers can seem cruel. When life is hard, we often ask, "Why are we being judged so cruelly? What did we do to deserve such a fate?" Nature, as well, can seem harsh and cruel—disease, illness, floods, hurricanes, earthquakes, volcanoes, etc. Nature can be so overwhelming that we are at a loss to understand. *Elohim* then alludes to the attribute of God that is sometimes made manifest in strict justice or nature—both of which can seem cruel.

The Shema comes to teach us that *Hashem Eloheynu*, these

two names of God, *Hashem*—the aspect of God of mercy and compassion—and *Eloheynu*—the aspect of God of nature and strict justice which can both seem cruel—are really *Hashem Echad*, one *Hashem*, one merciful and compassionate God. When life is hard and we are suffering, when we are unable to begin to understand what we did to deserve our fate, the *Shema* comes to teach us that although God sometimes appears in the guise of *Elohim*—the aspect of God of strict justice and nature—in reality He is always *Hashem*—the God of mercy.

The hardships in life, therefore, are really a good-not-yet-understood. We may not understand what is happening to us now, but there will come a time when we will be able to understand. It may be in a few days or months or years or a lifetime or even after this lifetime, but we will understand and see that God is always one Hashem, one merciful and compassionate God.

א   This unity of God is illustrated in the construction of the Hebrew letter *alef* that begins the name *Eloheynu*, the aspect of God manifested by strict justice and nature. Take a good look at the Hebrew letter *alef* above. When a Torah scribe writes an *alef*, he first draws a letter *yud* on the top right corner, then an upside-down *yud* on the bottom left-hand corner, and then a slanted *vav*, from top left to bottom right in the middle. *Yud*, the number ten, is the first letter of God's special four-letter name and therefore represents God's name. *Vav* is the number six and represents man who was created on the sixth day. The *alef*, the first letter of the name *Eloheynu*, is written with two *yud*s. Two *yud*s written together are often used to represent God's special four-letter name.[76] The two *yud*s are written on either side of the *vav*, the letter which is symbolic of man. What does this tell us? It tells us that, for the sake of man, God seems like an *alef*, like *Elohim* when life challenges him, but He is really the *yud*—*Hashem*, merciful and compassionate.[77]

To drive the point further, the *gematria*—the total number value of the two *yud*s and the *vav* that make up the construction of the letter *alef*—is 26 (*yud + yud + vav;* 10 + 10 + 6 = 26), which is also the *gematria* of ה-ו-ה-י/*Hashem* (*yud + hey + vav + hey*, 10 + 5 + 6 + 5 = 26). What it all comes down to is that hidden in the *alef* of *Eloheynu*, the name of God denoting strict justice and nature that can seem cruel, is *Hashem*, the God of mercy and compassion. This is a deep, deep secret, and when understood, it makes the challenges and hardships of life much easier to bear.

Let me illustrate with a scenario every parent has experienced. A parent will say, "I know that you think I'm being cruel and tough when I say that you must be home by 12:00 a.m., or you can't do this or that, or you must be punished for what you did, but I am really doing this to you because… I love you."

Studies reveal that children who are not disciplined feel a lack of love and often ask for discipline in different ways—often negative ways—to make sure they are loved. The *alef* of *Elohim*— the Supreme Parent—says to us, "If I look like an *alef* or *Elohim*, look closer, look deeper and you will see if I appear cruel or tough, it is because I really love you."

It sometimes appears that God is *Elohim*, but only because we need to be challenged so we can achieve our spiritual potential—so that our souls will be elevated on the ladder of growth. Another great spiritual truth, really a subject for another book, is that God never punishes. God only fixes! (See The *Amidah* Supplement, Part 3: "*Din*, Justice" for more on this.) If life seems overwhelming and cruel at times, it is because we need to learn something from the experience. If we had God's perspective, we would see a holy purpose behind all of life. In the moment of pain it is so hard to understand, but there will come a time in this lifetime or the next when we will understand *Hashem Echad,* that Hashem is One Merciful God and that everything He does is done with love![78]

If we are to feel any of the power of the six words of the *Shema*, we must maintain an awareness of the significance of each word as we recite the *Shema*. We should therefore say each of these six words slowly when we pray, pausing briefly to consider the concept behind our words before going on to the next word. This can take anywhere from 30 seconds to a full minute or more. Do not rush or feel pressured by a congregation that prays faster.

So far we have discussed the first four words: *Shema*, gather up the broken pieces to make oneness out of a broken world—and listen to God summoning you to a deeper place to become a vessel to spread His word; *Yisrael*, elevate yourself five levels to the Israel within you, to your higher self; *Hashem*, the merciful and compassionate aspect of God; and *Eloheynu*, the aspect of God denoting strict justice and nature that can seem cruel. However, these two names of God are really—as we will see in the last two words—*Hashem Echad*, One compassionate God!

One With God

יְ־הֹ־וָ־ה אֶחָד   The *Shema* ends with *Hashem Echad* (*Hashem* is One). When I was young I had some difficulty relating to this. After all, we live in a world that almost universally accepts the Judaic concept of monotheism.[79] I could understand this passage as being useful in reference to ancient times when most people worshipped many gods, but I wondered how it was still relevant to me? I was told it could refer to the worship of materialism, power, and other vain pursuits we so vehemently pursue, as being the "other gods" in our lives. But I later discovered there is much more to these two words.

When we say, "God is One," the understanding that this statement excludes other gods is certainly true, but superficial. "God is One" means He is absolutely One—One with everything. In other words, everything comes from God, and therefore there is a unity in everything. This is why the *Shema* is the first prayer a Jewish child learns and the last a Jew recites before death.

The Lubvitcher Rebbe once wrote in a letter to a scientist: "At the core of material existence, science has found a oneness of two opposite ideas: Quantity and quality…in simple language, matter and energy are one. Why? Because God is One, therefore the world is one…Indeed, science is rapidly approaching the inevitable conclusion that the entirety of existence is a singular ray emanating from a singular source."[80] The *Tanya*,[81] teaches a similar idea that nothing exists but God. God is not only the foundation of reality, He is the only reality: "God obscured and hid this…to make the world appear as an independently existing entity."

I once heard the astrophysicist Neil deGrasse Tyson[82] make a similar point that to me describes the oneness of God's creations in the physical world: "Recognize that the very molecules that make up your body, the atoms that construct the molecules are traceable to the crucibles that were once the centers of high mass stars that exploded their chemically enriched guts into the galaxy enriching pristine gas clouds with the chemistry of life. So we are all connected to each other biologically, to the earth chemically and to the rest of the universe atomically. That's kind of cool! That makes me smile and I actually feel quite large at the end of that. It's not that we're better than the universe; we're a part of the universe. We're in the universe and the universe is in us." As we learned in Chapter 2, the single source of all creation is God's loving energy.

In the mind of God   On a deeper level, everything is contained within God. When a writer creates a character in his mind, for example, the character is part of him—one with him—but it is not him. We and everything in the world are like the character in the mind of the writer in the sense that we exist in the mind of God. Unlike a writer's characters, we are independent; although some writers will tell you that their characters sometimes take on a mind of their own and go to places the writer had never before imagined. God has created us to be independent. We are not God, but on some level we are a part of God and God is a part of us.

When we recite the word *Echad* (One) at the end of the six words of the *Shema,* we should try to feel that Oneness of God, that unifying principle of God that connects all things.

Love   There is one more concept necessary to understand this sense of the Oneness of God and that is love. As we learned previously, God created the world with a *tzimtzum*—He constricted or diminished Himself in a sense, to make room for us and the world. It was a loving gesture—a model for any loving relationship. In order to allow love to enter our lives we must do a *tzimtzum* and make room for others. If we are full of ourselves, no love can be present. And just as we still maintain our sense of self when we make space for another within ourselves, even though God constricted Himself, God is not absent from this world. His essence totally permeates every space. He is One with the world and everything in it.

This connection between oneness and love can be further demonstrated in the *gematria*, the numerical value of the Hebrew letters, of the words אֶחָד/*echad* (one) and, אַהֲבָה/*ahava* (love). Both add up to 13 (*echad* is *alef* + *chet* + *dalet*: 1 + 8 + 4 = 13, and *ahava* is *alef* + *hey* + *vet* + *hey*: 1 + 5 + 2 + 5 = 13). As we learn from Kabbalah, when two words have the same numerical value, they share a similarity in essence. Oneness and love, therefore, are connected in a profound way.

Love is the power that breaks down barriers and unifies opposites. Two people who are deeply in love become one. If we add the numerical values of the words *echad* (one) and *ahava* (love), or if we add the numerical values of the two "ones" (*echad*) in a relationship, we get 26 which is the same *gematria* as the four-letter name of God י-ה-ו-ה *Hashem,* the loving and merciful name of God.

The blessing recited right before the recitation of this *Shema* verse is: "Blessed are You, Hashem, who chooses Your people Israel with love." (See Chapter 21, "The Greatest Love of All.") Immediately after the first verse of the *Shema* is the commandment, *V'ahavta,* "You shall love Hashem your God with all your heart, with all your soul, and with all your might."[83] This commandment speaks of the love we must have for God. Therefore, the *Shema* is sandwiched between two loves—God's love for us and our love for God. Both of these loves suggest the ultimate unity in the *Shema*.

THE BIG LETTERS   The word *Shema* ends with the letter *ayin*
and the word *echad,* at the end of the verse,
ends with the letter *dalet*:

שְׁמַ**ע** יִשְׂרָאֵל י-ה-ו-ה אֱלֹהֵינוּ י-ה-ו-ה אֶחָ**ד** :

These two letters are written in the Torah larger than the others
and signify a powerful coded message. When combined, the
letters spell the word: עֵד/*eyd*, meaning "witness." A witness is
someone who sees, who gives eyewitness testimony. When we
recite the *Shema* we give testimony that God exists, proclaiming
His Unity to the entire world in fulfillment of the Biblical[84] injunction, *Atem eydai* (You are to be My [God's] witnesses. Not
only are we to testify to our faith in reciting the *Shema*, but we
must also guard against betraying that faith—even inadvertent-
ly—by hedging our bets on the possibility of more than one God.[85]
Therefore the letter *ayin* (ע) is enlarged in order to distinguish it
from the *alef* (א), which would change the word שְׁמַע/*Shema* to
שְׁמָא, which means "perhaps."[86] The letter *dalet* (ד) is also enlarged
to distinguish it from the letter *reysh* (ר) which looks similar to
the *dalet* and would change the word אֶחָד/*echad* to אַחֵר/*acheyr,*
meaning "another," implying another god.[87] The enlarged letters
are to leave no doubt about the One True God.

The *ayin* and *dalet* can also be read as עַד, *ahd*, meaning
"until." This teaches that our belief in God can never be perfect.
We can only come "until" God, seeing a glimpse of Him—never
quite reaching Him. The *ayin* and *dalet* can also be read as עֹד/*ohd*
(still), perhaps signifying that despite all the times we experienced
God as Elohim, through all the suffering and persecutions we
endured, we "still" believe and declare that *Elohim* and *Hashem*
are the One merciful God in the world.

If we reverse the *ayin* and *dalet,* we get the word דַּע/*da*,
which means "know." "Knowing" is a higher form of belief. Knowing indicates experiencing and bonding intimately with God. The
Hebrew word דַּעַת/*Daat* means "knowledge," but the literal mean-

ing of this word is the intimate relationship in marriage, and so the Torah tells us: "Adam knew his wife Eve and she conceived."[88] The encoded word *da* (know) in the *Shema* sets for us a higher spiritual goal towards which we should all aspire: To know God by experiencing Him. This kind of knowing is a higher state than believing. One can say they believe the stock market will do better next year, but knowing this for a fact would make one's investment strategy much more successful. Knowing God by experiencing Him is, therefore, a much higher state than just believing.

אֶחָד   And finally, a time-honored practice recommended by the Talmud[89] is to recite the last word of the *Shema* verse, *echad*, elongating its pronunciation—*echaaaaaaaddd*—and emphasizing the letter *dalet*, the "d" sound, at the end. In doing so, one is to focus on "the Kingship of God in heaven and on earth and over the four directions of the skies." God rules in heaven and on the earth and in every direction. Rabeynu Yona[90] adds that we should focus on "the four corners of the earth...in the great abyss and in our own 248 organs"—i.e. within ourselves. Whoever does so, said Sumchos in the Talmud,[91] "will lengthen his days and his years."

What they all are trying to teach us is that the recitation of this last word of the Shema, *echad*, is the climax of the spiritual ascent of the Shema experience. When reciting this powerfully charged word, you should allow your soul to soar so you can feel the love of God and the uniqueness of your soul as it becomes one with God Who is One, and one with everything—for everything emanates from God's loving energy. After you begin to say *echad*, do not complete the word with the *dalet*, "d" sound, until you can feel that love and oneness in every fiber of your body and all the way to the very depths of your soul.

It is obvious that the *Shema* was constructed for the very purpose of bringing us to this heightened state of awareness. This is the reason the Torah teaches us that it should be recited evening and morning, "when you lie down and when you rise up".[92]

In reciting the *Shema* twice every day, we then live our lives in between with the special awareness of God's love for us and our oneness with God, and this can make our lives so much more wonderful and meaningful.

EXERCISE   Take a few moments now to absorb what you have read in the last three chapters. This is so important that I would suggest you take the time to read these again and even take notes. Remembering the wisdom and power in each of these six words is crucial to achieving an elevated state of connection as you recite the *Shema*. Set aside some quiet time—at least ten minutes—to be with God and to meditate on the six words of the *Shema*. Be careful to heed the warning of the Talmud[93] not to repeat the word *Shema*, and so do not recite it like a mantra. As I have suggested before, you will need to either remember the following instructions (go to www.DancingWithG-d.com to find an easy-to-use recorded version of this exercise) or to record it very slowly and then play it back as you do the exercise:

> Sit in a comfortable chair, place your feet firmly on the ground, close your eyes and relax. Breathe deeply through your nose and out of your mouth several times as we have learned (adding the three other types of breath if necessary to achieve a state of complete relaxation). Breathe in God's light filled with love and harmony. Breathe out all your cares and problems. Become more relaxed with each breath. Place your right hand over your eyes to help you focus, as is the custom while reciting the Shema. Now say the words of the Shema, dwelling on each word for about 10 to 15 seconds, focusing on its meaning:
>
> *Shema*—**Listen**, listen deeply with your heart, and know your mission is to gather the broken pieces of this world to Oneness, to become a vessel to spread the word of God you receive.

Yisrael—The Israel inside you that **struggles** with God, that nevertheless fights on behalf of God, that becomes a champion of God, that becomes straight with God, that sees God everywhere and in everything.

Ad-o-nai—Feel the warmth of God's **compassion** envelop you as you recall at least one way God has shown His compassion towards you.

Eloheynu—Feel the awe and the fear of the aspect of God's **strict justice** and **nature** that can seem cruel. Recall at least one time you felt God as *Elohim*. But know God is really...

Ad-o-nai Echaaaaaaad—**One compassionate God!** Get ready to say the word *Echad*. Hold the word *Echad* and don't finish reciting it until you feel the energy of God's love fill you to the point you feel one with Him and one with the world in every fiber of your being. Abide in this feeling of oneness for a few moments. Now open your eyes.

Do this exercise when you recite the *Shema* in your prayers and before you go to sleep at night. Before long the feeling of oneness with God that you experienced with the *Shema* will stay with you all day.

Shema Recitation Card   I have prepared a special card to help you as you begin to incorporate these concepts in your *Shema* recitation. Copy the page and cut it out to use until the deep understanding of the words of the *Shema* become a part of you. If and when you do not remember the concepts contained in one of the six words of the *Shema*, just open your eyes briefly and glance at the card to remind you. Do not worry; it will not break your holy spiritual state.

Shema Recitation Card

Shema—<u>Listen</u>, listen deeply with your heart, and know your mission is to gather the broken pieces of this world to Oneness, to <u>become a vessel</u> to spread the word of God you receive.

Yisrael—The Israel inside you that (1) <u>struggles with God</u>, that nevertheless (2) <u>fights on behalf of God</u>, that (3) becomes a <u>champion of God</u>, that (4) becomes <u>straight with God</u>, that (5) <u>sees God</u> everywhere and in everything.

Ad-o-nai—Feel the warmth of God's <u>compassion</u> envelope you as you recall at least one way God has shown His compassion towards you.

Eloheynu—Feel the awe and the fear of the aspect of God's <u>strict justice</u> and <u>nature</u> that can seem cruel. Recall at least one time when you felt God as *Elohim*. But know God is really...

Ad-o-nai Echaaaaaaad—<u>One compassionate God</u>! Hold the world *Echad* and don't finish reciting it until you feel the energy of God's love fill you to the point you feel one with Him and one with the world in every fiber of your being. Abide in this feeling of oneness for a moment.

A *SHEMA* STORY

Let me conclude this chapter on the Shema with a story told by Victor Fankl in his powerful book *Man's Search For Meaning*.[94] Frankl relates how he entered the Auschwitz concentration camp stripped of his status, his possessions, his clothes, and most of all, his wife and children. He was left alone and naked and told to proceed to the next room for a shower. Throughout his ordeal, Frankl always had kept with him, hidden in his coat, a copy of the manuscript of his first book. This manuscript meant everything to him. It was the only thing he had left that mattered. And now he was being told that he would be killed if he tried to take anything with him into the next room. Frankl knew he had a choice to make, a terrible choice—to leave behind the only shred of meaning left in his life or to forsake life altogether. Finally, Frankl chose life and decided to part with the manuscript and walked into the shower room.

After showering, he was given the worn out rags of a Jew who had not been so "lucky," who had not been selected for work, who had already been sent to the gas chamber immediately after his arrival at Auschwitz. Sorrowful over the loss of his manuscript, Frankl slowly dressed in his new clothes, trying to accept the fact that the last element of meaning had been drained from his life.

As he dressed, he felt something in his shirt pocket. He reached in and found a piece of paper with writing on it, and suddenly he began to cry. At the moment when it seemed life had lost all meaning, here was new meaning, new hope, new purpose. For here, in the clothes of a dead man, he found what a Jew had chosen to take with him into death's portals, what one person had carried to give meaning and purpose to the hell to which he had come. The piece of paper was a page from an old prayer book and on it were the words: *Shema Yisrael Hashem Eloheynu, Hashem Echad!*

This piece of paper had passed from one *Yisrael,* one Jew to another, uplifting him and sustaining him, making him feel truly one with God and the world, even in the blackest night. It did so for Frankl. If we open our hearts, the *Shema* can do this for us as well.

CHAPTER 8

The Rest of the Shema: Climbing to God

The recitation of the *Shema* is a Torah commandment, according to the Talmud,[95] to be recited every morning and evening. This is derived from the words contained in both of the first two paragraphs, "You shall speak of them" and "when you lie down and when you rise up."[96] The recitation of the last paragraph is derived from the words "I am Hashem your God Who took you out of the land of Egypt,"[97] as well as the commandment to remember the Exodus from Egypt.[98]

There is some debate as to which parts of the *Shema* actually constitute a Torah commandment and which are rabbinic in origin. Most authorities contend that only the first six words of the verse *Shema Yisrael Hashem Eloheynu Hashem Echad* is required by the Torah. This is one reason we devoted three chapters to probing its depths. For our purposes, it is sufficient just to know that the *Shema* is composed of three paragraphs from the Torah, so when we read the *Shema* it is God speaking to us from His Torah.

What is God's message to us in the *Shema*? God's message in the first verse is complex as we have seen. It was summarized in the exercise at the end of the previous chapter. In short, it is to strive to become one with God through an understanding of God's love, mercy and compassion.

What are the messages contained in the rest of the *Shema*?

We will unpack these paragraph by paragraph. But before we do, we need to take a look at a verse that is not from the Torah that was inserted by the sages after the six words, *Shema Yisrael Hashem Eloheynu Hashem Echad*, and before the rest of the paragraph that begins with the word *V'ahavta*:

בָּרוּךְ, שֵׁם כְּבוֹד מַלְכוּתוֹ, לְעוֹלָם וָעֶד:

Baruch Sheym k'vod malchuto l'olam va-ed

"Blessed is the Name of His glorious kingdom forever and ever."

This verse, although not appearing in the Torah, is very ancient. According to the Talmud,[99] it was the response in the Holy Temple whenever God's Holy Name— י-ה-ו-ה—was recited in a blessing—much like our use of the word *Amen* today. Its origins, according to the Talmud,[100] stem from the story of Father Jacob blessing his children. The Torah tells us Jacob wished to reveal to them what "will befall you in the End of Days."[101] The Talmud then tells us that at that moment, the *Shechina*, God's Divine Presence, departed from Jacob, who suspected this was because one of his children might be unworthy—like Abraham's son Ishmael or Isaac's son Esav—and God did not want Jacob to experience the pain of prophetically seeing this. All his sons then reassured him by proclaiming their faith in God by reciting, *Shema Yisrael* (Hear Israel [Jacob's other name]), *Hashem Eloheynu Hashem Echad* (Hashem is our God and Hashem is One). At that moment, says the Talmud, Jacob replied with this verse, *Baruch Sheym k'vod malchuto l'olam va-ed* (Blessed is the Name of His glorious kingdom forever and ever).

Rabbi Joseph Hertz[102] explains that the Roman Emperors demanded "divine honors"—i.e. that they be worshipped—and so the rabbis of that time inserted this verse after the *Shema* verse as Father Jacob did, so that a Jew would proclaim only Hashem is God and He alone is "the Sovereign" of our lives.

There was some controversy in the Talmud[103] as to whether

this verse ought to be recited silently—as is our custom. Noting that Moses did not include this verse in the Torah, the sages concluded it should be recited silently. The Midrash[104] maintains Moses learned this verse from the angels on Mt. Sinai and taught it to the Jewish people. Since we are on a lower spiritual level than the angels, this approach maintains, we dare not recite it aloud. But on Yom Kippur, when we are as sin-free as the angels, we do recite it aloud.

In the final analysis, this angelic verse, *Baruch Sheym k'vod malchuto l'olam va-ed* (Blessed is the Name of His glorious kingdom forever and ever), is a fitting response to the six words of the *Shema* proclaiming that God is One with everything and everyone as personified by His Name—ה-ו-ה-י—indicating that He was, He is and He always will be. In effect, we are blessing God that everything that comes forth from His Name—"His glorious kingdom"—be worthy of God's blessing. This puts an awesome responsibility upon us to make our world worthy of God's blessing.

וְאָהַבְתָּ אֵת יי אֱלֹהֶיךָ בְּכָל לְבָבְךָ וּבְכָל נַפְשְׁךָ וּבְכָל מְאֹדֶךָ: וְהָיוּ הַדְּבָרִים הָאֵלֶּה אֲשֶׁר אָנֹכִי מְצַוְּךָ הַיּוֹם עַל לְבָבֶךָ: וְשִׁנַּנְתָּם לְבָנֶיךָ וְדִבַּרְתָּ בָּם בְּשִׁבְתְּךָ בְּבֵיתֶךָ וּבְלֶכְתְּךָ בַדֶּרֶךְ וּבְשָׁכְבְּךָ וּבְקוּמֶךָ: וּקְשַׁרְתָּם לְאוֹת עַל יָדֶךָ וְהָיוּ לְטֹטָפֹת בֵּין עֵינֶיךָ: וּכְתַבְתָּם עַל מְזֻזוֹת בֵּיתֶךָ וּבִשְׁעָרֶיךָ:

V'ahavta eyt Adonai Elohecha b'chol l'vavcha, uv'chol nafshecha, uv'chol m'odecha. V'hayu had'varim haeyleh asher anochi m'tzavcha hayom al l'vavecha. V'shinantam l'vanecha v'dibart'cha bam, b'shivt'cha b'veytecha, uvlech-t'cha vaderech, uveh-shochb'cha uv-kumecha. Uk'shartam l'ot al yadecha, v'hayu l'totafot beyn eynecha. Uch-tavtam al m'zuzot beytecha uvish'arecha.

"And you shall love Hashem your God with all your heart, and with all your soul and with all your might. And these words that I command you today shall be in your heart. You shall teach them to your children and speak of them when you are sitting at home and when you walk on the way, and when you lie down and when you rise up. You shall bind them as a sign upon your hand and they shall be tefilin between your eyes. You shall write them upon the doorposts of your home and upon your gates."[105]

V'AHAVTA (And you shall love): This is the commandment to love God. The obvious question is that while we can understand how God can command someone to do or not to do something—like shake a *lulav* or not to light a fire on the Sabbath—how can God command emotions and feelings like love? Maimonides[106] answers with an intellectual approach. He suggests that this commandment to love God commands us to contemplate the awesomeness of God's actions, creations and wonders. Once we do so, he maintains, we cannot help but come to love God.

Taking this one step further, I would say that love is a choice.

Modern society has created the fairy tale that love is uncontrollable, that it is something that simply happens. And so we say, "She fell in love," as if love is some kind of a hole in the ground one does not see and falls into—in other words, she could not help herself. But the truth is, this is not love.

Love does not just happen. Real love is a choice and a commitment. Among human beings, love is an unconditional commitment to an imperfect person. And as you choose to love those who are not perfect, how can you not love God Who is? Shlomo Carlebach expressed it this way: "If a man loves a woman, he can do anything for her without any difficulty. So too, when someone loves God, it is easy for him to keep the Torah. He can do anything for God without any difficulty."[107] If we focus only on the hardships in our lives we might walk around angry with God. Alternatively, we can appreciate how much God has given us, remembering the times we were in trouble and He was there for us when we needed Him, and we will inevitably come to love Him.

On a deeper level, the commandment of *V'ahavta*, of loving God comes immediately after the words *Hashem Echad* (God is One) in the six opening words of the *Shema*. The love of God is then the immediate consequence of feeling the Oneness of God with yourself and everything in the world.[108] Serving God with this kind of love—as Rashi, the premier Biblical commentator[109] teaches—is a far higher state than serving God from fear.[110]

HASHEM ELOHECHA, "Hashem your God": Hashem, as we have learned in Chapter 6, denotes the aspect of God's mercy and *Elohim* the aspect of God's strict judgment—when life is difficult and we feel we are being judged harshly. The use of both names of God in this command to love God, tells us we must love Him whether He deals mercifully or harshly with us because, as we have learned in Chapter 7, the *Shema* teaches us that *Hashem* and *Elohim* are really *Hashem Echad*, one *Hashem*, one merciful and compassionate God. Sometimes God appears to us as *Hashem*—when things are going well in our lives. And sometimes God appears to us as *Elohim*—when life is hard and we are suffering and we cannot begin to understand what we did to deserve our fate. However, although God sometimes appears in the guise of *Elohim*—the aspect of God of strict justice and nature—in reality, as we have learned, He is always *Hashem*—the God of mercy, because the hardships in life are really a good-not-yet-understood. So this verse implores us to love God when He comes to you as *Hashem* or as *Elohim*.

B'CHOL L'VAVCHA (with all your heart): The Talmud[111] points out that the word for heart used here, *l'vavcha*, is not written with one letter *beyt*, as is the common usage, but with two, signifying we should love God with our two hearts—namely both our good and evil inclinations.

How do we serve God with our evil inclinations? We need to channel our animal-like desires and passions into the service of God. Sexual drives need to be channeled into the building of a holy marriage and family. The Ten Commandments warns us not be jealous of our neighbor's possessions. But you can be jealous of another's learning so that you will strive to learn more. Hate not your fellowman but hate suffering, poverty and evil.

Uv'CHOL NAFSHECHA (and with all your soul): *Nefesh*, from the word *nafshecha,* refers to the animal aspect of the soul that animates life. In essence it refers to one's physical life. And so the Talmud[112] interprets this to mean we are to love God even if He (God) takes our life or even if we must sacrifice our life. The Talmud[113] tells the famous story of Rabbi Akiva who was publically tortured to death by the Romans for teaching Torah. Just before he died was the time to recite the *Shema.* The Jerusalem Talmud[114] tells us that Rabbi Akiva laughed. When the cruel Roman governor Turnus Rufus asked him if he was mocking him, Rabbi Akiva replied, "My whole life I have recited this verse, 'You shall love God with all your heart, with all your soul and with all your might.' I have loved God with all my heart; I have loved Him with all my might, but I was not certain till now if I could love Him with all my soul…and now 'all my soul' faces me and I see that I can, and so I recite the *Shema* and laugh." In the face of his torturous death Rabbi Akiva taught his most powerful lesson. This is an inspiring story that compels us to ask ourselves as we recite the words, *Uv'chol nafshecha* (with all your soul): How much are we willing to sacrifice for the sake of God and Jewish life?

Uv'CHOL M'ODECHA (and with all your might): The Hebrew word *M'od* literally means "very" or "very much." It is a word that amplifies. God tells us in the story of creation—after looking at everything He created—that it was *tov m'od* (very good).[115] It was not just "good;" it was "very good." *Uv'chol m'odecha* then literally means, "with all your very much," or in a more grammatically correct form, "with all your extra." Variously the commentators suggest it refers to "your might," or "your wealth," or "your talents."[116] When we recite these words we should do so with a silent vow to serve God with our very best, indicating to God that we love Him *m'od* (very much)!

V'HAYU HAD'VARIM HAEYLEH ASHER ANOCHI M'TZAVCHA HAYOM AL L'VAVECHA (And these words that I command you today shall be in your heart): To what do "these words which I command you today" refer? These words refer to the commandments of the Torah. This first paragraph of the *Shema* is the opening to the *HaMitzvah* (The Commandments) section[117] of Moses' final farewell speeches to the Jewish people, and the second paragraph of the *Shema* concludes the section with similar words. So "these words which I command you this day" certainly refer to the *mitzvot* (God's commandments). God wants us not to just blindly follow His commandments, but to keep them in our hearts and to understand these were given to us with great love.

Rashi teaches us something so absolutely beautiful about the usage of the word *hayom* (today) in this verse: "Let not these words be like an old edict to which a person does not think it so important. But rather they should be like a new one towards which everyone runs." In other words, look at this message from God as if it was given for you today. In fact, ask yourself every time you recite these words: What is God's message for me today that needs to be in my heart?![118]

V'SHINANTAM L'VANECHA V'DIBARTA BAM, B'SHIVT'CHA B'VEYTE-CHA, UVLECH-T'CHA VADERECH, UVEH-SHOCHB'CHA UV-KUMECHA (And you shall teach them to your children and speak of them when you are sitting at home and when you walk on the way, and when you lie down and when you rise up): The word *shinantam* (teach) is derived from the root word *shanan* (to sharpen).[119] It is undoubtedly connected to the word *sheyn* (tooth). The message is that when we teach our children Torah, it is not enough to just review the verses. You must teach them in a way that makes an indelible impression. The words *v'dibarta bam* (and speak of them), the Talmud[120] suggests, add that it be done "in any lan-

guage that you speak," so they will understand. And the words
uv'shochb'cha uv-kumecha (when you lie down and when you
rise up), as we have learned above, teach us the *Shema* is recited
evening and morning.

UK'SHARTAM L'OT AL YADECHA, V'HAYU L'TOTAFOT BEYN EYNECHA
(And you shall bind them as a sign upon your hand and they
shall be tefilin between your eyes): The pronoun "them" refers to
the previous words, "And these words which I command you,"
and so the black boxes of the *tefilin* contain scrolls of four Torah
passages[121] about the commandment of *tefilin*. They also teach
about the Oneness of God, the acceptance of His commandments
and how God redeems His people when necessary as He did in
Egypt—all fundamental principles of faith.

The observance of the commandment to put on *tefilin* is so
important that tradition suggests it encompasses all 613 commandments; if we can understand its meaning we can perceive the
deeper meaning of the others.[122] *Tefilin* are identified in this verse
as an *ot* (a sign). It is one of the special signs that identify a Jew,
such as circumcision, *tzitzit* and *mezuzah*. When one binds the
leather boxes of the *tefilin* on one's arm or head with the leather
straps tied to it, one is effectively binding oneself to God and His
Torah. The leather box on the arm is placed near the heart, sym-
bolizing that all one's strength and actions—symbolized by the
arm—and all one's passions—symbolized by the heart—as well as
one's intellect—symbolized by the *tefilin* on the head—be aligned
with God. In this way *tefilin* can certainly heighten one's prayer
experience. Although Jews only generally wear *tefilin* during the
weekday morning prayer service, it is not difficult to understand
why there are those who wear *tefilin* all day.

In order to reinforce one's awareness of this, it is customary
to take one hanging leather strap from the head *tefilin* and touch
the arm *tefilin* box when reciting "upon your hand," and then kiss
it, and then touch the head *tefilin* box when reciting, "between
your eyes," and kiss it. Binding the leather boxes of God's holy

words to your arm and head and then kissing them can be a very intimate experience with God—even without saying a word. It can feel almost like kissing God, or better, being one with God.

Women do not need to wear *tefilin* because their bodies are a constant reminder of their inherent unity with God—in being able to co-create another human being with Him. All female body parts that participate in such creation and the nurturing of a human being are a constant reminder of this. Looking at this in another way, Kabbalah teaches that a man's left hand represents the feminine element. The single hollow represents the womb, and the coils of the *tefilin* the umbilical cord. As Aryeh Kaplan writes: "What man partakes of with an object, a woman partakes of with her very body."[123] A woman's body is her *tefilin*!

Let's go deeper. Dr. Steven Schram, a PhD in chemistry, a chiropractor and acupuncturist, has written a fascinating article called: "*Tefillin*: An Ancient Acupuncture Point Prescription for Mental Clarity."[124] Schram points out that when worn properly the leather straps and boxes of the *tefilin* stimulate acupuncture points associated with improved concentration and inspiration. For example, the straps hit the point called "Heart 7" under the pinkie on the side of the wrist—a point used in Chinese medicine to treat every psychiatric disease. The spot on the nape of the neck, where the knot of the head *tefilin* hits, corresponds to acupuncture point "du-16" which "directly stimulates and nourishes the brain."

Schram was not a particularly observant Jew and had not worn *tefilin* since his *Bar Mitzvah* until a friend urged him to try. He went to his rabbi for a refresher course. For a while he would put them on in the morning sitting on his adjustment table. He would then say the *Shema* and meditate. But some time later, at an acupuncture seminar, he had an "aha" moment. He carefully mapped it all out and this became a lead article in the *Journal of Chinese Medicine*.

Kabbalah, as you would expect, takes this even further, telling us that one who wears *tefilin* is, "enveloped by the Supernal Mind, and the Divine Presence does not depart from him." As

Aryeh Kaplan wrote in his book on *tefilin:* "When a man wears *tefilin,* he therefore binds himself to the very highest spiritual level. He achieves a closeness to God that even the deepest meditation could not accomplish...his very thoughts are elevated close to God... But even the physical act in itself can bring man to the loftiest heights."[125]

A man once came to Rabbi Yitzchok Yaakov Weiss, the *Minchat Yitzchak,* with a most unusual *tefilin* question. He had served in the Israeli army. During that time, he had a tattoo put on his left arm. The tattoo—of all things—was of a naked woman. The man later decided to become religious and wanted to start putting on *tefilin.* The question was: Could he put his *tefilin* on his left arm over the tattoo of the naked woman? Or would it be better to put it on his right arm?

The Talmud[126] takes note of an earlier verse[127] that says the *tefilin* should be placed on the arm, *yadcha,* which is spelled in a peculiar way—ending in the additional letter *hey.* The superfluous *hey,* when combined with the *chaf—* the usual ending letter—alludes to the word *keyha,* meaning "weak." This indicates that the *tefilin* must be put on the *yad keyhah,* the weaker arm—the left, for most. Rabbi Weiss ruled the man had no choice but to put his *tefilin* on his left arm, even though it bears the tattoo of a naked woman.

The problem, however, is that a man should not *daven* or say a blessing before a naked woman because this might lead to thoughts inappropriate for the *tefilin* experience. To counter this problem, Rabbi Weiss recommended that the man expose only as much of his arm as is necessary to wrap the *tefilin;* wear the smallest size *tefilin* in order to minimize the contact between the *tefilin* and the tattoo; and when saying the blessing, keep the entire arm covered.[128]

This adds up to a great message. The image of this man wrapping his *tefilin* over a tattoo of a naked woman—while bizarre—demonstrates the power of Torah. Despite how far this man had strayed from a life of Torah, goodness and compassion—as indicated by his tattoo—there was still room for him to return. No matter how far a person wanders, the Torah can still reunite us with Hashem. And *tefilin* can play an important part in returning to God.

How difficult it must be each morning for this former Israeli soldier to wrap his *tefilin* around his arm. But how great is his reward for confronting his past deeds and covering them over with such a *mitzvah*! No matter what that arm had done before, the *tefilin* on that arm is able to elevate him to great heights of connection with God.

Why put on *tefilin*? As the Torah tells us, *l'maan tih'yeh Torat Hashem b'ficha* (so that the Torah of God shall be in your mouth),[129] so that you will be inspired and live an inspired life. Is this not a great way to start the day?

Uch-tavtam al m'zuzot beytecha uvish'arecha (And you shall write them upon the doorposts of your home and upon your gates): This is the *mitzvah* of *mezuzah*. Following the command to love God in the *Shema* are three action commandments. Two—*tefilin* and *mezuzah*—follow immediately in this first paragraph of the *Shema* and are repeated in the second paragraph, and *tzitzit* in the last paragraph of the *Shema*. By surrounding yourself and your home with symbols of God and His Torah, your awareness and closeness to God is enhanced. And so the Talmud[130] declares: "Whosoever has *tefilin* on his head and arm, *tzitzit* on his clothes and a *mezuzah* on his door is assured not to sin."

A *mezuzah* is a small parchment scroll upon which are written the first two paragraphs of the *Shema*. It is placed in a small box[131] and affixed to every doorpost (with exceptions like bathrooms) of one's home on the upper third of the right side of the door as you enter the room. The scroll is written on parchment by a scribe in the manner of writing a Torah. The scroll thus has a great degree of holiness and that holiness is brought into the home. When one kisses the *mezuzah* upon entering one's home and upon leaving, and upon entering and leaving every room—as is customary—one is constantly reminded of the Oneness of God with everything in the world and His unbounding love for us. It literally brings the protective power of the *Shechina* into our homes.

The Talmud, Rabbinic, Chassidic and Kabbalistic literature are filled with stories of the protective power of the *mezuzah*. The most famous comes from the Jerusalem Talmud.[132]

The Parthian King Ardavan (2nd century) sent Rabbi Yehuda Hanasi—the key leader of the Jewish people and author of the Mishnah—a priceless gem, with the request, "Let me have in return an article as valuable as this." So he sent the king a *mezuzah*.

The king became very upset upon receiving the *mezuzah* and sent back word, "I gave you a priceless object, and you return to me something worth but a *folar*?"

Rabbi Yehuda replied, "My desirable things and thy desirable things are not to be compared. You sent me something which I must guard, while I sent you something which guards you while you sleep." The Talmud then tells us that the king personally experienced its power when his daughter became very ill. The *mezuzuah* was affixed to the doorpost of her room and she soon was healed.

Jewish literature is filled with wondrous stories of the protective power of the *mezuzah*. Let me just share a few true modern stories.[133]

The first is about a young boy who complained of severe headaches. His parents took him to several doctors to try to diagnose and cure the problem. Finally an ophthalmologist told them the young boy needed surgery immediately or he would risk losing sight in one eye. The father called his rabbi asking him to say a *Mishebeyrach* healing prayer for his son in the morning when the Torah would be read. The rabbi said, "Of course," but told the father to check his son's *mezuzah* immediately. The father explained he just had all the *mezuzot* in his home checked. (Jewish practice is to check at least twice every seven years.) The rabbi implored him to recheck anyway. The scribe, who the rabbi recommended, examined the *mezuzah* from the son's bedroom and found it had a serious defect that rendered it not kosher. The father replaced the mezuzah the next morning.

Later that day the parents brought their son to the hospital for a final check before surgery. After the examination, the ophthalmologist informed them he saw a small improvement in their son's eye and wanted to delay the surgery for now. After a couple of weeks, the headaches were gone and the eye was completely healed. The doctor was dumbfounded. It was miraculous! I saw a copy of this *mezuzah* and the ones in the stories below. What was the defect in the son's old *mezuzah*? The word *eynecha*, "your eyes," was misspelled! See the illustration below from: http://campsci.com/mezuzah/mzpart1.htm#ACP.

Figure 1: the second word on the last line עיניכם should be עיניך.

Then there is the story of a cute toddler who, at age two, still did not talk. His parents had taken him to several specialists, but to no avail. After his third birthday his parents became more desperate every day. One night the father's rabbi approached him after evening services in the synagogue because the father appeared so distraught. The father poured out his heart telling the rabbi about his son. The rabbi told him that he must check the *mezuzah* on his son's door. Yes, it had a significant defect. The word *v'dibarta* (and you shall speak) was misspelled. Two days after a new *mezuzah* was affixed to the door, the child began to speak!

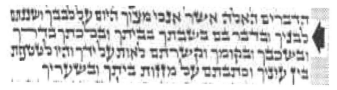

Figure 2: the second word on the second line ‏ובדבר‎ should be ‏ודברת‎.

The next story is about a man who had suffered two mild heart attacks. He had given his *mezuzot* to be checked after each attack, but no problem was found. After his cardiologist told him he was in danger of a third heart attack, someone suggested that the man send his *mezuzot* to be checked with the new computerized scan. He did and the word *l'vavchem* (your heart) was found to have a small, but significant defect. I have personally heard many stories of people with heart conditions who went to the previous Lubavitcher Rebbe and after he advised them to check their *mezuzot* such defects in the word for "heart" were found. They immediately replaced the *mezuzah* and their medical problems were diminished.

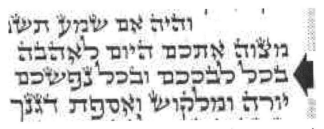

Figure 3: the second word on the third line לבככם should be לבבכם.

My last story is about a young man who was taken in by a cult. The parents sought the advice of a famous Kabbalist who told them to check the *mezuzah* on the doorpost of his room. A defect in the word *echad,* which speaks about the Oneness of God was found. The last letter of the word *echad,* the *dalet,* ד, had the upper right-hand corner chipped off so it looked like the letter *reysh,* ר. The reading of the word *echad,* אֶחָד, was then changed to read *acheyr,* אַחֵר, which indicates another god. Not long after replacing the *mezuzah* with a kosher one, the young man returned to his family and to his Jewish studies.

The *V'ahavta* paragraph of the *Shema* opens with the commandment to love God. Showing our love of God by following the commandments—especially those that follow, like teaching your children, *tefilin* and *mezuzah*—evokes a loving response from God as He then showers us with His protecting love.

Keeping Me On Track:
What's My Reward

The theme of the second paragraph of the *Shema* is a plea to keep our relationship with God strong through following His commandments—commandments given to us out of God's great love for us. The Talmud[134] teaches that this paragraph comes after the first paragraph of the *Shema* because we must first accept the *ol malcut Shamayim*, literally, "the yoke of the reign of Heaven," before we can accept the *ol mitzvot* (the yoke of the commandments). We must first come to a belief and a relationship with God before we can appreciate the gift of His commandments and how these give meaning and dimension to our lives.

וְהָיָה אִם שָׁמֹעַ תִּשְׁמְעוּ אֶל מִצְוֹתַי אֲשֶׁר אָנֹכִי מְצַוֶּה אֶתְכֶם
הַיּוֹם לְאַהֲבָה אֶת יְיָ אֱלֹהֵיכֶם וּלְעָבְדוֹ בְּכָל לְבַבְכֶם וּבְכָל
נַפְשְׁכֶם: וְנָתַתִּי מְטַר אַרְצְכֶם בְּעִתּוֹ יוֹרֶה וּמַלְקוֹשׁ וְאָסַפְתָּ דְגָנֶךָ
וְתִירֹשְׁךָ וְיִצְהָרֶךָ: וְנָתַתִּי עֵשֶׂב בְּשָׂדְךָ לִבְהֶמְתֶּךָ וְאָכַלְתָּ וְשָׂבָעְתָּ:
הִשָּׁמְרוּ לָכֶם פֶּן יִפְתֶּה לְבַבְכֶם וְסַרְתֶּם וַעֲבַדְתֶּם אֱלֹהִים אֲחֵרִים
וְהִשְׁתַּחֲוִיתֶם לָהֶם: וְחָרָה אַף יְיָ בָּכֶם וְעָצַר אֶת הַשָּׁמַיִם וְלֹא יִהְיֶה
מָטָר וְהָאֲדָמָה לֹא תִתֵּן אֶת יְבוּלָהּ וַאֲבַדְתֶּם מְהֵרָה מֵעַל הָאָרֶץ
הַטֹּבָה אֲשֶׁר יְיָ נֹתֵן לָכֶם: וְשַׂמְתֶּם אֶת דְּבָרַי אֵלֶּה עַל לְבַבְכֶם
וְעַל נַפְשְׁכֶם וּקְשַׁרְתֶּם אֹתָם לְאוֹת עַל יֶדְכֶם וְהָיוּ לְטוֹטָפֹת בֵּין
עֵינֵיכֶם: וְלִמַּדְתֶּם אֹתָם אֶת בְּנֵיכֶם לְדַבֵּר בָּם בְּשִׁבְתְּךָ בְּבֵיתֶךָ
וּבְלֶכְתְּךָ בַדֶּרֶךְ וּבְשָׁכְבְּךָ וּבְקוּמֶךָ: וּכְתַבְתָּם עַל מְזוּזוֹת בֵּיתֶךָ
וּבִשְׁעָרֶיךָ: לְמַעַן יִרְבּוּ יְמֵיכֶם וִימֵי בְנֵיכֶם עַל הָאֲדָמָה אֲשֶׁר נִשְׁבַּע
יְיָ לַאֲבֹתֵיכֶם לָתֵת לָהֶם כִּימֵי הַשָּׁמַיִם עַל הָאָרֶץ:

"And it shall come to pass that if you will diligently
listen to My commandments which I command you
today to love Hashem your God and to worship Him
with all your heart and with all your soul, then I will
give rain for your land in its season—the autumn rain
and the spring rain—that you may gather in your grain,
your wine and your oil. And I will give grass in your
fields for your cattle and you shall eat and be satisfied.
Guard yourselves lest your hearts be seduced and you
turn and worship other gods and bow down to them.
Then the anger of God will flare against you and the
heavens will shut so that there will be no rain and the
land will not yield its produce and you will quickly perish from off the good land that Hashem has given you.
Therefore, place these, My words, on your hearts and
on your souls. You shall bind them for a sign upon your
hands and they shall be *tefilin* between your eyes. And
you shall teach them to your children, to speak to them
when you sit in your home, when you travel on the way
and when you lie down and when you rise up. And you
shall write them upon the doorposts of your homes
and upon its gates, so that your days may be multiplied
and the days of your children on the land that Hashem swore to your fathers to give to them as long as the
heavens are above the earth."[135]

*V'HAYA IM SHAMO-A TISHM'U EL MITZVOTAI ASHER ANOCHI
M'TZAVEH ETCHEM HAYOM* (And it shall come to pass if you diligently listen to My commandments that I command you today):
The use of the word "listen" implies that the commandments have
a message for us to hear. The first obvious message is that these are
mitzvotai (My [God's] commandments). One should not observe
God's commandments merely out of nostalgia for family customs
or because one is influenced by a compelling logical explanation
of how a particular commandment will better one's life. One

should observe God's commandments—as the following words of the verse indicate—*L'AHAVA ET HASHEM ELOHEYCHEM*, (out of love of Hashem your God.) And this love should lead us to trust that God, as the ultimate Super Parent, loves us completely and has only our best interests in mind. So if God tells us to do something and, after considering all that He has done and does for us, how can we not come to the conclusion that it is in our best interests to listen?

HAYOM (today): Rashi, in an exquisite comment similar to the one he made on the word *hayom*/today in the first paragraph, tells us "that the commandments should be as new to you as though you heard them this day." In other words, observe God's commandments with enthusiasm as if you just heard God tell them to you. Prayer, as we will soon learn, needs *kavana* (focus and intention) to be truly effective, but so does the observance of every *mitzvah*. When we do a *mitzvah* with enthusiasm, focus and intention, two essential things happen: The *mitzvah* experience is heightened as our relationship with God is strengthened, and our children, family and community who see our enthusiasm in the observance of God's commandments will in turn be encouraged to be enthusiastic in their observance as well. Enthusiasm is contagious.

UL'AVDO B'CHOL L'VAVCHEM UV'CHOL NAFSH'CHEM (And to worship Him with all your heart and with all your soul): This is similar to the first paragraph of the *Shema* where we are told, "And you shall love Hashem your God with all your heart, and with all your soul." The difference here is this second paragraph of the *Shema* is written in the plural form. So when God here tells us "to worship Him with all your heart and with all your soul," He is then telling us that beyond the personal service of the heart, God wants us to gather with others to worship Him.

In the communal prayer of the collective heart and soul, our prayer experience can soar as the power of each soul lifts the other.[136] The Midrash[137] further states: *T'filatan shel Tzibur eyna chozeret l'olam reykam* (The prayers of a congregation are never returned empty).

V'NATATI M'TAR ARTZ'CHEM B'ITO YOREH UMALKOSH, V'ASAFTA D'GANECHA V'TIROSHCHA V'YITZ-HARECHA (Then I will give rain for your land in its season, the autumn and spring rains, so that you may gather in your grain, your wine and your oil): The verses in the Torah preceding this second paragraph of the *Shema* speak about the unique relationship between rain, the Land of Israel and the people of Israel. It tells us how the Land of Israel is not like the land of Egypt which could be watered by kicking the earth with one's foot against the banks of the Nile River, allowing the waters to flow into the fields. The Land of Israel is a land where "the rain from Heaven you shall drink," and "the eyes of God are always upon it." [138] In other words, if the people of Israel want water for their land—if they want to be blessed with prosperity—they have to look to Heaven and earn it with the fulfillment of God's commandments and their prayers.

Note the usage of the term *m'tar* for rain instead of the more commonly used word *geshem*. The Malbim, in his commentary[139] suggests the term *geshem* denotes the natural process of rain in the physical world—the process of evaporation forming rain clouds. The word *gashmi-ut*, similarly, denotes physicality and materialism, while *m'tar* is something that transcends the natural processes and is a gift from God. Rain, therefore, in this passage is a metaphor for the gifts from God that we need, gifts we ask Him to shower upon us. The verse, therefore, switches from the plural in the word *artz'chem* (your land) to the singular in the words *d'ganecha v'tiroshcha v'yitz-harecha* (your grain, your wine and your oil) to emphasize that although the blessings of rain will be showered upon the land and its people, each individual will benefit.

V'NATATI EYSEV B'SADCHA LIVHEMTECHA, V'ACHALTA V'SAVATA. (And I will give grass in your fields for your cattle and you shall eat and be satisfied.): Judaism teaches we must be sensitive to animals and hence the prohibition[140] of *tzaar baaley chayim*, of causing undue pain to any animal. The Torah, therefore, commands us to send the mother bird away before taking her eggs or chicks from the nest and not to muzzle an ox in his threshing.[141] And the Talmud learns from the above verse that you must feed your animals first and then you can eat.[142]

HISHAMRU LACHEM PEN YIFTEH L'VAVCHEM V'SARTEM VAA-VAD'TEM ELOHIM ACHEYRIM V'HISHTACHAVITEM LAHEM (Guard yourselves lest your hearts be seduced and you turn and worship other gods and bow down to them): One cannot help but notice how the warning, "Guard yourselves," follows the words, "you shall eat and be satisfied." It is because when one is satisfied and prosperous there is the human tendency to forget God and even others who helped you get there. So be careful and do not let your heart be seduced away from God and turn to other gods. It is hard for the modern mind to comprehend how luring the seduction of idolatry was in the Biblical world. It was fun, especially the fertility rites filled with seductive music—not unlike today's rock concerts—and with great pageantry and drunken orgies. After mentioning this in one of my lectures, a congregant jokingly said it sounds like I'm talking about spring break from many American colleges. Be careful, the Torah warns us, this will only bring you down and stain your holy soul. In today's world, we are subjected to the lure of cults, drugs and a culture of hedonism. This can all be very seductive. So be careful, this passage in the *Shema* warns us; it is just not worth it!

V'CHARA AF HASHEM BACHEM V'ATZAR ET HASHAMAYIM V'LO YI-H'YEH MATAR V'HA-ADAMA LO TITEYN ET Y'VULA VA-AVAD'TEM M'HEYRA MEYAL HAARETZ HATOVA ASHER HASHEM NOTEYN LACHEM. (Then the anger of God will flare against you and the heavens will shut so that there will be no rain and the land will not yield its produce and you will quickly perish from off the good land that Hashem has given you): What does it mean when the Torah tells us that "the anger of God will flare"? God does not have human emotions. Does God really get angry?

Actions have consequences, and the Torah is trying to drive this point home. It is true that God does not get angry in the same way we do, but one of the consequences of distancing ourselves from God is that God may correspondingly distance Himself from us. I once saw a billboard sponsored by a dental association that read, "Ignore your teeth and they'll go away!" If we ignore God, we face the real possibility He would ignore us and go away—i.e. no longer protect us as He had previously. Then we would be much more vulnerable to life's challenges. This is what the Torah calls a *hesteyr panim* (a hiding of God's face). [143]

This second paragraph of the *Shema* seems like a classical example of reward and punishment. But reward and punishment are not such simple concepts in Jewish thought. Upon first reading this passage it would seem that if one is faithful and religiously follows God's commandments, then one will be amply rewarded. And if one ignores God's commandments, one will have a hard and difficult life. Does this mean that one who scrupulously follows all the *mitzvot* will not get cancer? Clearly we have seen truly pious people suffer great illness. Clearly there were very devout people who were slaughtered in Hitler's ovens. Does this also mean there are no evil rich people in this world? Clearly this passage must have another meaning.

Who is the Torah addressing in this second paragraph of the *Shema*? Let us examine the opening words again: *V'haya im shamo-a tishm'u* (And it shall come to pass that if you will diligently listen). The word *tishm'u* (listen) is written in the plural, as is most of this paragraph, signifying it is not the individual who is being addressed, but the whole people of Israel. In other words, if the Jewish people will obey God's commandments, they will be rewarded; the rains will fall as needed and the land will respond yielding its produce. It is a collective reward for the Jewish people as a whole and not necessarily for any individual. For a more thorough discussion of the issue of the suffering of individuals, see *The Amidah* Supplement, Part 1: *Gevurot*.

V'SAMTEM ET D'VARAI EYLEH AL L'VAVCHEM V'AL NAFSH'CHEM UK'SHARTEM OTAM L'OT AL YEDCHEM V'HAYU L'TOTAFOT BEYN EYNEYCHEM. V'LIMADTEM OTAM ET B'NEYCHEM, L'DABEYR BAM B'SHIVTECHA B'VEYTECHA, UVLECHT'CHA VADERECH, UV'SHACHB'CHA UVKUMECHA. UCH'TAVTAM AL M'ZUZOT BEYTE-CHA UVISH'ARECHA (Therefore, place these, My words, on your hearts and on your souls. You shall bind them for a sign upon your hands and they shall be *tefilin* between your eyes. And you shall teach them to your children, to speak to them when you sit in your home, when you travel on the way and when you lie down and when you rise up. And you shall write them upon the doorposts of your homes and upon its gates): The theme of this second paragraph of the *Shema*, as we have learned, is a plea to keep our relationship with God strong by following His commandments. God uses different approaches to motivate us. First there is the promise of blessing if we obey and the threat of punishment—a hiding of God's face—if we reject God.

Then God throws in three commandments, which if observed will help us remember to do the right thing. The first is teaching our children Torah. If you teach your children in a way that really gets to them, you cannot be unaffected by the process yourself. You will grow through the teaching as they grow through the learning. It should be noted that "teaching your children" in this verse is in the plural, telling us we all share the responsibility of supporting communal Jewish education. The second commandment is the daily use of *tefilin,* which has scrolls of Torah inside and physically binds us to God. And the third is the *mezuzah* which reminds us of our relationship with God as we enter and leave our homes and every room within, day and night.

L'MAAN YIRBU Y'MEYCHEM VIMEY V'NEYCHEM AL HAADAMA ASHER NISHBA HASHEM LA-AVOTEYCHEM LATEYT LAHEM KIMEY HA-SHAMAYIM AL HAARETZ (So that your days may be multiplied and the days of your children on the land that Hashem swore to your fathers to give to them as long as the heavens are above the earth): This is the ultimate reward—that the people of Israel will fulfill their destiny and be God's people—i.e. the people of Israel observing the Torah of Israel in the Land of Israel. This verse is similar to the fifth commandment, "Honor your father and your mother," in that both offer the reward, "your days may be lengthened on the land that Hashem your God gave to you."[144] Just as honoring your parents lengthens ones days, how much more so does honoring the Ultimate Parent—God?

The Talmud[145] points out that this verse does not say, "on the land that Hashem swore to your fathers to give to *you*," but, "to give to *them*"—i.e. "your fathers." The Talmud, therefore, maintains this is the source for the Resurrection of the Dead in the Torah—that our fathers, Abraham, Isaac and Jacob, will live again on the land they did not get to fully see or enjoy in their lifetimes. For a more detailed discussion of Resurrection of the Dead, see The *Amidah* Supplement, Part 1: *Gevurot*.

Let me add a closing thought on the phrase, *L'maan yirbu y'meychem* (So that your days may be multiplied). The word *yirbu* (multiplied) also means "expanded" or "made greater." In addition to the promise to the people of Israel that being faithful to God will multiply their days on the Land of Israel, perhaps there lies a message here for all of us—even those of us who do not live in the Land of Israel. Perhaps this phrase also contains the meaning "So that your days may be expanded or made greater." The message, therefore, for all of us is that in the very process of being faithful to God and following His commandments, our personal lives are expanded and made greater—even if they are not actually made longer!

Tzitzit: Tie a String Around Your Finger

lthough the first two paragraphs of the *Shema* follow the same sequence appearing in the Torah—both from the book of Deuteronomy—this final paragraph of the *Shema* is out of sequence and actually appears earlier, in the book of Numbers. Nevertheless, it is placed last because its content, according to the Talmud,[146] contains five basic ideas of Judaism that beautifully connect it with the first two paragraphs and forms a fitting completion of the *Shema* as a statement of our faith.

וַיֹּאמֶר יְיָ אֶל מֹשֶׁה לֵּאמֹר: דַּבֵּר אֶל בְּנֵי יִשְׂרָאֵל וְאָמַרְתָּ אֲלֵהֶם
וְעָשׂוּ לָהֶם צִיצִת עַל כַּנְפֵי בִגְדֵיהֶם לְדֹרֹתָם וְנָתְנוּ עַל צִיצִת הַכָּנָף
פְּתִיל תְּכֵלֶת: וְהָיָה לָכֶם לְצִיצִת וּרְאִיתֶם אֹתוֹ וּזְכַרְתֶּם אֶת כָּל
מִצְוֹת יְיָ וַעֲשִׂיתֶם אֹתָם וְלֹא תָתוּרוּ אַחֲרֵי לְבַבְכֶם וְאַחֲרֵי עֵינֵיכֶם
אֲשֶׁר אַתֶּם זֹנִים אַחֲרֵיהֶם: לְמַעַן תִּזְכְּרוּ וַעֲשִׂיתֶם אֶת כָּל מִצְוֹתָי
וִהְיִיתֶם קְדֹשִׁים לֵאלֹהֵיכֶם: אֲנִי יְיָ אֱלֹהֵיכֶם אֲשֶׁר הוֹצֵאתִי אֶתְכֶם
מֵאֶרֶץ מִצְרַיִם לִהְיוֹת לָכֶם לֵאלֹהִים אֲנִי יְיָ אֱלֹהֵיכֶם:

"And Hashem said to Moses to say: Speak to the Children of Israel, and say unto them, they shall make for themselves *tzitzit* on the corners of their garments, for all generations; and they shall put on the *tzitzit* of each corner a thread of blue. And it shall be for you *tzitzit* that when you look upon it, you shall remember all the commandments of Hashem and do them; and you shall not follow after your hearts and your eyes, after which you stray. So that you shall remember and do all My commandments, and you shall be holy onto your God. I am Hashem your God, Who took you out from the land of Egypt to be your God; I am Hashem your God."[147]

VA-YOMEYR HASHEM EL MOSHE LEYMOR: DABEYR EL B'NEY YIS-RAEL, V'AMARTA ALEYHEM, V'ASU LAHEM TZITZIT (And Hashem said to Moses to say: Speak to the Children of Israel, and say unto them, they shall make for themselves *tzitzit*.): What are *tzitzit*? According to Rashi on this verse, they are "strings that hang," for anything that hangs from the body like a lock of hair is call a *tzitz*—and *tzitzit* hang from the clothes on the body. In addition, Rashi tells us these fringes are called *tzitzit* from the root word *tzitz*, meaning "something to look at," telling us their function is to be looked at. Similarly, the headplate of the High Priest's turban worn for all to see in the Temple with its message "Holy to Hashem" is called a *tzitz*.

AL KANFEY VIGDEYHEM L'DOROTAM (on the corners of their garments, for all generations): Human beings wear clothes—animals do not. Covering your body with clothes de-emphasizes your animal nature and reaffirms that the real you is not your body but your eternal soul. Clothing is very personal for most people because what is worn says something about them. This is why policemen and firemen wear special uniforms and doctors and nurses have special attire. When they wear these special clothes, they are identified in a special way, but it is not much different with the clothes most of us wear. One can dress simply or ostentatiously. One can wear different clothes for leisure, for work, for coming to the synagogue on Shabbat or for a wedding.

Jews dress in special ways. Each Chassidic sect has its unique way of dressing. Today's yeshiva world generally dresses in white shirts and black pants or black suits with their *tzitzit* hanging out for all to see. Everyone agrees that a Jew should dress in a way that reflects modesty and not in a suggestive manner—for he is created in the image of God. When a Jew wears *tzitzit* on his body, he literally wears holiness—helping to fulfill the injunction two verses later, *vih'yitem kedoshim lEyloheychem* (you shall be holy onto your God).

The Torah teaches that *tzitzit* are to be put on garments of four corners.[148] But what if one does not typically wear a garment with four corners like a cloak or a poncho? Technically, one then does not have to wear *tzitzit*. However, since the verse also contains the word *l'dorotam* (for all generations), the Jewish people have accepted upon themselves the strong custom for all generations of wearing *tzitzit* nevertheless, and this is why a Jew dons a *tallit* every morning before he prays. Most people who wear *tzitzit* the rest of the day wear a simple four-cornered garment under their shirt called a *tallit katan*, (a little *tallit*) or *arba kanfot* (four corners). Some wear these with the fringes hanging out and some tuck them in. There are Jews—Chasidim generally fall into this category—who wear such a garment on top of their shirt so that it is visible.

EXERCISE: "IT'S A WRAP"   When one wraps himself in a *tallit*, with its holy coded strings, knots and windings, in preparation for prayer, if one wraps himself with proper focus, one can actually feel its holiness and the Presence of God wrapped around him. Are you skeptical? Try the following exercise:

> Take your *tallit* in your hands and recite the blessing: *Baruch Ata Adonai, Eloheynu Melech ha-olam, asher kid'shanu b'mitzvotav v'tzivanu l'hitateyf batzitzit* (Blessed are You, Hashem our God, King of the universe, Who has sanctified us with His commandments and commanded us to wrap ourselves in *tzitzit*).

Now take the holy, coded *tallit*, and with your hands
held high holding the *talit*, wrap it around your body, especially covering your head. Feel yourself surrounded in holiness. Close your eyes for at least ten seconds and scream
Rebbe Nachman's silent scream. Without making a sound,
tense all the muscles of your body with a silent scream
from the depths of your heart and soul—a scream that
expresses all the frustrations you are facing on your path
in life and all your hopes for redemption. Hold that tensed
scream for about ten seconds and then let go, allowing your
hands to return to a normal posture and your *tallit* to fall
into its proper place on your body. Notice how you feel.
Most probably your body will tingle from the experience
because you have felt the holiness and the Presence of God
wrapped around you, and you feel that God has heard your
frustrations and hopes—even without saying a word. It is a
prayer without words that connects you to God before you
begin to pray. If you are a woman and therefor do not wear
a *tallit* for prayer, you can modify the exercise before you
pray by simply closing your eyes while you tense your body
for the silent scream.

V'NATNU AL TZITZIT HAKANAF P'TIL T'CHEYLET (And they shall
put on the *tzitzit* of each corner a thread of blue.): The *tzitzit*
fringes are made from four strands of wool[149] folded over after
being threaded through a hole in the corner of a garment to form
eight strands. One strand is longer than the others so that coded
windings an knots can be made in the *tzitzit*. According to this
verse, this larger strand should be "a thread of blue."

So how is it that most *tzitzit* today are completely white? It
is because the blue color came from a special dye made from the
chilazon snail[150] whose identity was lost. There have been attempts
in our time to rediscover the identity of the *chilazon* snail. In the
late 19th century the Radziner Rebbe thought it came from the
Sepia Officinalis or cuttlefish. Today, the prevailing opinion is

that it is from the Murex Trunculus snail because archeologists have discovered remnants of several dye making factories along the Mediterranean coastline in Israel with piles of shells of this species. Why is a "thread of blue" important? The Talmud[151] tells us it is because "blue resembles the sea, and the sea resembles the heaven and heaven resembles the Throne of Glory." In other words, the blue color on the *tzitzit* is to get us to focus our thoughts on God in heaven.

Question: Why not make all the strands blue? Because the Torah does not want us to be so immersed in thoughts of God that we not live in this world. There is one thread of blue tied around the other seven[152] so that the seven days of the week are intertwined with the concept of holiness. Looking at the one blue strand among the seven white ones as the next verse commands, one should be inspired to take that which the blue represents—the holiness of God—and bring it into the everyday.[153]

THE FLAG OF ISRAEL   David Wolffsohn, a banker from Lithuania, who succeeded Theodore Herzl as president of the World Zionist Organization, records in a jubilee volume celebrating the 25th anniversary of the First Zionist Congress, that during the first Zionist Congress it was unanimously decided the Israeli flag be blue and white, the same colors as the *tzitzit*. He writes, "We already have a flag, white and blue—the *tallit* …. This *tallit* is our symbol. Let us take the *tallit* out from its case and unfurl it before the eyes of Israel and before the eyes of all the nations."

V'HAYA LACHEM L'TZITZIT UR'ITEM OTO UZCHARTEM ET KOL MITZVOT HASHEM VA-ASITEM OTAM (And it shall be for you *tzitzit* that when you look upon it, you shall remember all the commandments of Hashem and do them): If the function of *tzitzit* is to be looked at, what are we supposed to learn from looking at them? *Tzitzit*, like *tefilin* and *mezuzah*, is a *mitzvah* given to us by God to help us—as we live in a world filled with distractions—to not lose sight of Him. But the Torah tells us that *tzitzit* go even further and help us to remember all the other *mitzvot*. How? By means of an elaborate code of knots and windings. When the four strands are placed through the hole in a corner of a garment to make *tzitzit*, each side of the four strands is tied together to form two knots, and then seven windings are made with the larger strand on the remaining seven strands, another two knots and eight windings, another two knots and eleven windings, another two knots and thirteen windings and then a final two knots.

The first three sets of windings—seven, eight and eleven— add up to 26, which is the *gematria* (the numerical equivalent of the letters) of the Name of Hashem (ה-ו-ה-י = *yud* + *hey* + *vav* + *hey*, 10 + 5 + 6 + 5 = 26). The last set of windings is 13, which is the *gematria* of the word *echad*, "one" (אֶחָד = *alef* + *chet* + *dalet*, 1 + 8 + 4 = 13). The Sephardic custom is to wind ten, five, six and five with a total of 26—the *gematria* of Hashem's Name. Thus the windings, like *tefilin* and *mezuzah*, help us to be mindful there is a God in this world and He is One.

TIE A STRING AROUND YOUR FINGER   Do you remember this piece of advice your parents or a friend told you when you were a child and needed to remember something? *Tzitzit*, in a sense, serve this purpose. Rashi[154] points out that the word *tzitzit* in its full form has a *gematria* of 600 (צִיצִת = *tzadi* + *yud* + *tzadi* + *yud* + *taf*, 90 + 10 + 90 +10 + 400 = 600). If you add this six hundred to the eight strands on each of the *tzitzit* (four doubled by folding them over from the hole on each corner) as well as its five sets of knots (separating the windings) it gives us a total of 613 which is the number of the commandments in the Torah. And so the Talmud[155] teaches that the observance of this *mitzvah* is so important it is "equal to all the other *mitzvot* combined."

So when we gaze upon the *tzitzit*, as this verse commands us and see the *tzitzit* with its strands and knots, we should remember all the 613 commandments of God. But it is not enough just to remember the commandments. Our verse demands: "you shall remember all the commandments of Hashem *and do them.*" It is not sufficient to nostalgically recall the observances of Jewish life and be a Jew at heart. To have a meaningful relationship with God one must act like a Jew.

On a deeper level, the Talmud[156] takes note of the word *oto* (it) in the above phrase, "when you look upon it." The simple meaning is that "it" refers to the *tzitzit.* However, *oto* is in the singular form. So the Talmud suggests, based on another verse with the similar usage,[157] that *oto* can also mean "Him", and therefore, here it can refer to God. This suggests that when we act like a Jew and we follow the commandments of God with enthusiasm and focus, we can rise to a level of experiencing God akin to "seeing Him"—to the extent this is humanly possible.

There is a beautiful custom universally followed that requires more than just gazing upon the *tzitzit* as we recite the *Shema.* The practice is that every time we recite the word *tzitzit* in this passage, we kiss the *tzitzit* we have previously gathered in our hands in preparation for reciting the *Shema.* It is a custom that demonstrates—in a demonstratively emotional way—our love for the infinite God and His gift to us of 613 commandments.

V'LO TATURU ACHAREY L'VAVCHEM V'ACHAREY EYNEYCHEM ASHER ATEM ZONIM ACHAREYHEM. (And you shall not follow after your hearts and your eyes, after which you stray.): It is interesting that the Ibn Ezra[158] suggests it is more important to wear *tzitzit* during the rest of the day than during the time of prayer so that the *tzitzit* help us refrain from sin.

Clearly, *tzitzit* is considered by our tradition as an important tool in avoiding sin. The Talmud[159] has a great story beautifully illustrating this.

There was once a man who was scrupulous in his observance of the *mitzvah* of tzitzit. However, he was not immune to the temptations of the world. He had heard of a certain prostitute in one of the towns by the sea who was so beautiful and skillful that she charged 400 gold denars for her services. He sent her the money and scheduled a time to be with her. When he was led into her chamber, she was lying on a gold bed fully naked waiting for him. He was so excited and began to remove his clothes, when all of a sudden the fringes of his *tzitzit* flipped up and struck him in the face. He jumped off the bed and sat on the floor. The prostitute was insulted and demanded to know what flaw he saw in her that caused him to do this.

The man explained, "Never have I seen a woman as beautiful as you. But there is a *mitzvah* that God has commanded us called *tzitzit* . . . Now the *tzitzit* appeared before me as four witnesses testifying against me."

The woman demanded that he identify himself and his teacher and the name of the school where he studied Torah. This same woman came to his teacher, Rabbi Chiya, and studied with him for conversion and later married this man. Such is the power of *tzitzit* in preventing sin.

HEAVENLY FLAK JACKETS   During the War in Gaza in 2009, there was a great spiritual hunger among Israeli soldiers—most of whom were from secular backgrounds. Several *minyanim* (prayer groups) were hastily formed in the field and well attended. Before boarding buses into Gaza, a great many soldiers stationed at the border stopped to put on *tefilin* and were handed free *tzitzit* for their prayers. So many went into battle wearing their *tzitzit* that Israeli Army rabbis referred to them as "heavenly flak jackets"! Miraculously, not one of them was killed in battle!

L'MAAN TIZK'RU VA-ASITEM ET KOL MITZVOTAI, V'HIYITEM K'DOSHIM LEYLOHEYCHEM. (So that you shall remember and do all My commandments, and you shall be holy unto your God): What is the purpose of remembering and observing God's commandments? What is the purpose of reciting these passages of the *Shema*? *V'hiyitem k'doshim lEyloheychem* (and you shall be holy unto your God). Each of us is a *neshama*, a holy soul. The *Shema* pleads with us to keep our holy soul one with God and not to stain it by straying from God and His commandments.

ANI HASHEM ELOHEYCHEM ASHER HOTZEYTI ETCHEM MEY-ERETZ MITZRAYIM L'HIYOT LACHEM LEYLOHIM, ANI HASHEM ELOHEY-CHEM (I am Hashem your God, Who took you out from the land of Egypt to be your God; I am Hashem your God): With the recitation of this verse in the morning and evening *Shema*, we fulfill the commandment to remember the departure from Egypt day and night. The Talmud[160] teaches that this *mitzvah* applies at night as well from the extra word "all" in the verse: "So that you will remember the day of your Exodus from the land of Egypt all the days of your life."[161] It is because of the *mitzvah* of remembering the Exodus from Egypt at night that this paragraph is included in the evening *Shema*.

Why is it so important to remember the Exodus from Egypt? First of all, in Egypt we had no choice in how we lived our lives. We were slaves and had to do the bidding of our masters. When God took us out He was telling us a human being is not a slave. A human being must be free to choose his own life.

Also, the Exodus from Egypt is so important to remember because it is a paradigm. The children of Israel became a people in Egypt. They were oppressed and enslaved. It was the first time they, as a people, were in trouble and God came to their rescue. It set the paradigm for the future of Jewish history. The children of Israel cried out to God to save them and He did. He did it then and, hopefully, He will do it again in our time.[162]

The word מִצְרַיִם/*Mitzrayim* (Egypt) comes from the root צַר/*tzar* (narrow). *Mitzrayim* literally means, "narrow places". So this verse can also be understood as, "I am Hashem your God Who took you out from the narrow places to be your God." We all have our "narrow places"—places where we feel so squeezed we do not see how we can make it through. God is telling us, as He did in Egypt, that He will be with us and take us out of the narrow places we find ourselves in. In the meantime we need to hold the words of Rebbe Nachman close to our hearts: *Kol ha-olam kulo gesher tzar m'eod, v'ha-ikar lo l'facheyd klal* (All the world is a very narrow bridge, and the essential thing is not to be afraid at all). So as we recite this passage we might think about our own *Mitzrayim*, our own narrow places, with the hope God will take us out from there as well.

Notice that God introduces Himself twice in this last verse as *Ani Hashem Eloheychem* (I am Hashem your God). *Hashem*, as we pointed out in Chapter 6, "God's Name," denotes the Godly attribute of mercy; and *Elohim*, the attribute of strict justice and nature that can seem cruel. What God is saying to us is, "I can be Hashem to you—kind and sweet—or I can be *Elohim*—which can seem harsh. It is up to you. Your actions have consequences. The last words of the *Shema, Ani Hashem Eloheychem* (I am Hashem your God), form a perfect close to the *Shema* as it reaffirms its beginning, *Shema Yisrael Hashem Eloheynu Hashem Echad* (Listen Israel, Hashem is our God, Hashem is One)! Hashem and *Elohim* are really One *Hashem*, One loving and compassionate God. No wonder the *Shema* in our prayers is always followed by the word *emet* (truth)!

The Amidah: Increase Your Intimacy With God

The *Amidah*, recited soon after the *Shema*, is our opportunity to become intimate with God. With the recitation of the *Shema* we had the opportunity to feel truly one with God. In the *Amidah* we can feel the *Shechina*, the very Presence of God. And, in doing so, we can seize this unique opportunity to pour out our hearts to Him—praising Him, thanking Him and asking for His help in our lives.

The focus of the *Shema* is to become one with God through understanding God's mercy and compassion—i.e., even when God's judgment seems harsh, or when we have trouble understanding why life is so hard, there is a loving and compassionate God behind it all, symbolized by God's main name (Hashem/‎י-‎ה-ו-ה).

The *Amidah* is more specific. The *Amidah* offers a more intimate connection with God through our personal lives. It is our opportunity to *stand* (the *Amidah* literally means "standing") before God and pour out our hearts asking Him to help us in our lives.[163]

HEAVENLY DIALOGUE   The *Amidah* and the *Shema* are the two most important prayers and, taken together, form the core of our liturgy. The *Shema* is composed of three messages from God as recorded in the Torah. Even though we are mouthing the words, these are God's words. So in actuality, God is speaking His message to us, and as the name *Shema* implies, we listen. Our lips, therefore, become God's vehicle to relay His message to us. We mouth the words so we can listen to them.

The *Amidah*, on the other hand, is composed of 19 blessings (originally 18, hence its common name *Shemona Esrey* which means "18")—19 prayers and petitions to God. So when we recite the *Amidah*, it is our turn to speak to God; and if we do so with a sincere heart, God listens.

And so when we recite the Shema God speaks to us, and when we recite the Amidah we speak to God—thus completing a holy dialogue. Perhaps this is why the Talmud refers to the *Amidah* as *"haTefila,"* or "the Prayer." In fact, it is the prayer of prayers—the most extraordinary opportunity to connect with God!

The *Amidah* has a definite and ancient structure created by the Men of the Great Assembly[164] who were the bridge between the last prophets of the Bible and the first rabbis (3rd to 4th century BCE). Great prophets—such as Chaggai, Zechariah and Malachi—wrote some of the blessings of the *Amidah*.[165] The point is, as Arye Kaplan beautifully expresses it,[166] "The same spiritual energy that went into the writing of the Bible went into the writing of the *Amidah*." There is great holiness in every verse, in every word and in every letter. It was written with such potential that everyone—regardless of the circumstances of their lives—can find themselves in these prayers. If you can unpack some of that spiritual energy when you recite the *Amidah*, your prayer experience can be amazingly powerful.[167]

By reciting the *Amidah* with proper *kavana* (focus and intention), you can achieve an intimacy with God you could not ever have imagined; and as your connection with God becomes more and more intense through this spiritual practice, it can actually change your life as your soul experiences significant growth.

Once a congregant asked me, "Rabbi, we recite the same prayers over and over every Shabbat. It's so repetitive, even boring. Can't we substitute some new ones into the service?"

Now this man came to shul regularly, so it was obvious to me he was not being facetious. He was sincerely seeking a more meaningful prayer experience, and so I gently suggested, "Yes, we can add new prayers, but they will most likely become repetitive after awhile as well. What all of us need to understand is that the prayers of the *Siddur* (Jewish prayer book) were precisely formulated—among other things—to be templates through which we bring to God our own personal prayers. This is what *avoda* (worshipping God) is all about. For example, when we recite the prayer in the *Amidah* asking God to heal the sick, each of us should add a personal prayer for those we know who are in need of God's healing. When we say the prayer asking God for prosperity, we should add a personal prayer, not only for our own prosperity, but also for those we know who are in need." This congregant subsequently took a greater interest in learning about Jewish prayer so that praying would be a more effective experience for him.

The problem with our prayer experience is not the prayers we recite, but an inability to understand the great spiritual power the prayers contain and how to access that power.

For this reason the Talmud[168] cautions us: "He who makes his recitation of the *Amidah* a mechanical task, his prayer is not a prayer of heartfelt supplication." And so when we recite the *Amidah*—not in a mechanical way—but with a heart filled with awe and appreciation, adding our personal prayers, the prayer experience becomes not just another religious obligation, but an opportunity to re-energize our souls as we connect with God. And if we do this every morning, it will no doubt, help us face the day ahead. No matter what the challenges the day may bring, we will face these strengthened by the spiritual connection we made earlier—a connection that stays with us throughout the day. If we recite the *Amidah* three times a day as prescribed by our tradition, we will make such a strong connection with God that we will never feel alone!

It is like a young child who goes to a park with his mother.

The child wants to climb the monkey bars, slide down the slide and play with the other children. He feels comfortable doing all this, even wandering into a field by himself, as long as he can still see his mother. He can go far because as long as he knows mother is watching, he knows he is okay. We are the children of God. As long as we can feel that our Ultimate Parent—God—is with us, watching us as we face the trials of life, we know we will be okay. There is no better way of achieving that spiritual level, of being able to carry that feeling with you always, than by reciting the *Amidah* three times each day with *kavana!* But even if you only do this once a day, you still will find its effects transforming.

Maimonides writes:[169] "Any prayer that is not recited with *kavana* is not prayer. If one prays without *kavana*, one must repeat his prayers with *kavana*." In the Talmud[170] we are told: "Rabbi Yochanan said: 'I saw Rabbi Yannai pray and then pray again.' As Rabbi Yirmiyah said to Rabbi Zeira: "Perhaps originally he did not have *kavana*." If Rabbi Yanai of the ancient Talmud had trouble concentrating on his prayers, what should we say today about ourselves? We live in a world of constant distractions including televisions, computers, Smartphones, IPads and tablets where we email, text, tweet, Facebook, etc. throughout the day.

"Okay," you may say, "I'll pray. Just tell me how." First, if you are unfamiliar with it, you must commit yourself to study and learn the *Amidah*.

I suggest you begin with the first blessing which, according to the Talmud,[171] is so crucial it must be recited with *kavana*, even if you cannot sustain that intense concentration for the whole *Amidah*. The first blessing is called *Avot* (Fathers) because it calls upon God's close relationship with our Forefathers to advocate on our behalf in our prayers to God. It is your opening, your door to God for your personal prayers. So take hold of it, open it, and feel your heart and soul expand as you draw closer to God.

This blessing is so essential it always begins the *Amidah*, whether it is the weekday *Amidah* or a special Sabbath or festival *Amidah*. The *Avot* blessing is only 42 words and can be readily learned by heart, even if you are not fluent in Hebrew and need to use transliteration. Reciting this in Hebrew is important in order to access the full power of the prayer, so try to learn it, even if you do not read Hebrew yet. Here is the Hebrew text followed by a transliteration and translation:

בָּרוּךְ אַתָּה יי אֱלֹהֵינוּ וֵאלֹהֵי אֲבוֹתֵינוּ. אֱלֹהֵי אַבְרָהָם. אֱלֹהֵי
יִצְחָק. וֵאלֹהֵי יַעֲקֹב. הָאֵל הַגָּדוֹל הַגִּבּוֹר וְהַנּוֹרָא אֵל עֶלְיוֹן. גּוֹמֵל
חֲסָדִים טוֹבִים. וְקוֹנֵה הַכֹּל. וְזוֹכֵר חַסְדֵי אָבוֹת. וּמֵבִיא גוֹאֵל
לִבְנֵי בְנֵיהֶם לְמַעַן שְׁמוֹ בְּאַהֲבָה: מֶלֶךְ עוֹזֵר וּמוֹשִׁיעַ וּמָגֵן: בָּרוּךְ
אַתָּה יי, מָגֵן אַבְרָהָם:

Baruch Ata Adonai, Eloheynu vEylohey Avoteynu, Elo-
hey Avraham, Elohey Yitzchak, Veylohey Yaakov; Ha-
Eyl hagadol hagibor v'hanora Eyl Elyon; gomeyl chasad-
im tovim, v'koney hakol, v'zocheyr chasdey avot, umeyvi
go-eyl livney v'neyhem l'ma-an sh'mo b'ahava. Melech
ozeyr umoshi-a umageyn. Baruch Ata Adonai, Mageyn
Avraham.

"Blessed are You Hashem, our God, and God of our fathers; the God of Abraham, the God of Isaac and the God of Jacob; the great, the mighty and the awesome God, God the most High; Who does beneficial acts of kindness, and is the owner of all things; who remembers the kindness of the fathers, and will bring a redeemer to their children's children for the sake of His Name, with love. He is King, Helper, Savior and Shield. Blessed are You Hashem, the Shield of Abraham."

If the task of memorizing or fluently reading this paragraph becomes difficult, then at least memorize the four words of increasing intimacy as presented in Chapter 15. In Chapter 14 we will unpack some of the power of this *beracha*, but first we must deal with a unique problem in the creation of prayer.

CHAPTER 12

Too Awesome For Praises

How do we describe God?
The sages were immediately confronted with a crucial problem in creating this first blessing of the *Amidah*—a fundamental problem for the creation of prayer in general. The problem is how to describe God.

The answer to this question has determined the content and structure of Jewish prayer, to a great extent.[172] And it all centers around a famous verse from the Torah that is included in our prayers: *Mi chamocha ba-eylim Hashem; mi kamocha ne'edar ba-kodesh; norah t'hilot, osey feleh* (Who is like You, Hashem, among the powers of the world; who is like You, glorious in holiness, too awesome for praises, doing wonders?) This verse comes from the *Shirat HaYam*, "The Song of the Sea," which Moses and the Children of Israel sang[173] after crossing the Red Sea.

The song begins: *Ashira la-Hashem ki ga-o ga-a*, which is usually translated as, "I shall sing to Hashem, for He is highly exalted." The word *ga-o*, however, literally means "higher." The doubling of the word to *ga-o ga-a* would then mean "higher than high." We have heard of cleaner than clean and brighter than bright (in commercials for Mr. Clean). How about higher than high?

Rashi comments: *Ki ga-o ga-a al kol hashirot* (For He is exalted beyond all praise) *v'al kol ma sheh-akaleys Bo* (and all that we may laud on Him) *od yeysh Bo tosefet* (there is still more to be added about Him). In other words, *ki ga-o ga-a* then means, "for He [God] is higher than high, beyond anything we can say about Him."

If this is the case, is it permitted to compose prayers of praise to God? The answer may surprise you. Let me explain with a story from the Talmud[174] about a student who was leading the prayer service, and in the first blessing of the repetition of the *Amidah* after the words of praise *Ha-Eyl hagadol hagibor v'hanorah* (the great, mighty and awesome God), he added, "the glorious, the potent, the feared, the strong, the powerful, the sure and the honored God." His teacher, Rabbi Chanina, waited until he had finished the *Amidah* and then admonished him, asking: "Did you complete all the praises of your Master?"

What was it that had so upset Rabbi Chanina? The Talmud explains with a parable about a king that had many thousands of gold dinars and was insulted by someone praising him for having silver dinars. He should have mentioned the king's gold dinars which are much more valuable and, therefore, more praiseworthy. But let me give you a more contemporary illustration. If a young man wanted to arrange a blind date for a friend, the friend would probably ask, "What is she like?" If the response was, "Well, she has a good personality," the friend might make the assumption she is probably not very attractive because if she was attractive this would have been mentioned. Suppose he was told three more things about her, such as she has a good personality, her father has money, and she goes to a certain school. What she looks like still would be a mystery. The omission is in itself a statement.

What the Talmud is saying is we dare not reduce the qualities of the Infinite God to a few adjectives. But if praise is one of the three major categories of prayer, how can Jewish prayer ever offer prayers praising God? The Talmud is teaching us here that there must be more of a limitation on prayers of praise than petition or thanksgiving. We can request what we need, and we certainly should thank God and show appreciation for what He has given us, but prayers of praise are generally forbidden because, as Rabbi Chanina asks, "Did you complete all the praises of your Master?"

Since we cannot possibly say all there is about how amazing God is, we are better off not saying anything about God. For whatever we say diminishes God by what we leave out.

Later in the "Song of the Sea," Moses sings the famous verse that is repeated in our morning and evening prayers: *Mi chamocha ba-eylim Hashem; mi kamocha ne'edar bakodesh; norah t'hilot, osey feleh* (Who is like You, Hashem, among the powers of the world; who is like You, glorious in holiness, too awesome for praises, doing wonders?)

Let us take a closer look at the last four words: *nora t'hilot, osey feleh* (too awesome for praises, doing wonders). Rashi comments on *nora t'hilot*(to awesome for praises): "People are afraid to tell Your praises lest they be too few; as it is written,[175] 'To You, silence is praise.'" In other words, one of the greatest praises you can give God is silence—to stand in awe.

So how is it the *Siddur* has prayers of praise? How could Moses have sung the "Song of the Sea" in praise of God? There are two ways in which it is permissible to offer praise of God. The one given in this passage in the Talmud is the key to almost all of the *Siddur*. Rabbi Chanina tells his student: "Had not Moses mentioned [the three words of praise—*hagadol, hagibor, v'hanora*] and the Men of the Great Assembly inserted them into the *Amidah*, we would not be able to recite them!"[176]

You may not have realized this, but the prayers of praise we find in the *Siddur* consist almost entirely of quotes from the Bible. So when we say these prayers we are not making up things to describe God, we are using the Word of God to describe Him, and we are permitted to do this—at least to the extent the Men of the Great Assembly advised.[177] How did David create Psalms of praise that make up a significant part of the *Siddur*? David had *Ruach Hakodesh* (Divine Inspiration), and therefore his words have the status of God's own words. Moses, who spoke to God face to face, had an even more direct connection to God and his words reflected this.

We find the second method of permissible praise in Maimonides' *Guide To The Perplexed*[178]: "Here let it become clear to you that every description [of God] that we describe Him with is either a description of action or … negation." Maimonides writes in technical philosophical language on this subject, so let me explain by returning to the example of our blind date. When the friend asks the young man what this girl is like, if the answer is, "She has a great personality," the friend understands something about her from what is not being said. But what if the friend is told she is a great girl and then shares a story or two about her? Maybe this girl was once passing a homeless person and she stopped and bought him a meal, or perhaps she volunteers as a "big sister" to an orphan. In telling what she has done, we need not mention her attributes. Even though God is *nora t'hilot* (too awesome for praises), we can describe Him as *osey feleh* (One who does wonders). We can describe what He does.

With this in mind, in the "Song of the Sea"—which is also part of the morning service—Moses begins, *Ashira laHashem ki ga-o ga-a* (I will sing unto Hashem although [translating *ki* as 'although'] He is above all exaltation, He is higher than high.) How? The verse continues, *sus v'rochbo rama vayam* (a horse and a rider [the Egyptians] He threw into the sea). Moses praises God by telling us that He saved us from the Egyptians by drowning them in the sea before they could harm us. In other words, we can praise God by describing the wonderful things that He does—like creating the world, the Exodus from Egypt, healing the sick, raising up those who fall, etc. And so we have prayers in the *Siddur* that describe God by describing His acts of kindness and compassion.

A perfect illustration of both principles is the first blessing of the *Amidah*. After mentioning that God is the God of our fathers Abraham, Isaac and Jacob, God is described as, *Ha-Eyl haGadol haGibor v'haNora*, (the Great, the Mighty and the Awesome God). This is a direct quote from a verse in the Torah[179] where Moses describes God to the Jewish people as they prepare to enter the Promised Land. Then God is described in this blessing by what

He does: *Gomeyl chasadim tovim, v'koney hakol, v'zocheyr chasdey avot, umeyvi go-eyl livney v'neyhem l'ma-an sh'mo b'ahava. Melech ozeyr umoshi-a umageyn.* (Who does beneficial acts of kindness, and is the acquirer of all things; who remembers the kindness of the Fathers, and will bring a redeemer to their children's children for the sake of His Name, with love. He is King, Helper, Savior and Shield.)

We will comment on each of these descriptions of God in chapter 14.

CHAPTER 13

Step Right Up and Find God

The *Amidah* is the holiest of prayers. Its recitation creates a special opportunity to draw closer to God and speak before Him, knowing He is not only listening, but eagerly awaiting the prayers of our hearts and the intimacy they can bring. When it is time to recite the *Amidah*, Jewish tradition recommends that we picture ourselves about to speak before the King of kings, and so before we approach God—out of awe to the King—we first take three steps backward and only then approach[180] the King, as was customary in royal courts, by taking three small humble steps forward drawing nearer and nearer to God.

On a deeper level, taking three steps forward before we begin this holiest of prayers reminds us of Moses as he approached God at Mt. Sinai, ascending through three increasingly difficult barriers—through *choshech*, then *anan*, and finally, *arafeyl*.[181]

Choshech means "darkness." Sometimes life appears dark and we cannot seem to find our way. Moses teaches us to trust, step forward through the darkness, and find God. *Anan* is a "cloud." While darkness is the absence of light and really not much of a barrier, a cloud not only blocks our vision, its moisture physically slows us down. When life pulls us away from our path to God, Moses is telling us to stay on the path, and that we can find God. *Arafeyl*, is sometimes translated as a "mist" or a "thick cloud" or "thick darkness." Whatever it is, obviously it is an increasingly difficult barrier.

What are your barriers to God? For some people, the barrier is that they don't feel worthy enough for God to answer their prayers. Others might have had really difficult challenges in their lives and are filled with anger over how unfairly life has treated them. Why should they have to pray for things to get better? God should make things better because it is only fair! Still others feel a strong need to be so self-sufficient they would rather deal with life's problems on their own. And then there are those that think, "God should know what I need, so why do I need to pray?"

Whatever your barriers are, Moses' message is clear. No matter what barriers confront us, no matter what temptations life challenges us with, we can pierce every barrier. In the end, every barrier to God is no worse than a mist that cannot stop us from finding Him if we but step forward.[182]

> The Baal Shem Tov illustrates this point with a marvelous parable. A wise king once wanted to test his subjects' loyalty and devotion. Making use of optical illusions, he made barriers, walls, towers and gates, and ordered treasures to be placed near each gate. He then made a proclamation that whoever came to see him in his palace would be richly rewarded. When his subjects came to the palace, some went through one gate and others through two or three, but when they saw the treasures, they simply took them and returned home. Only the king's son—with his intense desire to be with his father—pushed further and further beyond the barriers until he found his father and realized there really never were any barriers at all. It was nothing more than an illusion.[183] God sometimes seems hidden behind many barriers, but these are no more than an illusion. God is always near and waiting for His children to find Him.

So as you take those three steps forward (after having taken three steps back), do it slowly with focus and intention. With each step imagine yourself piercing through your own increasingly difficult barriers to God. After you take the third and last step imagine yourself having passed through all your barriers and you are now standing before the King of kings, before your God Who is ready and eager to listen to your prayers. Now recite the preliminary verse found in any Siddur just before the *Amidah*, *Hashem s'fatai tiftach, ufi yagid t'hilatecha* (God open my lips that my mouth may speak Your praise)[184] and begin the *Amidah*. In the *Minchah* (afternoon) and *Musaf Amidah* the verse, *Ki sheym Hashem ekra, havu godeyl l'Eyloheinu* (When I call upon God's Name, give greatness to our God) is added.[185]

EXERCISE   Do this *Amidah* exercise while standing as you would when reciting the *Amidah*. Make sure you have a clear space behind you. Go to www.DancingWithG-d.com to find an easy-to-use recorded version of this exercise, or record this exercise as you did the others:

> Close your eyes and relax. Take several deep breaths as you have learned in previous exercises. Slowly breathe in and out—in and out—repeating ten times. Pause.
>
> Look inside yourself and search deep within for that hunger, that need to connect with God. Feel the yearning well up inside you to find God—the King of kings. Take three short steps backwards with humility as you begin to feel how awesome God is. Pause.
>
> As you contemplate approaching God, take a moment to think about your barriers to God. What keeps you from coming closer to God? Know that no matter what the barriers are, you can pierce every one. Pause.
>
> Moses identified three increasingly difficult barriers to God: *choshech* (darkness), *anan* (cloud), and *arafeyl* (mist). Before you take each of the three steps forward towards God, recite one of these barrier words, and as you recite each one, let it represent your own increasingly difficult barriers. Say the word, "*choshech*," and take a step forward while thinking of piercing those lesser barriers. Say, "*anan*,"

and take a second step forward while thinking of piercing your stronger barriers. And finally say, "*arafeyl*," and take the final step forward to God as you pierce right through all your strongest barriers to God.

Now imagine yourself standing right before God with no barrier separating you and God. Feel the awesome power of His Presence and know that He is ready to receive your prayers. Take a minute to thank God for all He has blessed you with in your life. Pause. Now take a few more moments to tell God whatever it is you want to tell Him. Pause. Ask Him to help you with whatever you need help with. Pause. And finally, take a few more moments just to abide with God in His Presence—feeling the warmth of His presence. Pause.

When you are finished, take three steps back in humility before the Presence of God. Now open your eyes.

This exercise is designed to simulate an *Amidah* experience. As you learn more about the *Amidah* and add more elements of understanding, your *Amidah* experience will become a highlight of each day. Before we begin describing the power of the words of this first blessing of the *Amidah*, a word or two is in order concerning how to recite these words.

The *Amidah* should be recited in a quiet whisper, as we learn from the story of Hannah.[186]

Hannah was one of two wives of Elkanah, and on holidays they would go to Shilo to celebrate.[187] This was before the establishment of the first Temple. The *Mishkan*—the portable "Tabernacle" built during the time of Moses—was at that time set up at Shilo. The people went there to worship God. Hannah was barren and every time they would come to Shilo she would see all the families with their children and this must have tormented her. To make matters worse, the Bible[188] tells us her rival wife, Penina, who had many children, would taunt Hannah about her childlessness.

One day, at a celebratory meal, Hannah could not take it any longer; she left her family and went into the Sanctuary of God and prayed. The text[189] tells us not only what she prayed, but how she prayed: "Hannah was speaking from her heart—only her lips moved, but her voice was not heard."

In the Talmud[190] Rav Hamnuna taught: "How many important laws (of prayer) can be learned from Hannah's prayer! 'Hannah was speaking from her heart,' teaches that one must pray with *kavana,* with focus and concentration. From the passage, 'only her lips moved,' we learn it is necessary to pronounce the words of prayer with one's lips. 'But her voice was not heard,' teaches that it is forbidden to raise one's voice loudly in prayer above the other worshippers."[191] So when we pray, we should direct our voice inward rather than outward.[192]

Another passage from the Talmud recommends how fast or slow the *Amidah* should be recited. The Talmud[193] relates that the *Chasidim Harishonim* (the first pious ones) *hayu shohin sha-a achat umitpal'lin,* which is usually translated as, "would tarry for one hour and then pray."[194] Later, the Talmud[195] explains this to mean they took an hour before the *Amidah* as preparation for prayer, an hour to recite the *Amidah,* and another hour after the *Amidah* in meditation to wind down. But why did they need an hour to recite the *Amidah* when one fluent in prayer can recite it in less than five minutes? Because if it is said any faster, one might miss some of the feeling and spiritual power of the words.

The *Amidah* contains approximately 500 words. Aryeh Kaplan[196] notes that if the *Chasidim Harishonim* (the first pious ones) took an hour—or about 3,600 seconds—to recite the *Amidah,* then they did so at a pace of approximately one word every seven seconds. Most of us are not so spiritually disciplined to be able to maintain such focus for an entire hour, but we might be able to do this for the first blessing, since it contains only 42 words. In fact, the Talmud[197] teaches that being focused while we recite this first blessing is crucial. We might also be able to conjure up this kind of focus for a few other selected passages of the *Amidah* that more personally relate to us, like the blessing for healing or the blessing for forgiveness. Each word contains such holiness and opportunity for connection with God that we should not let it pass us by without noticing. Fortunately, the power of the *Amidah* is such that if somehow we lose focus for a few words, we can always find great holiness and opportunity for connection in the next word.

> The story is told of two Chasidim. One prayed with great speed. He could get through his morning prayers in a matter of minutes. The second man, who took a much longer time to pray, said to his friend, "When I pray, I just love the words of the prayers; they mean so much to me, that I savor each and every word. That's why I take so long to *daven* (pray)."
>
> "Oh," said the other. "For me it is different. When I pray, I love the words so much, that after I say each word I just cannot wait to get to the next one."

Moses prayed for the sins of Israel for 40 days,[198] while he offered only a short prayer of five words for his sister Miriam.[199] There is no set amount of time we should spend praying. What is important is that our prayers be heartfelt and meaningful. As Rabbi Yehuda asked in the Midrash,[200] "How long must one stand in prayer? Until one's heart aches!"

Let us turn now to this first blessing, called *Avot* (Fathers or Ancestors) and see if we can unpack some of the holiness in each of its words. For those readers not yet fluent in prayer, I suggest you skip to Chapter 15, "Four Words of Increasing Intimacy," and return after you have integrated its contents into your daily prayer experience. The purpose of this book is to facilitate your connecting with God, and for the beginner—or even for most regular *daveners* (Yiddish for "those who pray")—Chapter 15 should be mastered first.

Avot: For the Sake of Our Ancestors

T he *Avot* blessing begins: *Baruch Ata Hashem*, "Blessed are You Hashem." Note the first word of the *Amidah* is *baruch* (blessed). If you think about it, how very strange it is to think of blessing God. With what can we bless Him? We can bless each other that God should provide us with wealth or health or wisdom. But what does God lack that we can bless Him with? And who can provide God with something He needs? God does not need anything! The word *baruch* must, therefore, have another meaning.

There is a story of an old woman who comes to synagogue on Rosh Hashanah. In the middle of the *Amidah* she pauses and says to God, "Dear God, thank You; thank You; thank You! I had such a wonderful year. Thank God my health is fine. Thank God my children are fine. Thank God the business my late husband left me is doing well enough that I have all that I need. So I thank You, dear God, for a wonderful year. But before I ask You to bless me in the coming year, I want to bless You in the New Year. So with what can I bless You…with wealth? The whole world is Yours. With health? I guess you can take care of Yourself." She pauses to think for a moment and then says, "God, I bless You that in the New Year You should have *nachas* (joy) from Your children!"

God desires a closeness, a relationship with us. But God chooses not to control us so that we may freely choose to be in this relationship—thereby creating the potential of a much stronger relationship. Emerging from this is the understanding that our relationship with God is the one thing that is uncertain, the one thing He does not control. As the Talmud[201] teaches: *Hakol bidey Shamayim, chutz miyirat Shamayim.* (Everything is in the control of Heaven, with the exception of the fear of Heaven!)

In the Talmud,[202] Rabbi Yishmael ben Elisha, who was the High Priest, relates that once when he went into the Holy of Holies God asked him for a blessing. Faced with the same challenge as the old woman in the story he had a very different response: "May it be Your will that Your mercy conquer Your anger and that Your mercy overcome Your attributes of strictness, and that You behave toward Your children with the attribute of mercy, and for their sakes that You go beyond the boundary of strict justice."

And so when we bless God, we are saying He should have a strong relationship with His children—that His children should yearn to be close to Him—and this, according to Rabbi Yishmael, comes about in part, because of His mercy and compassion. It is also a nod to us to behave in such a way that will make God proud—i.e., treating each other with compassion and kindness, and by observing His Torah.[203]

The word *baruch,* "blessed," has the same root—ברכ—as בְּרֵכָה/*breycha* (a pool of water). It also shares the same root as בֶּרֶךְ /*berech* (knee). A בְּרֵכָה/*breycha* (a pool of water) is a source of water which nourishes and sustains life and is thus a source of blessing—especially in Israel where water is a precious commodity. We are able to walk and move by bending the knee. The knee, therefore, is a source of movement, activity and much of life itself—undoubtedly a source of blessing. When we say the word *baruch* at the beginning of a blessing, we are acknowledging God as the source of all life, of all movement, of all blessing. And so when we say the word *baruch* at the beginning of the *Amidah,* we bend the knee and bow before God, the source of all blessing.

Following after *baruch* in almost every blessing is: *Ata Hashem* (You God). Why do we need both words? Either would seem to suffice. And who are we to call God "You?" When addressing a king, one always says "Your Majesty." When addressing a president we say, "Mr. President." When addressing a judge we say "Your Honor." The difference is that God—unlike earthly kings, presidents and judges—wants an intimate relationship with us. This is also why we address God as if He were a Person and not just as a "Force." God hears our cries and knows the yearnings of our hearts. He, therefore, allows us to address Him as our Divine Parent, our Guide.[204] Rabbi Yisrael of Koznitz taught that to say, "You God" in a prayer is to acknowledge that God is right in front of us, that we are speaking to Him and He is listening.[205]

And not just that God is in the place we are, but that God is in the moment. He is in the spark of gratitude for food expressed in a blessing for food. When we light Shabbat candles, when we say Kiddush over the wine and say *"Baruch Ata Hashem"* we are recognizing the presence of God in our homes at that moment and in what we are doing. In the life of a practicing Jew it happens in a hundred little ways every day. Any time we do something that calls for a *beracha* we assert that God is present. We are saying "I am doing this because God is real and He is motivating me. He is helping me to create a moment of holiness, and when I do this holy act I am one with Him." So every time you make a *beracha* try to feel the presence of God with you as you bless Him.

Baruch Ata Hashem is a response to that powerful yearning within each of us to experience God. When we recite these words as we begin the *Amidah*, we should focus on feeling the closeness of God. He is in the air that we breathe, within our bodies, and deep within our souls. We should feel the awe, love and power of His presence. After bending the knee on the recitation of the word *baruch*, we bow as we say *Ata* (You.)

Hashem, as we have learned in chapter 6, "God's Name," is the Name of God denoting the divine attribute of mercy. It is the four-letter Name of God— ה-ו-ה-י —written with the Hebrew letters—*yud, hey, vav* and *hey*—so filled with mystery that no one knows how to pronounce it. Its secret pronunciation was only recited by the High Priest in the days of the Holy Temple on Yom Kippur. The sages have decreed that because this Holy Name must not be pronounced even as we pray, we should substitute *Adonai* (my Lord) in our prayers.

The sages[206] point out that the Holy Name ה-ו-ה-י/ *yud, hey, vav,* and *hey* is a contraction of the Hebrew words הָיָה, הֹוֶה, יְהְיֶה/*haya, hoveh, y'hiyeh*—(was, is, will be) indicating Hashem was, is and always will be; He is the Source of everything that was, is and will be.

When we pray, we should be aware that God transcends time as He transcends space. He only relates to us in time and space to make it possible to have a relationship with Him, but His mercy is so great it can transcend even the laws of nature which He created. Since it is impossible to picture God in our mind when we pray, I sometimes try to picture just the four letters of His name—ה-י ה-ו. As I feel closer and closer to God in my prayers, these letters appear to get closer and closer until they surround me.

According to Kabbalah,[207] when we say Hashem's name in this formula, *Baruch Ata Hashem (Adonai)*, if we are receptive to it, something absolutely marvelous and wonderful can happen. The *Shefa* (the overflowing abundance of God's energy), can radiate from above and fill us with His light. This light penetrates within us, even to those uncharted places within us that are dark and confused, helping us to find God even there. What is important to understand is that with God's *Shefa* anything is possible. If we are open to this radiant flow from above and allow it to penetrate through us into the world, it will set the stage for us to petition God for our needs in the rest of the *Amidah* that follows.

EXERCISE FOR THE FIRST THREE WORDS To practice what you have learned about these first three words of the *Amidah,* go to www.DancingWithG-d.com to find an easy-to-use recorded version of this exercise, or you will again need to record the exercise. This exercise should be done while standing up:

> Close your eyes and breathe in and out (ten times) as we have learned—getting more relaxed with each breath. Pause. Take three short steps backward, feeling ever so humble before God, followed by three steps forward. With each forward step, recite one of Moses' increasing barriers to God. Let it represent your own increasing barriers, as you pierce through each one: *choshech* (darkness), pause … *anan* (cloud), pause … and *arafeyl* (mist). Pause.
>
> Now bend your knees and say the word *Baruch*, thinking to yourself, 'I am bending the knee before You God, the Source of all blessing, because Your mercy and compassion are endless. You should be blessed that we, Your children, yearn to be close to You.'
>
> Now say the word *Ata*, thinking to yourself, 'I bow before You Who is with me now as I am speaking directly to You—not just here in the place where I am, but in this holy moment.'
>
> Finally, slowly straighten up as you say *Hashem* (*Adonai*), thinking to yourself, 'You are a compassionate God, who fills me with Your *Shefa*, Your merciful abundant energy and light. With God's *Shefa*, anything is possible.'
>
> You are now filled with God's *Shefa* and light. Ask God for help in your life, and then thank Him for everything He has blessed you with. Pause. Now ask Him to help you with whatever you need help. Pause. Take a moment or two to abide in the light. Pause. Take three steps backward, withdrawing from God's presence and open your eyes. (When using this exercise in prayer, wait until the end of the *Amidah* to take three steps back.)

The next word, *Eloheynu*, is generally translated as "our God." As we explained in chapter 6, this name for God denotes the aspect of God of nature and strict justice. This aspect of God can seem cruel at times; yet there is a compelling characteristic to the formulation of this name. Aryeh Kaplan[208] makes a great point about saying "our God," instead of just "God," when he writes: "This shows the extent to which God allows us to relate to Him and draw close. As far above us as He is, He allows us to address Him as 'our God,'—as if, in a sense, He belonged to us. This is perhaps the greatest gift and miracle of all—that God allows us to call Him 'ours'…that He lets us in!"

More than just "our God," the prayer continues in its description of God: *Eloheynu vEylohey Avoteynu* (our God and God of our Fathers) *Elohey Avraham, Elohey Yitzchak, vEylohey Yaakov* (God of Abraham, God of Isaac, and God of Jacob). This formulation, say the sages,[209] is so holy because its origin is in the Torah itself.[210] It defines God for us as being the God of our Patriarchs. It was they, after all, who had the most intimate and powerful relationship with Him. This recitation expresses our yearning to have this kind of relationship with God as well.

There is a dispute in the Talmud[211] concerning the source of the requirement of Jewish practice to pray three times a day. Rabbi Joshua ben Levi argues that our prayers replace the three daily sacrifices commanded in the Torah that we can no longer offer because the Temple was destroyed. Thus we see the rules for the proper times of prayer are based on the Temple sacrifices. Scriptural support for this approach can be seen in the verse from Hosea:[212] "And let us render in place of the bulls the offering of our lips."

Rabbi Yossi ben Chaninah says the three daily prayer services follow the prayers of the three Patriarchs, who each prayed at different times of the day—morning, afternoon and night— Abraham, Isaac and Jacob, respectively. The verses from the Torah he cites to support his approach, show how each of the three Patriarchs brought his own personality to his prayer. Abraham's early morning *Shacharit*, for example, was to save the wicked of Sodom. Abraham, the eternal optimist, thought he could wake up with the sun and change the world. He did not simply plead with God, he argued with Him: "Will You sweep away the innocent along with the guilty? ...Shall not the Judge of all the earth deal justly?" Abraham also introduced the concept of one God to the world, beginning a new spiritual path, and so he prayed at the beginning of the day—the morning.

Isaac's *Minchah* in the afternoon is more contemplative. Isaac was passive—things happened to him. Perhaps he relived the nightmare of Mount Moriah every day, when his father had to be restrained from executing him upon God's command. His mother died before he was ready to face life without her. His wife was chosen for him. He reopened the wells his father had dug. As the sun began to set, he prayed while he contemplated the meaning of his day and his life.

Jacob's evening *Maariv* is a cry for help. His brother Esav, as we have discussed, was coming to kill him. Jacob could not sleep so he cried out, "Please, God, get me through the night. Save me!"[213] Jacob, even surrounded by family, was lonely. He was hated by his brother; separated from his parents for over 20 years; his beloved wife Rachel died in childbirth; and his favorite son was presumed dead. His prayer is a cry of anguish in the night.

It is because each of our three Patriarchs had such a unique experience of God, that the *Amidah* addresses God as "the God of Abraham, the God of Isaac and the God of Jacob," not the "God of Abraham, Isaac and Jacob." It reveals that Abraham's experience of God was not the same as Isaac's or Jacob's. Every human being experiences God differently.

Are you wondering who is right? Does praying the *Amidah* three times a day follow the sacrifices or the Patriarchs? The answer is both! The Patriarchs instituted the three prayer services, but it was through the Temple sacrifices that these evolved into the service of our hearts.[214]

The next four words are a quote from the Torah[215] where Moses describes God as *Ha-Eyl haGadol haGibor v'haNora* (the great, mighty and awesome God). The word *Eyl* (*ha* means "the") is generic for God in Hebrew and therefore can be used to refer even to false gods, as in *elohim acheyrim* (other gods). In Chapter 6, "God's Name," we learned that Eyl means "power," and its plural form, *Elohim,* literally means "These Powers." The Torah also uses *Elohim* to refer to judges because judges have the power to decide the fate of those standing before them.

As the source of all power in the world, God as *Elohim* then refers to God's attribute of *midat hadin* (strict justice). This also is the name of God used in the Creation story, hence it denotes God as revealed in nature. Both strict justice and nature, as we have pointed out, can seem cruel. The *Shema* comes to teach us that underneath the seeming hardships in our lives is God's compassion and He is One Compassionate God.

However, the short form for the word God, *Eyl,* used in this prayer, also expresses *midat harachamim* (God's compassion) in the Torah. When God reveals His attributes of mercy to Moses, He describes Himself as *Eyl Rachum v'Chanun* (God, Merciful and Gracious).[216] *Eyl,* in the singular, then denotes the ultimate power of the world—God's love. After expressing our yearning for an intimate relationship with God with the recitation of the Patriarchs and their God, we recite the word *haEyl,* and are then in effect saying, "Merciful God, help us to draw closer to You."

HaGadol means "The Greatest!" The first to discover God as The Greatest was Abraham, and that is why he is called the father of monotheism. Greatness, in Kabbalah, is the attribute of *chesed* (loving kindness). In Psalm 145:8 *(Ashrei)* God is described as *g'dal chesed* (great in kindness). When we say the word *haGadol* in this prayer, we should focus on God as The Greatest—the greatest in power and might and the greatest in kindness. How fortunate we are that God so great should care or even pay any attention to us. Just as Abraham—as prominent a person as he was—achieved greatness by emulating God with his running to care for even the poorest and most needy, so should we.

Gibor is might and strength, but it is not physical strength. When speaking of physical strength in classical Hebrew we use the word *koach*. Isaac is the paradigm example of strength in Kabbalah, even though he fights no wars as did Abraham, or threatening strangers as did Jacob. In fact, Isaac's strength lies in his ability to withhold his urge to confront and retaliate when provoked. He avoids conflict and maintains his Godliness even in a hostile environment.

The Talmud[217] asks: *Eyzehu gibor* (Who is a *gibor*, who is mighty?) *Hakoveysh et yitzro* (He who conquers his desires/urges). God is undoubtedly the strongest and the mightiest. What is the greatest demonstration of God's strength and might? It is not the destruction of His enemies. It was not how He rained plagues upon the Egyptians. Although these were truly amazing demonstrations of His might, they do not compare to the might of God when He relaxes His control over us and allows us to exercise our free will—even when we disobey Him. God's greatest strength is revealed when He withholds punishment and forgives us, and so when we say the word *gibor* in this prayer, we should focus on God's might which has no limit, especially His power to grant us free will and forgiveness.

And finally, the last of the four words Moses uses to describe God is *Nora* (awesome). Only the contemplation of God can induce such an intense state of wonder, joy and fear all at once. It is the experience of Jacob: he awoke from his amazing dream of angels ascending and descending on a ladder to heaven declaring, *Ma nora hamakom hazeh* (How awesome is this place!)[218] When we say *Nora* in this prayer we should feel, "How awesome is it to stand before God in prayer!"

Note that after mentioning the three Patriarchs and feeling a desire to come close to their experience of God, this prayer points us on the path to do just that—i.e., by emulating the dominant attribute of each: Abraham—kindness, Isaac—inner strength, and Jacob—awe.

The first *beracha* continues by describing God as *Eyl Elyon* (God the most High). What does this mean? It means God is "higher than high," so high above everything else He is beyond our understanding. The human mind cannot possibly fathom the essence of God or understand why He does what He does or why He even bothers to help and to care about us. This *Eyl Elyon,* this Higher-than-High God loves each and every one of us. He is therefore, *Gomeyl chasadim tovim,* "One Who does good acts of kindness and love" for us. So when we recite these words we should focus on how we experience God's kindness, love and goodness.

Next, God is defined as the *Koney hakol* (the owner of all). The word *koney* really means "one who acquires," hence the word *Kanita* means "you bought." A person usually buys only the things he desires and does not buy the things he does not want. To say God "buys," or "acquires" us, is saying He made us because He desires to have us in His life, and just as a master must take care of his servants, God must take care of us!

Perhaps another approach, more faithful to the text, is that even though God is *Koney hakol* (One who acquires everything), there is nothing He lacks and He has nothing to gain from helping us. Nevertheless He is *Gomeyl chasadim tovim,* He does good acts of kindness and love for us for no reason other than because He loves us! Still another exquisite approach[219] is to take the meaning of *koney* from its similarity to the word *tikun* (repair). *Koney hakol* would then mean God repairs all things—especially us.

V'zocheyr chasdey avot (and He remembers the kindness of the fathers). Have you ever found that after having bought something, you got tired of it, especially if it did not live up to your expectations? What did you do? You probably discarded it or gave it away. We often fail to live up to God's expectations of what we should be, of living up to the Divine potential God implanted within us. And so the Talmud[220] advises us to implore God to help us, to remain close to us and not discard us, to protect us by reminding Him of the merit and acts of *chesed,* love and kindness our forefathers performed. We beg Him: *Umeyvi go-eyl livney v'neyhem* (bring a Redeemer to their children's children), *l'ma-an sh'mo b'ahava* (for the sake of His Name, with love).

Why "for the sake of His Name?" What does God's Name have to do with bringing a *go-eyl,* a redeemer, to the children of our forefathers? Perhaps it is because one of God's names, as seen in our prayers—in the seventh blessing of the daily *Amidah*—is *Go-eyl Yisrael* (Redeemer of Israel). And so, for the sake of His Name *Go-eyl Yisrael,* God will fulfill this promise with love.

B'ahava (with love): God's love is the key, the cornerstone, the foundation of everything. It is the reason God created us, and it is this great love for us that spans the generations from our Forefathers to ourselves, keeping God's faith in us strong. God patiently waits for us to live up to the potential He has implanted within us just as our Forefathers did! So as we recite this word, *b'ahava* (with love), let us try to feel the power of God's love within us.

It is interesting to note that Moses' four descriptive words, *HaEyl haGadol haGibor v'haNora* (God, Who is the Great, the Mighty and the Awesome), are defined in the words that follow:

HaEyl, (the God) is defined as *Eyl Elyon* (God on High).

HaGadol (the Great), is defined as *gomeyl chasadim tovim* (Who does beneficial acts of chesed, kindness).

HaGibor (the Mighty), is defined as *v'koney hakol* (and the Owner of all things); and,

V'haNora (the Awesome) is defined as *v'zocheyr chasdey avot, umeyvi go-eyl livney v'neyhem l'ma-an sh'mo b'ahava* (and He remembers the kindness of the Fathers and brings a Redeemer to their children's children for the sake of His Name, with love).

All, as we have learned, are different facets of God's unbounded love!

CHAPTER 15

Four Words of Increasing Intimacy

T he main path for increasing your intimacy with God, "the key to the entire *Amidah*," in the words of Aryeh Kaplan, can be found in the last four words preceding the signature *beracha* of this first blessing. As I suggested earlier, even before you make use of your understanding of the words of the *Amidah* explained in the previous chapter, you should master these four words, for they can help you immediately ascend to an intimate prayer relationship with God.

מֶלֶךְ עוֹזֵר וּמוֹשִׁיעַ וּמָגֵן
Melech, Ozeyr, uMoshi-a uMageyn
King, Helper, Savior and Shield

These are four terms of increasing intimacy with God. In our explanation of the six words at the beginning of the *Shema*, we climbed the ladder to our higher selves as we recited the word *Yisrael* while focusing on five of its meanings that correspond to the five levels of the soul.

This sets the stage for an amazing *Shema* experience every time. With these four words in the first blessing of the *Amidah*, you can climb the ladder higher and higher towards God. As you recite these words and become so connected to Him in the process, you actually will feel He is eagerly waiting to hear your prayers, which follow in the rest of the *Amidah*.

Words are insufficient to tell you how important this is and how it can change your life. Yes, change your life!

Remember the analogy of the mother and child on the playground? The child may find other children there and make friends. The child may even go off with these friends into an adjacent field, but he will not go so far that he cannot still see his mother. It is because he knows that when his mother is watching he is safe and he will be okay. When we recite these four words, we can feel spiritually and—as we will soon see—even physically connected to God. These words remind us in a concrete way—in a way we can actually feel—that God is here with us.

I cannot stress enough how crucial this is. If you achieve this feeling when you pray in the morning, this feeling can stay with you throughout your day. Just like the child on the playground, you will feel that God—your Ultimate Parent—is watching over you and that you are safe, and if you pray again in the afternoon and in the evening as prescribed by our tradition, you will always feel God's closeness. You will always feel God is with you and, therefore you will be better able to face the trials of life. There is no better way of achieving this spiritual level, of being able to carry this remarkable feeling with you always, than by reciting the *Amidah* three times each day with *kavana,* with focus! But even if you can only do this once a day, you still will find its effects transforming.

When we rise to this heightened state of consciousness with the recitation of these four words, this sets the stage for an extraordinary personal *Amidah* experience. We feel God's closeness, ask for His help in our lives with the knowledge that He is really listening, and thank Him for His mercies. Let us now unpack these four words of increasing intimacy with God.

מֶלֶךְ/*MELECH* (KING)   God is first addressed in these four words as a *Melech*, King. A king can seem somewhat distant. After all, a king sets the rules, and he rules over his subjects by rewarding and exacting punishment. There is, therefore, a sense of awe and fear subjects have for their king—hardly the ingredients for a close relationship, but they submit to this relationship with the faith that their king will protect them. We want God to be our King. We want Him to set the rules and rule over our world. Try to imagine, if you can, what the universe would be like without the law of gravity. It would be total chaos and we would cease to exist! God creates all the laws of nature and rules over these to keep us safe. God rules over us, not in order to be distant, He does so as an act of great love.

The word *Melech*, the mystics teach, has a hidden spiritual component contained within its holy letters: מ-ל-ך /*mem, lamed, chaf*. Mem (מ), the mystics teach,[221] is the first letter of *Melech* and stands for the Hebrew word מֹחַ/*mo-ach* (brain). *Lamed* (ל), is the second letter of *Melech* and stands for לֵב/*leyv* (heart). *Chaf* (ך), the third letter, stands for כַּבֵד/*kaveyd* (liver). With this in mind, when reciting the letter *mem*, making the sound מֶ/*meh*—the first syllable of the word *Melech*—you should focus on opening your *mo-ach,* your mind, to be a vessel to receive the light of God. Feel it descend upon you into your brain like a Divine laser from Heaven. Feel the power of the light fill your mind expanding its powers of inspiration and intellect.

As you say the sound לֶ/*leh*—the second syllable of the word *Melech*—open your *leyv,* your heart, to be a vessel to receive the light of God as the light flows down from your mind into your heart. Allow it to flow continuously from God to your mind and then into your heart. Feel the power of the light fill your heart with its Godly attributes of mercy, kindness and love.

Then as you say the sound ך/*ch*—the final sound of the word *Melech* (not "ch" as in "chin," but the guttural "kh" as in the common Hebrew and Yiddish word for "life", "*chayim*")—open your *kaveyd,* your liver, to be a vessel to receive the light of God as it flows down from your heart. The liver is a crucial organ in that the blood—which contains the *nefesh*, the animal aspect of the soul—is cleansed in the liver and distributed to the entire body.

It is fascinating to note that *kaveyd* has a *gematria* (numerology) of 26 (20 + 2 + 4) which, we have learned, is the same as the Name of Hashem. As the light enters your liver, let it spiritually cleanse your blood and attach itself, thereby spreading the light—with its healing powers—to your entire body. Through the continuous channel of the brain, heart and liver, you will then be filled with God's light! You can achieve an amazing state of consciousness just in the recitation of this first word *Melech*!

עוֹזֵר/Ozeyr (Helper) The next word in this series of increasingly intimate descriptions of God's relationship with us is *Ozeyr* (Helper). Everyone is familiar with the expression "God helps those who help themselves." This is probably the most often quoted "Biblical" phrase that is not found in the Bible. It is actually a quote by Ben Franklin from his *Poor Richard's Almanac* of 1757. The Jewish take on this is you should not just wait around expecting God to answer your prayers. Take the initiative and do what you can to bring your prayers to fulfillment and God will help your efforts.[222] As the Talmud[223] teaches: *B'derech sheh-adam rotzeh leyleych, ba molichin oto* (In the direction a person wants to go, God will lead him). God will help bring your dreams to completion if you make every effort to do so.

If God puts a dream in your heart, He will certainly help you bring it to fulfillment. It does not matter how long this takes; God can still bring it to pass. How many of us have given up on a dream? How many of us have given up on a child or a relationship? Maybe you are tempted to give up on the thought that you could become learned or you could achieve financial success. You need to feel God is your Helper, and so as you say this word *Ozeyr,* think to yourself: "I'm going to start each day believing and expecting every promise God put in my heart, and God will help me bring it to fruition."

Do not give in to despair, to the thought "My dreams will never work out." Sometimes life tests us, trying to get us to give up, leaving us to think: "It didn't work out. I didn't get the promotion. I didn't qualify for the new home. I'll never find the time to study Torah. It's never going to happen. Just forget it!" Time, on the other end, is pulling. The longer it gets, the more we hear all the negative voices saying, "You don't have what it takes; the doctor's report says you are not going to make it." But if you are going to be the person God made you to be, you must have the attitude that nothing is going to cause you to give up. Do not ever give up on praying for the fulfillment of your dreams.

There is a story[224] of a *tzadik* (a holy man) who dies and goes straight to heaven. The angels greet him and tell him he is welcome in heaven; in fact they were waiting for him. They also tell him God gave them instructions to make him feel especially at home as quickly as possible and to give him a tour of the whole heavenly realm right away. One of the angels then takes the *tzadik* from place to place, from room to room and from hall to hall. The *tzadik* sees so many wonderful sights—many holy men and women engaging in creative holy activities, houses of study and such. Suddenly he notices the angel quickly walking by a closed door without opening it. He asks, "What's inside?"

The angel responds, "You don't want to know."

"But I want to see everything," says the *tzadik*. After a while he gets the angel to open the door. Inside is a huge room resembling a post office warehouse with shelf after shelf of packages that are addressed and ready to be delivered.

"What's this?" asks the *tzadik*.

The angel tells him, "There are certain people who have prayed and prayed for a long time for something and lost patience with their prayers. We were about to send them what they prayed for, and then we cancelled the package because they suddenly stopped praying!"

Rebbe Nachman (1772-1810) taught *By Gut, iz alles meglach* (By God everything is possible).[225] The only thing that can block the dreams God puts in us, teaches Rebbe Nachman, is our negativity—when we quit believing our dreams are going to happen. It may seem impossible—like Abraham and Sarah having a child in their old age—but God can make a way even when it looks like there is no way! So get rid of your negative thoughts. When you say this word *Ozeyr* in the *Amidah*, envision your dreams fulfilled. Know that God is your Supreme Helper, but you need to take the first steps and make the effort!

מוֹשִׁיעַ/*Moshi'a* (Savior)   The third word in this series is *Moshi'a* (Savior). There are times in our lives when life becomes so hard we are at a loss to know what we can do to help ourselves. In fact, sometimes there may be nothing we can do. We may have been diagnosed with a serious illness for which there is no known effective treatment. Our child may have rebelled and run off. The economy may have soured and we were fired from a job through no fault of our own, and even after we have searched and searched, we are still unemployed. Whatever the circumstances, there will be times when life gets so hard we feel powerless to change it. This is the time, teaches Rabbi Yitzchak Benzecry, that God comes to us as our *Moshi'a*, as "the One who saves us"—*b'lo hishtatfut ko-ach acheyr* (without the participation of any other power).[226] Just when we think we cannot go on, something unexpected may happen from "left field" that changes everything. This is God as our *Moshi'a*. We need to call upon God, imploring Him to be our *Moshi'a* and save us.

This is what happened at the Red Sea. After the devastation of the Ten Plagues—especially the last, the slaying of the Egyptians' firstborn—Pharaoh had practically thrown the Jewish people out of Egypt. Soon he had a change of heart and ran after them to bring back this great source of cheap labor. With all the chariots of Egypt, his horsemen and his army, he pursued them, catching up with them at the shore of the Red Sea. The Torah[227] tells us: *Vayiru m'od* (They [the Jewish people] were so terrified) *vayitz'aku v'ney Yisrael el Hashem* (The Children of Israel cried out to God!)"

Rashi comments: *Tafsu um'nut avotam* (They seized upon the craft of their fathers), by which he means prayer. In other words, it was not until they "cried out to God" that God saved them. This is a crucial lesson. We must never think that because God knows our circumstances and because He loves us He will automatically save us when we are in need. No, even when we feel powerless, we must not wait for God's help. We must ask for it—even beg for it! This is God manifesting as *Moshi'a*, our Savior.

CHAPTER 16

Shield of Abraham

The final word in these four terms of increasing intimacy with God is מָגֵן/*Mageyn* (Shield). What is a shield? A shield is something that protects us from danger—whether it is a tool or a warrior or bulletproof glass. God here is identified as the Supreme Shield protecting us even when we do not know it, even before a potential tragedy happens.[228]

Were you or someone you know ever involved in a terrible accident and somehow, miraculously, just walked away suffering little or no injury? This is God manifesting as our *Mageyn*. Did you ever make a wrong turn or for no reason take a different path and could not figure out why? This could be God as your *Mageyn* protecting you from some misfortune that was waiting. Sometimes we think we know exactly what we want and God stops us from achieving it to protect us. The best path to serenity in life is to understand God watches over us and protects us in a hundred different ways every day—in ways we will never know— no matter what happens. God, as *Mageyn*, manifests the ultimate demonstration of His love for us.

If we had a way to physically feel God as our shield, if we could physically feel God's love, this would be truly incredible— especially at times when we need, more than ever, to feel the comfort of God's love. In reality this is not possible because we cannot fully know or experience any aspect of God—even His love. Nevertheless, I have developed an exercise that might help us approach this experience. While we cannot physically feel the

Shechina, the feminine, loving, protecting Presence of God, we can perhaps feel the presence of our own eternal soul, which is forever joined with God.

Let me explain. There is a concept in Jewish Law called *dalet amot,* the space of four *amot.* An *amah,* according to most scholars, is a measurement between 18 and 24 inches;[229] so four *amot* equals six to eight feet. If someone comes this close to you, Jewish law teaches, they are in your space, and the closer they get, the more intensely they are in your space. This is why it is considered rude for someone to stand too close while they are speaking with you. Did you ever have the experience of sitting in a chair and someone silently approaches from behind, and somehow you know someone is there? How did you know? They were in your space.

This concept of *dalet amot,* of personal space, continues even after death. If one comes within four *amot* of a grave, one becomes *tamey,* or spiritually impure. Why? Because your soul is larger than your body and can extend this far, and even though your eternal soul departs at the moment of death, there still remains an aspect of your *nefesh,* your animal soul, buried with your body that can render you *tamey.* A *kohen,* or priest, since he is commanded by the Torah to avoid *tumah* (spiritual impurity) from death, must therefore stay on the road—more than four *amot* away from any grave—when he visits a cemetery.

Photographers can now photograph the auras around people. This is called "Kirlian photography." Are these auras a reflection or a measure of our souls? Possibly! Does the thought of having a part of you extend beyond your physical body seem really weird and hard to accept?

Research conducted at the HeartMath® Institute (HMI)[230] demonstrates that the human heart has an electromagnetic field extending beyond the body that is an important carrier of information. Take a look at the heart's electromagnetic field in the diagram below from the HeartMath® Institute or HMI. The heart's electromagnetic field—by far the most powerful rhythmic field produced by the human body—not only envelops every cell of the body but also extends in all directions into the space around us. The cardiac field can be measured several feet away from the body by sensitive devices.

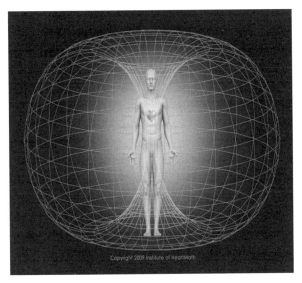

Figure 4: The Heart's Electromagnetic Field

This electromagnetic field, according to the HMI, is not necessarily the same as the auras surrounding us, but demonstrates there is something of us that extends beyond our physical bodies and it is, in fact, measurable.

The simple exercise that follows, I believe, can help us physically feel this "something" beyond ourselves that surrounds us all the time. Is it our aura? Perhaps, but I believe whatever it is also presents an extension of our souls joined with God. I have found more than 80 percent of the people who try this exercise are successful with it. If it does not work for you after several attempts, do not worry. This does not mean you lack a soul; rather, this method of sensing it does not work for you.

Exercise   Read the directions in the following paragraph before you do the exercise. It is simple and therefore does not need to be recorded:

> Sensitize your hands by rubbing them together for a moment. Spread your hands apart as far as they will go and close your eyes. Now bring them together very very slowly, stopping as soon as you feel the slightest resistance. Once you have stopped, think for a moment or two about what you are feeling. Open your eyes.

What was it you felt? It is my contention you felt an extension of your holy soul! And your holy soul is linked with God. Though it is not there physically, you were able to physically sense it. When I say this word *Mageyn* at the end of these four words of increasing intimacy, and I close my eyes and do this exercise, I can physically feel the connection, sensing my soul and, by extension, God's protective shield. I can feel God is in front of me, surrounding me and protecting me. For me this is a physical way of feeling God's love, and it can be for you as well. I need to feel this every day—in fact three times a day. Like the child in the playground, by sensing God's presence through my extended soul as I recite the word *Mageyn* in the *Amidah* three times a day, I am reassured He is watching and I know I will be fine.

Next comes the signature blessing of this first *beracha*: *Baruch Ata Adonai, Mageyn Avraham* (Blessed are You, Hashem, Shield of Abraham). We bow at the beginning and the end of this blessing.[231] We bend our knees as we say the word *Baruch*; we bow as we say *Ata*; and we rise as we say *Hashem* (*Adonai*), God's holy name, feeling the *Shefa*, the flow of God's light into us. For more on the meaning of bowing as a powerful silent prayer in itself, see the next chapter, "The Posture of Prayer."

The expression *Mageyn Avraham* (Shield of Abraham) is an allusion to the verse,[232] *Al tira Avram, Anochi mageyn lach* (Do not fear Avram, I [God] am your shield). Abraham saved his nephew Lot by miraculously defeating an alliance of much larger forces. Perhaps Abraham feared the surviving neighbors would attack him in revenge. Or perhaps, as Rashi comments, he feared he would be punished by God for killing many others in this rescue mission. God then reassures him, "Fear not, Avram, I am your shield." The Midrash[233] elaborates further and has God saying, "Even if all the nations in the world gathered against you I will fight against them." God promises to be the *Mageyn Avraham* (The Shield of Abraham). This promise is quite a legacy. No wonder it was made the theme of the first blessing of the *Amidah*.

As you recite this signature blessing, continue with your hands apart—as you did with the preceding four words of increasing intimacy—feeling your connection with God as your Shield; and as you do so, appreciate this added dimension of God as a Shield of the Jewish people. God shields us, not only for our own sake, but for the sake of His eternal covenant with Abraham our Father. Slowly pulling your hands together and actually feeling this shield between your hands can be so powerful it can open you up every time you pray to have an intimate experience with God—an experience you never before dreamed you could achieve.

The intimacy achieved in this simple act should last throughout your recitation of the *Amidah*, and the spiritual and tactual memory of such intimacy can last the whole day, so you always feel you are in the presence of God. Living in such a state can be a transformative experience and can literally change your life!

CHAPTER 17

The Posture of Prayer

I t is essential in trying to enhance your prayer experience to understand how vital proper posture is. This is something we usually take for granted, but we should not. How one stands is important in life. In sports, for example, whether it is baseball, tennis, or football, proper posture is vital to peak performance. Sloppy posture in social situations makes one seem less attractive and appealing. If one is in the armed services, standing properly at attention shows respect and honor for a superior officer. If one has an audience with a king or the president, certainly one would try not to stand in too casual a manner. Standing before God, the King of kings, in prayer while asking for life, health and sustenance, certainly calls for standing in a manner that projects awe, respect, honor and humility.

What is the proper posture of prayer?

Generally, we learn from Abraham who stood before God in prayer,[234] that standing is the preferred posture—especially in prayers where we address God directly, as in the *Amidah*, or to sanctify His name, as in the *Kaddish*. And so we traditionally stand for the *Amidah* and the *Kedusha* of the *Amidah*; the To-rah service (standing for the taking out and returning the holy Torah as a sign of respect); when the Holy Ark is opened; the lifting of the Torah; the *Aleynu*; the *Kaddish*; *Baruch She-amar* at the beginning of the *P'sukey D'zimra* and *Vay'vareych David* till *Yishtabach* at the end of the *P'sukey D'zimra*; *Barchu*; *Hallel*; *Yizkor*; the Blessing of the New Month; and other special prayers.

Since the prayer services can be long, it is permissible to

sit for the other prayers. Since the *Shema* is composed of three passages from the Torah, its recitation is akin to studying Torah, and therefore, can be recited in the posture of study which includes being seated.

When reciting the *Amidah*, one should stand with one's feet together facing Jerusalem. In the military, one stands at attention before a superior officer with one's feet together. Standing in this manner while reciting the *Amidah* would indicate we are standing at attention before the Supreme Commander who made His Presence most manifest in Jerusalem.

The Talmud[235] goes even further and tells us that standing with our feet together is the stance of the angels and in prayer one should try to emulate the angels. In the *Merkavah* (Chariot) vision of Ezekiel, which is one of the prime sources of Kabbalah mysticism, the prophet describes a fantastic image of several angels declaring the famous verse of praise *Baruch kevod Hashem mimekomo* (Blessed be the glory of Hashem from His place). We will discuss this verse in Chapter 20, "The Biggest Blessing." But for our purpose now, which is to discern the proper posture for prayer, in describing the feet of the *Chayot* angels reciting this verse, the text[236] tells us: *v'ragleyhem regel y'shara* (and their feet were [like] a straight foot). Therefore, when we praise God in our main prayer, the *Amidah*, our feet should be like a single straight foot, i.e., feet together.[237]

For the *Amidah* and *Kedusha* prayers, our feet should be together, but our knees should be slightly bent following the verse in Isaiah,[238] "To Me every knee shall bend," with the head slightly bowed. This is a posture that projects, both inwardly and outwardly, a feeling of awe and humility—a posture begging God for help.[239] It is best, if you can, not to use your hands to hold the *Siddur* for important prayers like the first paragraph of the *Amidah* so that you can either hold them out in front of you in a beseeching manner—which will facilitate the *Mageyn* (Shield) exercise—or fold your hands over your heart.[240] Therefore, it is recommended to memorize these prayers or have some sort of stand or desk to hold your *Siddur* in front of you. When you sit in prayer and recite passages that are most meaningful for you, you can place your *Siddur* in your lap as you fold your hands over your heart or out in front in a beseeching manner.

SHUCKLEN (SHAKING/SWAYING)   Whoever visits a traditional Jewish service cannot help but notice the unique dance-like motions of the bodies of the worshippers during prayer. This is typically referred to by the Yiddish term *shucklen* (shaking/swaying). Such movement is not prescribed or required by Jewish law, yet it is an effective way for the worshipper to physically help himself to focus on his prayers. Some worshippers sway back and forth or side to side very gently, while others exhibit more rapid motions. Such movements of the body can help the worshipper block out distractions.

There is some dispute as to the origin of this custom. Yehuda Halevi (12th century) in his epic work *The Kuzari*,[241] gives us an historical approach that can seem almost comical to the uninformed reader. Before the 16th century and the development of printing, books were handwritten and very rare. Yehuda Halevi tells us that people studying Torah together would form a semicircle around a book and each would take a turn bending down to read a passage and come up to give the next reader a turn. This up and down motion of study was then used for reading from prayer books as well. The Abudarham (14th century), following the *Midrash*,[242] maintains it comes from Psalm 35:10: "All my limbs will say, 'God, who is like You.'" Similarly, the Zohar[243] teaches that a person *shuckels* during prayer because the soul is aroused and reaches up towards its source as a fire dances beyond the wick.

Interestingly, many of our holiest sages would sway very little or not at all while reciting the most intimate passages of the *Amidah*, especially when adding their own prayers. They were so inwardly focused that *shucklen,* for them, was a distraction. Expressed in spiritual terms, we can say they had moved from *hitor'rut* (arousal), to *d'veykut* (the state of cleaving to God) a higher state. The recommendation from Jewish tradition seems to be to find what works for you, i.e., find your own dance with God.[244]

LIFT UP YOUR HANDS   A time honored custom, mentioned frequently in the Bible,[245] is lifting up one's hands during prayer. The Talmud[246] interprets Psalm 63:5, "In Your Name I shall lift My hands," as referring to the recitation of the *Amidah*. So, lifting one's hands while reciting the *Amidah* is a time honored practice. It may go against the image of the staid and stoic posture of most Jews in the synagogues of today, and therefore, may even seem somewhat strange and possibly weird. Nevertheless, it has been an effective spiritual practice among Jews since Biblical times. Gesturing with your hands as you speak to God can be an important part of the dance of prayer.

> It happened quite unexpectedly about twenty-five years ago. I was in deep prayer reciting the *Amidah* one morning in shul, and I lifted my hands out in front of me, gesturing to God. All of a sudden I was blinded by an indescribable light that seemed to descend from above and reflect off my somewhat outstretched hands like a laser towards my eyes. My eyes were closed in prayer, but somehow this amazing light penetrated and seemed to fill me with light. I was elated, overwhelmed, and never felt closer to God. Since then I have continued to hold my hands somewhat outstretched as I recite the *Amidah*. Although I do not always reach the intensity of that moment, I draw upon that experience and continue to use my hands as holy reflectors of God's light as I pray.

You may not have this laser-like experience if you try it. But if you imagine God's light reflecting off your hands and filling you with light as you pray, you can develop this as an effective part of your prayer experience.

In Chapter 15, "Four Words of Increasing Intimacy," I described the exercise of pulling your hands apart and then moving them ever so slowly together until you feel the slightest resistance. What you feel, I contend, is an extension of your holy soul linked with God. When you say the word *Mageyn* (shield), at the end of the four words of increasing intimacy in the first paragraph of the *Amidah*, or *Mageyn Avraham* in the signature blessing of that paragraph, if your hands are already lifted out somewhat in front of you, you have but to turn your hands, ever so slightly, towards one another to feel God's protecting shield. You can actually feel God in front of you, surrounding you and protecting you. This is a physical and powerful way of feeling God's love.

If this does not seem to work after a few tries, do not quit. Keep trying because actually feeling this connection to God, filling yourself with His light and with His shield between your hands can be so powerful it can open you up every time you pray to have an intimate experience with God that should last throughout your recitation of the *Amidah*. As I have noted previously, the spiritual and tactual memory of this can last the whole day so you always feel that you are in the Presence of God.

A WORD ABOUT BOWING   Bowing can be an extraordinarily intimate experience, a prayer experience more powerful than any with words. When you bow before God, you free yourself from your ego and the need to be in control, while opening yourself up to new possibilities and blessings. The Midrash[247] goes as far as to say that "everything happens with the merit of bowing," and proceeds to list several things that happened in Jewish history because people bowed and humbled themselves before God and opened up new blessings: the return of Abraham and Isaac from the Akeda, the Exodus from Egypt, the giving of the Torah, the holy Temple.

In the ancient world, bowing was a sign of respect and friendship. When one bowed before another, one put oneself in a very vulnerable position, and the deeper the bow, the more vulnerable one was. This was a statement of trust because the one bowed before could easily hurt or kill the one bowing. This is similar to the custom of shaking hands as a sign of friendship. Shaking hands usually joins the dominant hands—the right for most—of two people, leaving them bare and vulnerable without a weapon.

When we bow as we recite the *Amidah*, the Talmud[248] tells us to bend our knees with the word *Baruch,* bow from the waist on the word *Ata* and raise up our torso back to its original position as we say *Hashem,* God's name. Everyone knows it is forbidden to bow to false gods; however, because of the custom of raising our torso and head when we recite God's name, some mistakenly believe it is forbidden to bow when we recite God's name. It is not! The Talmud explains we raise our torso before we mention God's name because of the verse from Psalm 146:8, "God straightens the bent," and from a verse in Malachi[249] that states, "Before My Name he was humbled." In other words, we should humble ourselves or bow before mentioning God's name; and it is no sin to bow while reciting any of God's names.

The Talmud[250] stipulates we should bow at the beginning and at the end of this first blessing of the *Amidah—Avot—*and at the beginning and end of the *Modim,* the thanksgiving blessing, towards the end of the *Amidah.* As we have learned, the *Avot* blessing calls upon God's close relationship with our forefathers to advocate on our behalf in our prayers to Him. It defines our relationship with God through our ancestors and thereby becomes an important pathway to God for our prayers. The feeling of humility engendered by an appreciation of the greatness of our forebears makes this a perfect place to bow and feel our vulnerability before God.

In the *Modim* blessing we thank God for His mercies that He extends to us, "at all times, evening, morning and afternoon," without which we could not live. Bowing from the waist as we recite this blessing brings home to us in a powerful way—a way no words can convey—our ultimate vulnerability. It makes no difference how much wealth, position or power we have acquired. We are still so vulnerable, as we exclaim in this blessing: "Our lives are in Your hands and our souls are entrusted to You."

After prescribing where we should bow in the *Amidah*, the Talmud then makes two exceptions: one for the *Kohen Gadol*, the High Priest of the Temple of old, and the other for a king. The

Kohen Gadol, teaches the Talmud, should bow at the end of every blessing in the *Amidah.* A King should bow at the beginning and end of every blessing. One opinion in the Talmud goes as far as to say a king should bow at the beginning of the *Amidah* and not get up till the end. Why do these two powerful leaders need to bow so much?

Rashi, in his commentary, helps us make sense of this when he explains: "The greater position one has, the more he must humble himself before God." In other words, the greater one's stature, the more one needs to feel that ultimately, before God, it is nothing! Before God all power is merely an illusion. What we perceive as power, wealth or prestige is a gift from God to us, given in order to help us do His work in this world. It says nothing about our worth or stature as human beings other than that God trusts us to use these gifts wisely.

When we bow, we acknowledge we do not control the world. The ultimate truth is that control, no matter how powerful we may be, is also only an illusion. In prayer, we ask God to change things as they are and make our lives better. If we were in control we would make these changes ourselves. But we are not! We bow before God Who is the One Who is in control, asking Him to make the changes—whether for health or wealth or whatever it is that we desire.

Bowing in prayer, allowing ourselves to feel vulnerable, is a powerful exercise for connecting with God; so when you bow before God in prayer, do not just do it perfunctorily—nodding your head. The Talmud[251] teaches that when we bow in prayer we should bow deeply—deeply enough so that the vertebrae of our spine protrudes, or so that we can see the flesh opposite our heart. Why? So that we can deeply feel the reality of our vulnerability before rising up again, thinking about how vulnerable we really are before God. He can do as He wishes with us. Bowing before Him, which is the posture of defenselessness, enables us to feel deeply, not only our ultimate vulnerability, but also to feel deeply our trust in Him and in His loving protection.[252]

A Bowing Exercise   Let me suggest a bowing exercise. You can do this either in a standing or sitting position. Read the following paragraph first and then proceed to www.DancingWithG-d.com to find an easy-to-use recorded version of this exercise, or slowly record it and play it back while you do the exercise:

> Close your eyes. Bow your head toward your waist and hold it there. Feel deeply your vulnerability. Let go of the illusion you are really in control of your life. Acknowledge the truth that it is really God Who is in control and that He has given you more than you deserve. Take a few moments for this humble feeling of vulnerability to take hold within you. Pause.
>
> While you are still bowed, give over whatever control you think you have of your world to God. Pause. Be grateful as you feel God's protecting love. Pause.
>
> Now let go of that last ounce of control you are still holding on to, while you let His love in so it touches every fiber of your being. Abide with God a few more moments as you are strengthened by His love.
>
> Now come up very slowly like a snake,[253] noticing how you feel both spiritually and physically. Open your eyes.

How do you feel? This can be a very emotional experience, especially if you have not really bowed before God or have not done this for some time. Embrace the emotion and use it to heighten your prayer experience.

Take a moment to review your experience. Without saying a word you probably felt a strong emotional bond with God, the source of everything, in a way you may have never felt before.

Bowing—done properly with focus and attention—is an intense prayer by itself without any words. It can facilitate an intensive meditative spiritual state that can connect you ever more strongly to God as well as to the message of the prayer you are reciting.

CHAPTER 18

Let's Start The Dance

Now that we have reviewed the basic elements of Jewish prayer, it is time to begin to pull them all together for a truly profound and meaningful prayer experience—to literally dance with God. It would be helpful if you could find the time to review chapters 5-7 and 11-16 before doing this exercise, but it should be meaningful nevertheless.

How is this a dance? You will sit and stand, move your hands over your eyes and later in an outward motion; you will recite and chant, move backward and forward, bow and rise up and embrace God. Each movement is pregnant with meaning. Taken together it is nothing short of a most intimate dance with God.

This exercise will be somewhat longer than the previous exercises in this book. They were designed to reinforce one or two prayer elements. This exercise will include all of the essential elements of Jewish prayer. Make sure you set aside enough time to absorb it all. Allow yourself a good 15 minutes of time alone to do it properly.

EXERCISE   As I have suggested with the previous exercises, go to www.DancingWithG-d.com to find an easy-to-use recorded version of this exercise, or record them very slowly and play them back as you do the exercise, leaving several seconds to contemplate after every pause indicated. We will begin this exercise in a seated position for the first verse of the *Shema* and then rise for the first blessing of the *Amidah*. You will need to have a space sufficient to take three small steps backward and forward. Let us begin in a seated position with your feet firmly on the ground and your hands on your knees:

> Close your eyes and relax. Breathe deeply in through your nose and out of your nose several times... pause... with each breath you become more relaxed. Breathe in through your mouth and out of your mouth several times again... pause... breathe in God's light-filled with love and harmony. Breathe out all your cares and problems, then breathe in through your mouth and out of your nose several times... pause... and finally, breathe in through your nose and out your mouth more several times... pause.
>
> Now place your right hand over your eyes to help you focus, as is the custom while reciting the Shema. We will say the six words of the first verse of the Shema, dwelling on each word for about 10 to 15 seconds, focusing on its meaning:
>
> *Shema*—<u>Listen</u>. Listen deeply with your heart that your mission is to gather the broken pieces of this world to Oneness, to become a vessel to spread the word of God you receive.
>
> *Yisrael*—Become your higher self, from the Israel inside you that <u>struggles</u> with God, that nevertheless fights on behalf of God, that becomes a champion of God, that becomes straight with God, to the Israel inside you that sees God everywhere and in everything.
>
> *Ad-o-nai*—Feel the warmth of God's <u>compassion</u> envelop you as you recall at least one way God has shown His compassion towards you.
>
> *Eloheynu*—Feel the awe and the fear of the aspect of God's <u>strict justice</u> and <u>nature</u> that can seem cruel. Recall at least one time you felt God as *Elohim*. But know God is really ...
>
> *Ad-o-nai Echaaaaaaad*—<u>One compassionate God</u>! Get

ready to say the word *Echad*. Hold the word *Echad* and don't finish reciting it until you feel the energy of God's love fill you to the point you feel one with Him and one with the world He created in every fiber of your being. Abide in this feeling of oneness for a few moments. Pause.

Now that you have risen to the Israel—the higher self—within you, feeling one with God and the world, it is time to stand before God for an intimate encounter with Him… Now that you are standing, look inside yourself and search deep within for that hunger, that need to connect with God. Feel the yearning well up inside you to find God—the King of kings. Slowly take three short steps backwards with humility as you begin to feel how awesome God is. Pause.

As you contemplate approaching God, take a moment to think about your barriers to God. What keeps you from coming closer to God? Know that no matter what the barriers are, you can pierce every one. Pause.

Moses identified three increasingly difficult barriers to God: *choshech* (darkness), *anan* (cloud), and *arafeyl* (mist). Before you take three steps forward towards God, recite each of these barrier words, and as you recite each one, let this represent your increasing barriers. Say the word "*choshech*," and take a step forward while thinking of piercing those lesser barriers. Say "*anan*," and take a second step forward while thinking of piercing your stronger barriers. And finally, say "*arafeyl*" and take the final step forward to God as you pierce right through all your strongest barriers to God.

Imagine yourself standing right before God with no barrier separating you and God. Feel the awesome power of His Presence and know that He is ready to receive your prayers. Bend your knees and say the word, "*Baruch*," thinking to yourself, 'I am bending the knee before You, God, the Source of all blessing, because Your mercy and compassion are endless. You should be so blessed that we,

Your children, yearn to be close to You."

Now say the word "*Ata*," thinking to yourself, "I bow before You Who is with me now as I am speaking directly to You—not just here in the place where I am, but in this holy moment."

And finally, slowly straighten up as you say *Adonai*, thinking to yourself, "You are a compassionate God, who fills me with Your *Shefa*, Your merciful abundant energy and light. With God's *Shefa* anything is possible."

Identify God as *Eloheynu* (our God) and *Elohey Avraham, Elohey Yitzchak, v'Eylohey Yaakov* (the God of Abraham, the God of Isaac and the God of Jacob), each having their own personal, profound experience of God. In other words, He is your God for you to uniquely and personally experience Him.

We now come to the four words of increasing intimacy with God. Say the word *Melech* (King), very slowly. Say *Meh*—think *mo-ach* (brain)—as the light from God begins to flow into your head expanding your mind. Pause. Then say the next syllable *leh*—and think *leyv* (heart)—as the light flows into your heart intensifying your capacity for love and compassion. Pause. Finally, say the last syllable *ch*—and think *kaveyd* (liver). As the light flows into your liver, let it spiritually cleanse your blood and flow with it to every part of your body with its healing powers. In effect, you will then be filled with God's light in an amazing state of consciousness. In this elevated state, feel gratitude to God that He is the ruler of the world and maintains the laws of the universe that sustain our world. Pause.

Now say the next word *Ozeyr* (Helper), and as you do, remember God will help you—even in your times of difficulty—to fulfill your dreams. But you must make the effort. Think of a dream you have that needs God's Help to fulfill. Pause.

Say the word *uMoshia* (Savior), connecting with God

Who saves you when you cannot save yourself, when life becomes so difficult you are at a loss to know what to do or when there is nothing we can do. Think of a time in your life where God has saved you from some difficulty. Pause.

Before you say the last word in this series, spread your hands apart. As you say the word *Mageyn* (Shield), bring your hands together until you feel the slightest resistance, and focus on feeling a connection with your soul and God's protective shield. Pause.

Keeping your hands in this position, bend your knees and say the word, *Baruch*…bow to the waist as you say the word, *Ata*…now slowly rise as you say God's name, *Adonai*. As you say the last words of the blessing, *Mageyn Avraham* (Shield of Abraham), bring your hands together enough to feel again this added dimension of God as a Shield of the Jewish people, knowing that as a human being created in the image of God and as a Jew, God is always with you to protect you. Pause.

Now think of those areas of your life or someone else's life close to you where God's help is needed. Take a few moments to ask God for His help … pause … and then say out loud (if you are in an appropriate space), "Hashem help me!" (You can substitute God for Hashem if that works better for you.) Say it again, "Hashem help me!" Repeat this again and again, louder and louder, until you feel your prayer was heard and felt. Pause. Now take a few more moments to tell God whatever it is you want to tell Him. Pause.

Take a minute to thank God for all He has blessed you with in your life. Pause. Ask God to bring peace to the world wherever this is needed, peace to the Jewish people and peace to your life. Finally, take a few more moments just to abide with God in His Presence—feeling the warmth of His presence. Pause.

When you are finished, take three steps back in humility before the Presence of God as you complete your dance with Him; then open your eyes.

Understand that this exercise should be done every time you pray—with the exception of the afternoon *Minchah* service that just has the *Amidah* at its core. Then it should be done without the recitation of the *Shema*. Eventually this exercise should be expanded to encompass every Jewish prayer experience and include the entirety of the Jewish liturgy of the morning, afternoon and evening services. Eventually, one should say the whole *P'sukey D'zimra* with all its Psalms, the whole *Shema* with all its blessings—both before and after—and all of the *Amidah*, including its after-prayers.

But I caution you not to dive so quickly into the sea of Jewish liturgy that you lose the intimacy of the dance. If your prayer routine is to pray mostly alone, then decide on the amount of time you reasonably can give to this daily (or hopefully, thrice-daily) encounter with God. If 15, 20 or 30 minutes is the time you can reasonably devote to this, begin with the above meditation and then add more prayers as time allows, and as suggested at the end of Chapter 1, in the section titled "For the Beginner." When you pray in the synagogue you can do your own prayer routine, perhaps beginning as you say the *Shema* with the congregation and proceding at your own pace. Eventually you will be able to fully align your prayers with the congregation.

CHAPTER 19

Holy Structure

In the beginning of this book we asked the question: "Does the *Siddur,* the prayer book—our prepared script of prayers—help or get in the way of connecting with God? Is there a point to sticking to a set scheduled text—three times a day? Why can't we just pray spontaneously when we feel like it?"

This, as we learned, was the famous debate during the Middle Ages between Maimonides and Nachmanides. For Nachmanides, prayer is "God, I need you."[254] For Maimonides, prayer is "God, I serve you."[255]

Who is right? Our tradition[256] says they are both right! Crisis can be a powerful incentive to pray, but you need not have a crisis in your life to find God. Should prayer not be spontaneous? Of course! However, without a formalized prayer service and a set time to pray, we might hardly ever get around to praying.

There is a story[257] told about Menachem Begin who, as Prime Minister, held a meeting in his house. A religious cabinet member asked to be excused and tucked himself into a corner to *daven* a speedy *minchah* service.

"What's the point?" Begin asked him. "Do you think praying like that accomplishes anything?"

"Perhaps not," the cabinet member honestly replied. "But at least I'm trying. If I keep trying three times a day, eventually I'll make some sort of connection. But if we never even go through the motions …"

This story has a great lesson. Even if we just go through the motions, there is a point to prayer! The more regularly we pray, the more our chances of making a connection with God increases! Just the vibrations of the holy letters, words and chants alone can align our bodies—if not our souls—with God. And when we pray, if we can muster a bit of *Kavanah* (focus and intention) in spite of the busy surroundings we may find ourselves in, we can profoundly connect with God.

The words, the music and the motions of prayer are all part of an elaborate holy dance we do with God. And this dance Partner is ready to dance with us at any time. It is ironic, however, that just knowing this Partner is ready might keep us from dancing with God.

I once came across a beautiful little book about Judaism called *Choose Life!*[258] The author, Ezriel Tauber, asks us to imagine a person was told he could go into the vault at Tiffany's and have one hour to grab all the gems he wanted. The hour begins, but since there is so much time, and he knows he can grab more than he will ever need in half the time, he decides to let himself take in the sights for just a few moments. Mirrored displays, majestic fountains, gourmet food, amusements, and interesting people surround him. There are so many beautiful sights he quickly loses himself. A half hour goes by, 40 minutes, 50 minutes, 55, 59 minutes go by, and all of a sudden he remembers: The hour, it's almost up! As the last minute strikes he sees a gem lying around and grabs it.

He leaves the store, goes to the jeweler next door, and asks how much it is worth. The jeweler looks at the stone and says excitedly, "You want to sell this?"

"Yes."

"I'll give you $100,000 dollars."

If you were this person, how would you feel, asks Tauber? At first you probably would be thrilled with your good fortune. Afterwards, however, the regret would sink in. "Was I crazy?" you will tell yourself over and over. "If in one moment I grabbed $100,000, in one hour I could have grabbed many millions worth of stones!'"

God is always available to hear our prayers. In fact, Kabbalah tells us He waits for us. Sometimes He waits and He waits. If we make God wait until we are in crisis, we will miss out on so many opportunities—each one a precious gem in itself—for connection. And then we may not know how to connect with God when we really need Him!

In God's great wisdom, He commanded us to recite the *Shema* every morning and evening, while the sages commanded us to pray the *Amidah* three times every day. Daily prayer then is not for God's sake. It is obviously for our sakes—so that we never go even half a day without feeling the Presence of God.

Over the centuries the sages[259] carefully crafted a prayer service to help us learn how to do this dance with God. The subsequent holy structure of the service we see formulated in the Talmud:[260] *Bashachar m'vareych shtayim lifaneha v'achat l'achareha, uva-erev shtayim l'faneha ushatayim l'achareha* (In the morning one says two blessings before it [the *Shema*] and one after it, and in the evening two before it and two after it).

The holy structure of Jewish liturgy is fairly straight forward. The *Amidah* prayer is recited three times a day—morning, afternoon and evening—in place of the daily sacrifices and/or the times our forefathers prayed (see Chapter 14, *Avot*). The *Shema* is recited twice daily after the phrase in its first paragraph: *uv'shachb'cha uvkumecha* (when you lie down and when you rise up), i.e., morning and evening. The *Shema* is recited before the *Amidah* because this is the direct word of God from His holy Torah and God's word, of course, takes precedence.[261]

As previously pointed out, when we recite the *Shema*—because this is the word of God—God speaks to us; while in the *Amidah*, we speak to God. This rounds out for us a unique holy dialogue with God. Jewish liturgy, therefore, consists of two main prayers: the *Shema* and the *Amidah*.

The sages carefully crafted special blessings to be recited before the *Shema* and special blessings to be recited after the *Shema* connecting to the *Amidah*. They prefaced it all with a call to prayer called the *Bar'chu*. The one leading the service—if a minyan quorum of ten is present—recites, בָּרְכוּ אֶת יי הַמְבֹרָךְ/ *Bar'chu et Hashem Ham'vorach* (Bless Hashem Who is blessed). In essence, he is saying, "Are you ready to pray together to God?" And the congregation responds, בָּרוּךְ יי הַמְבֹרָךְ לְעוֹלָם וָעֶד/*Baruch Hashem Ham'vorach l'olam va-ed* (Blessed be Hashem Who is blessed forever and ever), indicating, "Yes we're ready to pray!"

Let us now take a look at the blessings before and after the *Shema*; these are so important, the Talmud teaches that anyone who does not recite these—especially the first—does not fulfill his *Shema* obligation.[262]

The *Shema* is a statement of faith—Hashem is our God and He is One with everything. The themes of the blessings before and after the *Shema* expand on this statement of faith as they explore the basic principles of this faith. What are they? They are found in the Talmud in the Mishnah Sanhedrin 10:1: There is a God in the world; the Torah is a gift of love by God to the Jewish people; and God is faithful to be fair. For more on these three principles, see The *Amidah* Supplement, Part 1: *Gevurot*.

The word *Amen*—אָמֵן—as we will see in Chapter 22, is an acronym of three words: אֵל מֶלֶךְ נֶאֱמָן/*Eyl Melech Neh-ehman* (God, King, faithful). When we say *Amen*, we are not only saying we believe, we are also proclaiming what we believe. *Amen* is the shortened form for these same three basic principles of faith: *Eyl*, there is a God; *Melech*, God, our Ruler, gave us the Torah; and *Neh-ehman*, even if we do not see it now, we know God is faithful and whatever evils are in this world will be straightened out eventually.

The *Shema* itself has 245 words. The sages decreed the recitation of the *Shema* should have 248 words in order to correspond to the number of positive commandments and the organs of the body.[263]

The Midrash[264] tells us this is as if God is saying to us, "If you watch over all of the 248 words of My *Shema* that I have commanded you to recite, I will watch over the 248 parts of your body." So when we pray with a minyan, the one leading the service repeats the last two words of the *Shema*—אֱלֹהֵיכֶם ײ (Hashem your God)—and the first word of the following blessing—אֱמֶת (true)—to arrive at this special total. When praying privately, before we recite the *Shema*, which is a statement of our faith, in order to reach the special total of 248 words, we recite the three-word phrase containing the basic elements of our faith: אֵל מֶלֶךְ נֶאֱמָן/*Eyl Melech Neh-ehman* (God, King, faithful).

In fact, the six words of the *Shema* itself allude to these three basic principles. As we learned in Chapter 5, "*Shema*," the six words of the *Shema* contain the first two of the Ten Commandments. What did the Jewish people hear at Mt. Sinai when they received the Ten Commandments? They actually only heard the first two commandments.[265] They begged Moses to tell God to stop speaking to them directly because they feared they would die from the intense spiritual experience. They then asked Moses to get the remaining commandments from God for them—and he did. What is the first of these two commandments heard directly from God? *Anochi Hashem Elohecha* (I am Hashem your God [*Elohecha*]), which is found in the six words of *Shema Yisrael* in the words *Hashem Eloheynu* (Hashem is our God). The second commandment is *Lo yih'yeh l'cha elohim acheyrim al panai* (You shall not have any other gods before Me), which is restated in the positive at the end of the *Shema* verse with the words *Hashem Echad* (Hashem is One). The six words of the *Shema Yisrael* then contain the first two of the Ten Commandments.

Why are these two commandments singled out to be contained in the *Shema*? Because these two commandments are the ones actually heard (*Shema* means "hear") from God.

These three basic principles of faith are revealed in the *She-*

ma as follows: The *Shema* has an *Eyl* (God) meaning, as it says, *Hashem Eloheynu* (Hashem our God), referring to the first commandment: *Anochi Hashem Elohecha* (I am the Lord your God). The *Shema* has a *Melech* (Kingship) meaning, in that within the *Shema* God reveals His commandments—in this case the first two of the Ten Commandments.

Along comes Rashi[266] and reveals in his commentary the *Ne-ehman* (faithful) aspect—the third principle—referring to the future messianic times when God will straighten everything out: "Hashem, Who is our God now, but not the God of the other nations. In the future He will be the One God." And then Rashi quotes the famous verse we recite at the end of the *Aleynu* prayer, "On that day God will be One and His Name One."[267] So within the six words of the *Shema Yisrael* are the three basic principles of faith.

The themes of the blessings surrounding the *Shema* also contain these three basic principles of faith. The first blessing before the *Shema*—*Birkat Yotzeyr* (The Blessing of Creation)—as we will see in the next chapter, maintains there is a God Who created the world and everything within it, including good and evil. The second blessing—*Birkat Ahava* (The Blessing of Love)—as we will see in Chapter 21, demonstrates how much God loves us and cares about us by giving us His Torah. The blessing following the *Shema*—*Birkat Geula* (The Blessing of Redemption)—also in Chapter 21, blesses God Who is involved in His people's lives as the "Redeemer of Israel" Who rescues the Jewish people as He did in Egypt. The ultimate redemption, of course, is the coming of the Messiah—and hence the third principle.

In the evening we add another blessing, *Birkat Shalom* (The Blessing of Peace), right before the *Amidah* as an extension of *Birkat Ahava* (The Blessing of Love). It blesses God for guarding His people and bringing them peace. You will note no universally recognized names are given to the blessings surrounding the *Shema*. The names used in this book for these blessings are mainly for reference purposes.

The blessings before and after the evening *Shema* are shorter, with a slightly different nuance, but nevertheless stress the same basic themes as those of the morning *Shema*. For example, the second blessing, the blessing right before the *Shema* —*Birkat Ahava* (The Blessing of Love) of the morning— expresses appreciation for God's love and compassion in the past for giving us the Torah. The *Birkat Ahava* of the evening looks toward the future promising that "we will rejoice in the words of Your Torah and in its commandments."

In the next couple of chapters we will unpack some of the marvelous holy energy in the *Shema's* blessings. First we will study the very special first blessing before the morning *Shema*. This blessing is, in fact, the biggest blessing of all, containing a most powerful message for all of us as we prepare to recite the *Shema*.

The Biggest Blessing

W ho has never had to confront a crisis in faith? How do you stay connected to God when your life seems to be crumbling before you? Everyone faces a spiritual crisis at some point or another in life, and this is why the sages, in their great wisdom, made the basic principles of faith a recurring theme in Jewish liturgy—especially in the *Shema* and its accompanying blessings.

Lack of faith is hardly a new problem. More than 3,000 years ago, right after the Exodus from Egypt, the Children of Israel again and again displayed a striking lack of faith. The incidents of the Golden Calf[268] and the Spies[269] are just two examples of many. After all God had done for the Jewish people with the ten plagues, the parting of the Red Sea and the defeat of the greatest military power in the world (Egypt) how could they not believe God would be there for them as He promised?

But when you are in pain, when you are afraid, when you are beset by worry, it is hard to think rationally. It is then that Jewish tradition urges you to ask, why is this happening to me? It is hard to come to the understanding that whatever happens to you is a gift from God—that it is only for the best! This kind of realization must come before one faces a crisis and this is one of the main tasks of the daily recitation of the blessings of the *Shema*. The *Shema* is the ultimate statement of faith, and the blessings surrounding it speak to the foundations of this faith: There is a God Who created the world; God loves and cares about us as shown by His gift of the Torah; and God is fair and will redeem us when needed.

בָּרוּךְ אַתָּה יי אֱלֹהֵינוּ מֶלֶךְ הָעוֹלָם, יוֹצֵר אוֹר וּבוֹרֵא חֹשֶׁךְ, עֹשֶׂה שָׁלוֹם וּבוֹרֵא אֶת הַכֹּל:

הַמֵּאִיר לָאָרֶץ וְלַדָּרִים עָלֶיהָ בְּרַחֲמִים, וּבְטוּבוֹ מְחַדֵּשׁ בְּכָל יוֹם תָּמִיד מַעֲשֵׂה בְרֵאשִׁית: מָה רַבּוּ מַעֲשֶׂיךָ יי, כֻּלָּם בְּחָכְמָה עָשִׂיתָ, מָלְאָה הָאָרֶץ קִנְיָנֶךָ: הַמֶּלֶךְ הַמְרוֹמָם לְבַדּוֹ מֵאָז, הַמְשֻׁבָּח וְהַמְפֹאָר וְהַמִּתְנַשֵּׂא מִימוֹת עוֹלָם: אֱלֹהֵי עוֹלָם, בְּרַחֲמֶיךָ הָרַבִּים רַחֵם עָלֵינוּ, אֲדוֹן עֻזֵּנוּ, צוּר מִשְׂגַּבֵּנוּ, מָגֵן יִשְׁעֵנוּ, מִשְׂגָּב בַּעֲדֵנוּ:

אֵל בָּרוּךְ גְּדוֹל דֵּעָה, הֵכִין וּפָעַל זָהֳרֵי חַמָּה, טוֹב יָצַר כָּבוֹד לִשְׁמוֹ, מְאוֹרוֹת נָתַן סְבִיבוֹת עֻזּוֹ, פִּנּוֹת צְבָאָיו קְדוֹשִׁים, רוֹמְמֵי שַׁדַּי, תָּמִיד מְסַפְּרִים כְּבוֹד אֵל וּקְדֻשָּׁתוֹ: תִּתְבָּרֵךְ יי אֱלֹהֵינוּ עַל מַעֲשֵׂה יָדֶיךָ, וְעַל מְאוֹרֵי אוֹר שֶׁעָשִׂיתָ, יְפָאֲרוּךָ סֶּלָה:

תִּתְבָּרֵךְ צוּרֵנוּ מַלְכֵּנוּ וְגוֹאֲלֵנוּ בּוֹרֵא קְדוֹשִׁים, יִשְׁתַּבַּח שִׁמְךָ לָעַד מַלְכֵּנוּ, יוֹצֵר מְשָׁרְתִים וַאֲשֶׁר מְשָׁרְתָיו, כֻּלָּם עוֹמְדִים בְּרוּם עוֹלָם, וּמַשְׁמִיעִים בְּיִרְאָה יַחַד בְּקוֹל, דִּבְרֵי אֱלֹהִים חַיִּים וּמֶלֶךְ עוֹלָם: כֻּלָּם אֲהוּבִים, כֻּלָּם בְּרוּרִים, כֻּלָּם גִּבּוֹרִים, וְכֻלָּם עֹשִׂים בְּאֵימָה וּבְיִרְאָה רְצוֹן קוֹנָם: וְכֻלָּם פּוֹתְחִים אֶת פִּיהֶם בִּקְדֻשָּׁה וּבְטָהֳרָה, בְּשִׁירָה וּבְזִמְרָה, וּמְבָרְכִים וּמְשַׁבְּחִים וּמְפָאֲרִים וּמַעֲרִיצִים וּמַקְדִּישִׁים וּמַמְלִיכִים:

אֶת שֵׁם הָאֵל הַמֶּלֶךְ הַגָּדוֹל הַגִּבּוֹר וְהַנּוֹרָא, קָדוֹשׁ הוּא, וְכֻלָּם מְקַבְּלִים עֲלֵיהֶם עֹל מַלְכוּת שָׁמַיִם זֶה מִזֶּה, וְנוֹתְנִים רְשׁוּת זֶה לָזֶה לְהַקְדִּישׁ לְיוֹצְרָם בְּנַחַת רוּחַ, בְּשָׂפָה בְרוּרָה וּבִנְעִימָה, קְדוּשָׁה כֻּלָּם כְּאֶחָד, עוֹנִים וְאוֹמְרִים בְּיִרְאָה:

קָדוֹשׁ קָדוֹשׁ קָדוֹשׁ יי צְבָאוֹת, מְלֹא כָל הָאָרֶץ כְּבוֹדוֹ:

וְהָאוֹפַנִּים וְחַיּוֹת הַקֹּדֶשׁ בְּרַעַשׁ גָּדוֹל מִתְנַשְּׂאִים לְעֻמַּת שְׂרָפִים, לְעֻמָּתָם מְשַׁבְּחִים וְאוֹמְרִים:

בָּרוּךְ כְּבוֹד יי מִמְּקוֹמוֹ:

לָאֵל בָּרוּךְ נְעִימוֹת יִתֵּנוּ, לַמֶּלֶךְ אֵל חַי וְקַיָּם, זְמִירוֹת יֹאמֵרוּ
וְתִשְׁבָּחוֹת יַשְׁמִיעוּ, כִּי הוּא לְבַדּוֹ פּוֹעֵל גְּבוּרוֹת, עוֹשֶׂה חֲדָשׁוֹת,
בַּעַל מִלְחָמוֹת, זוֹרֵעַ צְדָקוֹת, מַצְמִיחַ יְשׁוּעוֹת, בּוֹרֵא רְפוּאוֹת,
נוֹרָא תְהִלּוֹת, אֲדוֹן הַנִּפְלָאוֹת, הַמְחַדֵּשׁ בְּטוּבוֹ בְּכָל יוֹם תָּמִיד
מַעֲשֵׂה בְרֵאשִׁית: כָּאָמוּר, לְעֹשֵׂה אוֹרִים גְּדֹלִים, כִּי לְעוֹלָם חַסְדּוֹ:
אוֹר חָדָשׁ עַל צִיּוֹן תָּאִיר וְנִזְכֶּה כֻלָּנוּ בִּמְהֵרָה לְאוֹרוֹ: בָּרוּךְ אַתָּה
יְיָ, יוֹצֵר הַמְּאוֹרוֹת:

Blessed are You, Lord our God, King of the Universe,
Who forms light and creates darkness, makes peace
and creates everything.

With compassion You give light to the earth and to all
that who dwell upon it. And in Your goodness You continuously renew the work of creation every day. How
great are Your deeds, Hashem. With wisdom You have
made them all. The earth is full of Your possessions.
You alone have been exalted, praised, glorified and uplifted from days of old. Eternal God, with Your great
compassion, be compassionate towards us. Lord of our
strength, our saving Shield, be our stronghold.

The blessed God, great in knowledge, Who designed
and worked on the rays of the sun. The Good One Who
fashioned honor for His Name, surrounding His power
with luminaries all around. The leaders of His hosts are
holy beings that exalt the Almighty. They continually
tell of the honor of God and His holiness. May You be
blessed, Hashem our God, for the praise of the work
of Your hands, and for the luminaries that You have
made. May they glorify You. Selah!

May You be blessed, our Rock, our King and our Redeemer, Creator of holy beings. May Your Name be
praised forever, our King, Fashioner of ministering

angels. And all of His ministering angels stand at the heights of the universe and declare in awe with one voice the words of the living God and King of the universe. They are all beloved, they are all flawless, they are all mighty. They all do the will of their Maker with fear and reverence. And they all open their mouths with holiness and purity, with song and melody, and bless and praise and glorify and revere and sanctify and proclaim the Kingship of...

The Name of the God, the great, mighty and awesome King, holy is He. They all accept upon themselves the Yoke of the Kingdom of Heaven, one from the other, and give permission to one another to sanctify the One Who formed them with a tranquil spirit, with pure speech and sweet melody. With holiness they all as one answer and say with awe:

Holy, Holy, Holy is God, Master of legions, the world is filled with His glory.

Then the *Ofanim* and *Chayot Hakodesh* angels with a loud noise raise themselves opposing the *Serafim* angels. Facing them they praise and say:

Blessed is the glory of God from His place.

To the blessed God they offer sweet melodies, to the King, the living and eternal God, they will say psalms and declare praises. For it is He alone Who works mighty deeds, makes new things, is Master of war, sows righteousness, causes salvation to sprout, creates healing, is awesome of praises. Lord of wonders, Who renews every day, perpetually, the work of creation. Blessed are You God, Creator of the lights.

The first blessing before the *Shema* in the morning *Shacharit* service is called *Birkat Yotzeyr* (the Blessing of Creation) and is perhaps the longest blessing in all of Jewish liturgy. It begins: *Baruch Ata Hashem, Eloheynu Melech haOlam, Yotzeyr or uVorey choshech, oseh shalom uvorey et hakol* (Blessed are You, Lord our God, King of the Universe, Who forms light and creates darkness, makes peace and creates everything). It ends with a signature blessing: *Baruch Ata Hashem, Yotzeyr hamorot* (Blessed are You God, Creator of the lights.)[270] Its length is an obvious indication of its importance, for its message sets the table as an introduction to the theme of the *Shema*.

What is the central theme of the *Shema*? The central theme is personified in the six words of the first verse which ends with the words, *Hashem Echad* (God is One). Its message is: There is only one Creator of the universe and everything is one with the Creator.

The most profound challenge to faith, to understanding and appreciating the Oneness of God and His creation—as we will learn in The *Amidah* Supplement, Part 1: *Gevurot*—is the problem of theodicy: why the righteous suffer and the wicked prosper. The ancient Persians solved this conundrum by following the belief of their prophet Zoroaster who taught there are two gods in the world: the god of light and the god of darkness, i.e., the god of good and the god of evil. The problem for us in our world today is not how can we believe in two gods—such a thought would not enter the modern mind. Our problem is trying to understand how one God can create both light and darkness, good and evil.

The beginning of the understanding of the Oneness of God in the *Shema* is to understand God is the Creator of both the good and what appears to be evil—illness, handicaps, poverty, and natural disasters like floods, earthquakes, drought, and other misfortunes. The bad in our lives, as we have learned in the chapters on the *Shema*, is usually a good not yet understood. Understanding God is behind all evil is a major step towards understanding the Oneness of God—everything is contained within God, even what appears to be evil. This first blessing preceding the *Shema*, therefore, has the Oneness of God as its theme and specifically mentions God as the *Yotzeyr or uVorey choshech*, the Creator of both light and darkness—good and evil.

After blessing God as the Creator of light and darkness, Who in His goodness renews continuously the work of Creation … after dwelling on the wonder of Creation (on the Sabbath the liturgy elaborates even more), the blessing tells us God's angels sing in Heaven with awe as they, *m'varchim, um'shabchim, um'faaritzim, umakdishim, umamlichim* (bless, praise, glorify, tell of God's might, declare God's holiness and His Kingship).

What do angels have to do with this theme of the Oneness of God? After all, the very existence of angels indicates a plurality of heavenly beings, not one.

To answer this we must understand what an angel really is. The commentators mention the prophets portraying angels as creatures to help us picture how God works, but the Hebrew for angel, *malach*, really means "messenger." Angels, as Maimonides[271] teaches, are the vehicles, the messengers, the forces, the natural laws of the universe whose task it is to fulfill the *ratzon Hashem* (the will, the desire of God). There are some angels created with *chesed* (kindness), to give a flow of kindness to the world, and there are other angels created with *din* (judgment) to bring hardship into the world—hardships that make us wonder why we are being judged so harshly.

This blessing proclaims every morning: *Kulam ahuvim, kulam b'rurim, kulam giborim* (They—the angels—are all beloved, they are all flawless, they are all mighty). This blessing says of all the angels coming to this world: *Kulam osim b'eyma uv'yira r'tzon konam* (They all do the will of their Maker with fear and reverence). It is all one thing—whether the messenger comes to give us things that are easy, desirable and pleasurable, or whether the messenger comes to give us a great challenge. The source of both is one—God! *Kulam potchim et pihem bikdusha uvtahara* (And they all open their mouths with holiness and purity). Every angel coming to this world, everything happening to you from Heaven, comes from the same source.

This blessing is not an easy part of the prayer service. If someone is lying in a hospital bed worrying about his health, it is not easy to say, *Kulam ahuvim* (The angels who brought this upon me are all beloved, all flawless…They all do the will of their Maker with fear and reverence). It is a great personal challenge for one who prays while he is ill.

The blessing continues: *V'chulam m'kablim aleyhem ol malchut shamayim zeh mizeh* (And they all accept upon themselves the yoke of the Kingdom of Heaven one from the other). *V'notnim r'shut zeh lazeh l'hakdish l'yotzram* (and they grant permission to one another to sanctify the One Who formed them). They are together in their missions. It is all one—all the challenges of life. *Kedusha kulam k'echad onim v'omrim b'yira* (With holiness they all as one answer and say with awe):

קָדוֹשׁ קָדוֹשׁ קָדוֹשׁ, יי צְבָאוֹת. מְלֹא כָל הָאָרֶץ כְּבוֹדוֹ

Kadosh, Kadosh, Kadosh, Hashem tz'va-ot,
m'lo chol haaretz k'vodo,
Holy, Holy, Holy is God, Master of legions,
the world is filled with His glory.

Recognizing it is all one—all that happens is from the same source—deserves the longest blessing in our liturgy, because it deserves the most careful and purposeful consideration every day!

There are angels doing things for us we are happy to receive, and there are angels putting before us moments of challenge and suffering. But *Kulam ahuvim* (They are all beloved) … *Kulam osim b'eyma uv'yira r'tzon konam* (They all do the will of their Maker with fear and reverence). They are all here for a purpose.

For the one to whom things are going well to say, *Kadosh, Kadosh, Kadosh* (Holy, Holy, Holy is God) is one thing. But for one who is in a hospital bed to say this is quite another thing. He is truly sanctifying the Name of God! Our task when reciting this first blessing before the *Shema* is to recognize everything comes with a purpose, and along with every challenge comes an opportunity to sanctify the Name of God. It is the largest blessing because it is the greatest challenge to our faith.

The *Baaley Musar*, the 19th century Jewish moralists, teach that we must not go to someone who experiences a tragedy and tell him/her, "It's all for the best." When a person is not well or is suffering with great worry over his/her family situation or business, you must not start preaching to the person that it is all for the best. When a person is in pain we must give him/her comfort.

In order to avoid a crisis in faith when confronted by hardships, in order to reach the level of faith of knowing whatever happens to us is for the best, we must be prepared beforehand by recognizing this truth when things are well, and only then will we be able to recognize this again—first with small challenges and then larger ones. And so to help us get to such a level of faith we say *every day* in our prayers: *Kulam ahuvim* (They are all beloved)—the angels we are happy to experience as well as the angels we are disappointed to experience—all of them are beloved … *Kulam osim b'eyma uv'yira r'tzon konam* (They all do will of their Maker with fear and reverence).

The blessing continues with a mini-*Kedusha*. *Kedusha* means "holiness." It is a compilation of the holiest verses found in the Bible in praise of God. While the *Kedusha* found in the *Amidah* contains from three to five of these verses—depending upon whether it is a weekday, Sabbath or holiday *Shacharit* or *Musaf Amidah*—the *Kedusha* of this blessing preceding the *Shema* contains only the two most holy verses because the contrast of these verses amplify its main theme.

These verses, along with their chapters in the Prophets Isaiah and Ezekiel, are the main sources for what is called *Merkavah Kabbalah* (Chariot Mysticism), because these are the most profound revelations found outside the Torah.

The first verse of angelic praise is from Isaiah.[272] In it the *Serafim* angels sing out: *Kadosh, Kadosh, Kadosh, Hashem Tz'va-*

ot, m'lo chol haaretz k'vodo (Holy, Holy, Holy is God, Master of
Legions, the whole world is filled with His glory). What does
M'lo chol haaretz k'vodo (the whole world is filled with His glory)
teach us? Wherever you might look, you will see God revealed
in the world because the whole world testifies to God's glory. On
the physical plane, if we seriously look at the world—from the
intricacies of the human body to the cycles of nature to the vast
ecosystems that sustain the earth—one cannot help but see God.
If we look deeper into interpersonal relationships, or into spiritual and mystical insights, we will find a deeper understanding
of God. The profound message of this verse is that God can be
found anywhere we look.

The second verse is from Ezekiel:[273]

בָּרוּךְ כְּבוֹד יְיָ מִמְּקוֹמוֹ

Baruch k'vod Hashem mimekomo
Blessed is the glory of God from His place

Our blessing tells us these words were recited by the *Ofanim*
and *Chayot Hakodesh* angels as mentioned in Ezekiel. It reads,
B'raash gadol mitnas'im l'umat Serafim (With a loud noise they
raise themselves opposing the *Serafim).* They, in effect, say to
the *Serafim* angels of Isaiah, "No, sometimes our pain is so great
that we cannot see the glory of God everywhere. Our world is
sometimes a world of *hester panim,* a world where God 'hides His
face,' and we cannot see Him. Nevertheless we praise God saying,
'Blessed be the glory of God from His place!' wherever that is."[274]

So we have one group of angels—the *Serafim*—who praise
God as a God who reveals Himself everywhere, and we have another group of angels—the *Ofanim* and *Chayot Hakodesh*—who
praise God, even though it seems as though God is hiding. We
recite both verses of praise so we might come to the realization
both are true. Both exist in our lives—sometimes one right after
the other. There are times when life is sweet, when we can see the
glory of God in the world, and so we feel like singing out loud

proclaiming, *Kadosh, Kadosh, Kadosh Hashem* (Holy, Holy, Holy is God…the whole world is filled with His Glory). And there are times when we sense God is hiding from us; so we say, "Blessed be the glory of God in His place"—wherever that is!

Angels—who are one dimensional—are unable to see both approaches, but we must try to see both. In the *Maariv* evening service, this blessing before the *Shema* contains the words, *uvitvuna m'shaneh itim, umachlif et haz'manim* (and with understanding [God] changes the seasons and switches the times). There are good and bad seasons and times in our lives and God can change and switch us from the bad times to the good or the reverse. The evening blessing continues, God is *goleyl or mipney choshech, v'choshech mipney or* (He removes the light before the darkness and the darkness before the light).

What a blessing this is! It is about the things that make us happy and the things that make us sad. What is the fitting conclusion of this blessing? *Ki hu l'vado po-eyl g'vurot, oseh chadashot, baal milchamot, zoreya tzedakot, matzmiach y'shuot, boey r'fu-ot* (For God alone works mighty deeds, makes new things, is a Master of war, sows righteousness, causes salvation to sprout, creates healing). God is One! Whatever happens, it is all for the good. Everything stems from God's compassion—even the pain we sometimes experience. It is all part of God's *r'fuah*, God's healing.

Ham'chadeysh b'tuvo b'chol yom tamid ma-asey v'reyshit (He renews every day, perpetually, the work of creation). In other words, it is only because of the continuous flow of God's loving energy that the world maintains itself. If God would take only one day off—even one minute—the whole world would cease to exist. The signature *beracha* of this blessing then states: *Baruch Ata Hashem, Yotzeyr haM'orot* (Blessed are You God, Who forms the lights), Who brings His light and love to the world. What a beautiful blessing this is. It is an acknowledgment of what is going on in our lives as well as a fitting preparation to the theme of the Oneness of God in the *Shema*.

What are the great times in our lives? Ask anyone and they

will tell you the good times are when things are going well. But at a funeral, when we really assess the value of the life before us, we tell how the deceased persevered through adversity, how he started out with nothing and made something of himself, how he did what was right even though it was not easy, how he faced illness with courage, how he was a *mentsh*, a "wonderful human being," even though he was suffering, those are the moments that bring greatness.

John James Audubon,[275] the famous naturalist and ornithologist of the 19th century, for whom the Audubon Society is named, once found a cocoon of an emperor moth when he was a small boy. He took it home so he could watch the moth come out of the cocoon. Soon a small opening appeared. He sat and watched the moth for several hours as the moth struggled to force its body through the little hole.

Then it seemed to stop making any progress. It appeared as if it had gotten as far as it could and could go no further. It seemed to be stuck. Out of compassion for one of God's creatures, he decided to help the moth, so he took a pair of scissors and snipped off the remaining bit of the cocoon. The moth then emerged easily, but it had a swollen body and small, shriveled wings.

He continued to watch the moth because he expected that at any moment, the wings would enlarge and expand to be able to support the body, which would contract in time. Neither happened! In fact, the little moth crawled around with a swollen body and shriveled wings, and then died. It never was able to fly.

Little Audubon went crying to his father who explained to him that the restricting cocoon and the struggle required for the moth to get through the tiny opening, was the way of forcing fluid from the body of the moth into its wings so it would be ready for flight once it achieved its freedom from the cocoon. Freedom and flight, life itself, would only come after the struggle. By depriving the moth of its necessary struggle, he deprived the moth of its life.

The term the Torah uses for the struggles of life is *nisayon* (test). Abraham's ultimate challenge—the *Akeyda,* the binding of Isaac—is introduced with the words: *Elohim nisa et Avraham* (And God tested Abraham).[276] It is called a test because through testing—through enduring and overcoming bitter, tough experiences—we grow. The root of *nisayon, nisa,* also means "to lift up." *Neys,* which commonly means "a miracle," can also mean "a banner or a flag or something lifted up."[277] When a person goes through a *nisayon,* a test, at the same time he is uplifted and elevated.

Ask an artist when he really learned to paint or a writer to write. He most likely will tell you, "first you must suffer and then you will understand." Without the tests of life, we would be like a person born with a silver spoon in his mouth who never learns how to walk because he did not want to fall, who never learns how to think because he never had to think, who never learns how to do anything because he never had to. What a fantastic concept!

The Chofetz Chaim (Rabbi Israel Meir haKohen, d. 1933) once met a student of his after many years and asked him how he was doing with his life. The student responded, "*Oy Shlect,* it is so bad."

The Chafetz Chaim reproved him saying, "*Chas V'sholom,* God forbid. You are forbidden to say that. You must not say life is bad. You can say life is bitter, but you must not say it is bad."

The student was surprised and asked, "I don't understand. Forgive me for saying this, but bad or bitter, what's the difference?"

The Chafetz Chaim was so upset. He said—and here comes the punch line—"You don't understand. A medicine may be bitter but it's never bad!"

Wow! Let's think through what the Chofetz Chaim was saying. Bitterness is a momentary sensation. It passes. A medicine can be bitter but this does not mean it is bad, because bad is a long-range effect. One takes medicine for his own good even if it is a bitter pill to swallow. There are experiences in life which may be bitter pills to swallow, but, as God tells us: *Ani Hashem Rofecha* (I am the Lord your Doctor)![278]

Sometimes struggles and adversity are exactly what we need. If we were to go through life without obstacles, we would be crippled. We are only as strong as we are because of our struggles. Conflict leads to growth, so do not regret the struggles when they come, for the struggles help the development and growth of our souls.

When we praise God in moments of darkness, we bring greatness upon ourselves. Our personal hardships are—and it may be hard to look at it this way, but it is true—our personal hardships are God's gift to us, tailor-made for our personal soul development. *Kulam ahuvim,* all the angels watching over us are beloved—those bringing good times and those bringing hardship. What is the ultimate Source of it all? As the concluding blessing tells us, the *Yotzeyr hamorot,* God who brings His light and love to the world. When we train ourselves to see this truth by reciting this blessing every day, and by recognizing its truth as we go through the rest of each day, we will give ourselves the strength and the tools to avoid the crises in faith when they threaten.

162

CHAPTER 21

The Greatest Love of All

How can we deepen our love for God? The obvious answer is to keep the laws of the Torah and our religious traditions because God's Torah is an expression of His love for us, His guide for us to have a better life.

Our traditions, on the other hand, are an expression of our love for God. Embellishing the commandments, going beyond the letter of the law and doing more than the Torah law requires, is a way of showing our love.

The second blessing, the one right before the *Shema*, is *Birkat Ahava* (The Blessing of Love). Its basic theme is that with love, God, Who created and relates to all, chose the Jews to be His Chosen People—chosen to model for the world how to have a relationship with God.

This is an amazing honor and privilege. The ultimate expression of the love personified in this blessing is God giving His Torah to the Jewish people—an act of great and eternal love.

This is expressed in the different openings of the morning and evening versions of this blessing: *Ahava Raba* (Great love) for the morning and *Ahavat Olam* (Eternal love) for the evenings. There is some discussion in the Talmud[279] about which of these phrases should be used to open these blessings, and although many Sephardim and Chasidim recite *Ahavat Olam* (Eternal Love) in the morning as well, tradition has it that most congregations recite *Ahava Raba* (Great love) in the morning and *Ahavat Olam* (Eternal love) in the evenings.

This is not just a matter of semantics. There is a beautiful lesson here. When two young people meet and express their great love for each other, they get married in the morning of their lives. The hope is their great love will deepen to the extent it becomes an everlasting love in the evening of their lives. God's love for us is eternal and it is up to us to work to deepen our love for Him every day so that, in turn, it becomes everlasting as well.

The minutia of Jewish law and tradition are, in this context, a dance of love we do with our Creator. God's love for us, expressed in giving us the Torah, is also the theme of the blessing recited before the reading of the Torah, blessing God, "Who has chosen us from among all the other nations and has given us His Torah." In fact, the *Shulchan Aruch* suggests this second blessing before the *Shema* can be substituted as a blessing before the study of Torah.[280]

אַהֲבָה רַבָּה אֲהַבְתָּנוּ יי אֱלֹהֵינוּ, חֶמְלָה גְדוֹלָה וִיתֵרָה חָמַלְתָּ עָלֵינוּ: אָבִינוּ מַלְכֵּנוּ, בַּעֲבוּר אֲבוֹתֵינוּ שֶׁבָּטְחוּ בְךָ, וַתְּלַמְּדֵם חֻקֵּי חַיִּים כֵּן תְּחָנֵּנוּ וּתְלַמְּדֵנוּ: אָבִינוּ הָאָב הָרַחֲמָן, הַמְרַחֵם, רַחֵם עָלֵינוּ, וְתֵן בְּלִבֵּנוּ לְהָבִין וּלְהַשְׂכִּיל, לִשְׁמֹעַ, לִלְמֹד וּלְלַמֵּד, לִשְׁמֹר וְלַעֲשׂוֹת וּלְקַיֵּם אֶת כָּל דִּבְרֵי תַלְמוּד תּוֹרָתֶךָ בְּאַהֲבָה: וְהָאֵר עֵינֵינוּ בְּתוֹרָתֶךָ, וְדַבֵּק לִבֵּנוּ בְּמִצְוֹתֶיךָ, וְיַחֵד לְבָבֵנוּ לְאַהֲבָה וּלְיִרְאָה אֶת שְׁמֶךָ, וְלֹא נֵבוֹשׁ לְעוֹלָם וָעֶד: כִּי בְשֵׁם קָדְשְׁךָ הַגָּדוֹל וְהַנּוֹרָא בָּטָחְנוּ, נָגִילָה וְנִשְׂמְחָה בִּישׁוּעָתֶךָ: וַהֲבִיאֵנוּ לְשָׁלוֹם מֵאַרְבַּע כַּנְפוֹת הָאָרֶץ. וְתוֹלִיכֵנוּ קוֹמְמִיּוּת לְאַרְצֵנוּ: כִּי אֵל פּוֹעֵל יְשׁוּעוֹת אָתָּה, וּבָנוּ בָחַרְתָּ מִכָּל עַם וְלָשׁוֹן, וְקֵרַבְתָּנוּ לְשִׁמְךָ הַגָּדוֹל סֶלָה בֶּאֱמֶת: לְהוֹדוֹת לְךָ וּלְיַחֶדְךָ בְּאַהֲבָה: בָּרוּךְ אַתָּה יי, הַבּוֹחֵר בְּעַמּוֹ יִשְׂרָאֵל בְּאַהֲבָה:

With great love You have loved us, Hashem our God. With great and exceeding compassion You have had compassion upon us. Our Father our King, for the sake of our Fathers who trusted in You, and to whom You have taught the laws of life, be gracious to us and teach us as well. Our Father, merciful Father, You Who are the epitome of mercy, have mercy upon us, instill in our hearts to understand and discern, to hear, to learn and to teach, to guard and do, and fulfill all the words of Your Torah with love. Enlighten our eyes with Your Torah and let our hearts cleave to Your commandments, and unify our hearts to love and be in awe of Your Name so that we never be ashamed. Because in Your holy, great and awesome Name we have trusted, may we be joyful and happy in your salvation. Bring us in peace from the four corners of the earth, and lead us with our heads held high to our land. For You are a God Who brings salvations. And You have chosen us from every people and tongue and have brought us near to Your great Name, selah, in truth, so that we may thank You and declare Your Oneness with love. Blessed are You, Hashem, Who chooses His people Israel with love.

The structure of the service with the juxtaposition of this Blessing of Love with the first two verses of the *Shema* is nothing short of exquisite. The verse in the Torah immediately following the six words of the *Shema Yisrael*—the statement of faith of the Jewish people—is *V'ahavta eyt Hashem Elohecha* (You shall love Hashem your God). Sandwiched between *Birkat Ahava*, the blessing expressing God's love for us, and the *V'ahavta* verse, where we are to express our love for God, is the *Shema Yisrael* expressing the Oneness of God and how we are an extension of His loving energy that eternally connects us.

This is lovingly expressed in the morning version of this blessing: "Our Father, merciful Father, You Who are the epitome of mercy, have mercy upon us, instill in our hearts to understand and discern, to hear, to learn and to teach, to guard and do, and fulfill all the words of Your Torah with love. Enlighten our eyes with Your Torah and let our hearts cleave (*dabeyk*) to Your commandments, and unify our hearts to love and be in awe of Your

Name."

The word *dabeyk* (cleave) sums up the spiritual energy of this prayer and points to why it so appropriately precedes the *Shema*. *D'veykut* (cleaving) signifies the intimacy of being one with God. The Chasidim speak of achieving a state of *d'veykut* in which one can, for the moment, lose a sense of self. It is like the mystical state of *ayin*, or nullification. The Torah[281] tells us, "And you who cling (*d'veykim*) to Hashem your God, you are all alive today." To feel fully alive, one must feel the intimacy that comes with attaching oneself to God.

When your soul sometimes feels like it is scattered, when so much of what is going on in your life is negative and you do not know where to turn or what to do, you can find a path through prayer and meditation to *d'veykut*, to unify yourself with God. This, in turn, will help unify your soul and enable you to access the holy energy God is always sending you so you can go on and find your way. And so before we recite the *Shema*—a statement of God's unity—we recite this blessing in an attempt to help us on this path.

Vahavi-eynu l'shalom mey-arba kanfot haaretz...l'artzeynu (Bring us in peace from the four corners of the earth...to our land). Here is a plea for God to help all His people to find Him in the land He has given to His people. When reciting these words, it is customary for men to gather the *tzitzit* from the four corners of the *tallit* they are wearing and to hold them during the recitation of the *Shema*. This is sort of a reenactment of the hope that we will be reunited with all our people in our land from the four corners of the earth to proclaim the love and Oneness of God to the world.

In the previous chapter we discussed the first blessing before the *Shema*, the *Birkat Yotzeyr* (The Blessing of Creation). So far in this chapter we discussed the next blessing, *Birkat Ahava* (The Blessing of Love). Let us now move to the blessings after the *Shema*: *Birkat Geula* (The Blessing of Redemption) and, for the evenings, *Hashkiveynu* (The Blessing of Peace).

Birkat Geula This blessing is fairly long because of its powerful message, but it is not technically a "long
blessing" because it does not begin with the formula, *Baruch Ata*.
Instead, this blessing begins with a word that confirms what came
before.[282] In fact, according to tradition, one concludes the recitation of the *Shema* with the first word of this blessing. Accordingly,
the *Shema* ends with the words, *Ani Hashem Eloheychem* (I am
Hashem your God); to which is added immediately the first word
of this Blessing of Redemption, *Emet* (Truth).

When one does this, one affirms the sacred truth of the
whole *Shema*. This is further affirmed in the next 15 words of the
morning blessing: "certain, correct, enduring, straight, faithful,
beloved, precious, pleasant, delightful, awesome, powerful, perfect, acceptable, good and beautiful." In fact, the whole first part
of this blessing confirms the truth of the *Shema*:

אֱמֶת וְיַצִּיב וְנָכוֹן וְקַיָּם וְיָשָׁר וְנֶאֱמָן וְאָהוּב וְחָבִיב וְנֶחְמָד וְנָעִים
וְנוֹרָא וְאַדִּיר וּמְתֻקָּן וּמְקֻבָּל וְטוֹב וְיָפֶה הַדָּבָר הַזֶּה עָלֵינוּ לְעוֹלָם
וָעֶד: אֱמֶת, אֱלֹהֵי עוֹלָם מַלְכֵּנוּ, צוּר יַעֲקֹב מָגֵן יִשְׁעֵנוּ, לְדֹר וָדֹר
הוּא קַיָּם וּשְׁמוֹ קַיָּם, וְכִסְאוֹ נָכוֹן, וּמַלְכוּתוֹ וֶאֱמוּנָתוֹ לָעַד קַיֶּמֶת:
וּדְבָרָיו חָיִים וְקַיָּמִים, נֶאֱמָנִים וְנֶחֱמָדִים לָעַד וּלְעוֹלְמֵי עוֹלָמִים,
עַל אֲבוֹתֵינוּ וְעָלֵינוּ, עַל בָּנֵינוּ וְעַל דּוֹרוֹתֵינוּ, וְעַל כָּל דּוֹרוֹת
זֶרַע יִשְׂרָאֵל עֲבָדֶיךָ:

עַל הָרִאשׁוֹנִים וְעַל הָאַחֲרוֹנִים, דָּבָר טוֹב וְקַיָּם לְעוֹלָם וָעֶד,
אֱמֶת וֶאֱמוּנָה, חֹק וְלֹא יַעֲבֹר, אֱמֶת שָׁאַתָּה הוּא יי אֱלֹהֵינוּ וֵאלֹהֵי
אֲבוֹתֵינוּ, מַלְכֵּנוּ מֶלֶךְ אֲבוֹתֵינוּ, גּוֹאֲלֵנוּ גּוֹאֵל אֲבוֹתֵינוּ, יוֹצְרֵנוּ
צוּר יְשׁוּעָתֵנוּ, פּוֹדֵנוּ וּמַצִּילֵנוּ מֵעוֹלָם הוּא שְׁמֶךָ, אֵין אֱלֹהִים
זוּלָתֶךָ:

עֶזְרַת אֲבוֹתֵינוּ אַתָּה הוּא מֵעוֹלָם, מָגֵן וּמוֹשִׁיעַ לִבְנֵיהֶם אַחֲרֵיהֶם
בְּכָל דּוֹר וָדוֹר: בְּרוּם עוֹלָם מוֹשָׁבֶךָ, וּמִשְׁפָּטֶיךָ וְצִדְקָתְךָ עַד
אַפְסֵי אָרֶץ: אַשְׁרֵי אִישׁ שֶׁיִּשְׁמַע לְמִצְוֹתֶיךָ וְתוֹרָתְךָ וּדְבָרְךָ יָשִׂים
עַל לִבּוֹ: אֱמֶת, אַתָּה הוּא אָדוֹן לְעַמֶּךָ, וּמֶלֶךְ גִּבּוֹר לָרִיב רִיבָם:
אֱמֶת, אַתָּה הוּא רִאשׁוֹן וְאַתָּה הוּא אַחֲרוֹן, וּמִבַּלְעָדֶיךָ אֵין לָנוּ

מֶֽלֶךְ גּוֹאֵל וּמוֹשִׁיעַ: מִמִּצְרַֽיִם גְּאַלְתָּֽנוּ יְיָ אֱלֹהֵֽינוּ, וּמִבֵּית עֲבָדִים
פְּדִיתָֽנוּ, כָּל בְּכוֹרֵיהֶם הָרָֽגְתָּ, וּבְכוֹרְךָ גָּאָֽלְתָּ, וְיַם סוּף בָּקַֽעְתָּ,
וְזֵדִים טִבַּֽעְתָּ, וִידִידִים הֶעֱבַֽרְתָּ, וַיְכַסּוּ מַֽיִם צָרֵיהֶם, אֶחָד מֵהֶם
לֹא נוֹתָר: עַל זֹאת שִׁבְּחוּ אֲהוּבִים וְרוֹמְמוּ אֵל, וְנָתְֽנוּ יְדִידִים
זְמִירוֹת שִׁירוֹת וְתִשְׁבָּחוֹת, בְּרָכוֹת וְהוֹדָאוֹת, לְמֶֽלֶךְ אֵל חַי וְקַיָּם:
רָם וְנִשָּׂא, גָּדוֹל וְנוֹרָא, מַשְׁפִּיל גֵּאִים, וּמַגְבִּֽיהַּ שְׁפָלִים, מוֹצִיא
אֲסִירִים, וּפוֹדֶה עֲנָוִים, וְעוֹזֵר דַּלִּים, וְעוֹנֶה לְעַמּוֹ בְּעֵת שַׁוְּעָם
אֵלָיו: תְּהִלּוֹת לְאֵל עֶלְיוֹן, בָּרוּךְ הוּא וּמְבֹרָךְ, מֹשֶׁה וּבְנֵי יִשְׂרָאֵל
לְךָ עָנוּ שִׁירָה בְּשִׂמְחָה רַבָּה, וְאָמְרוּ כֻלָּם:

מִי כָמֹֽכָה בָּאֵלִים, יְיָ, מִי כָּמֹֽכָה נֶאְדָּר בַּקֹּֽדֶשׁ, נוֹרָא תְהִלֹּת, עֹֽשֵׂה
פֶֽלֶא:

שִׁירָה חֲדָשָׁה שִׁבְּחוּ גְאוּלִים לְשִׁמְךָ עַל שְׂפַת הַיָּם, יַֽחַד כֻּלָּם הוֹדוּ
וְהִמְלִֽיכוּ וְאָמְרוּ: יְיָ יִמְלֹךְ לְעוֹלָם וָעֶד:

צוּר יִשְׂרָאֵל, קֽוּמָה בְּעֶזְרַת יִשְׂרָאֵל, וּפְדֵה כִנְאֻמֶֽךָ יְהוּדָה וְיִשְׂרָאֵל
גֹּאֲלֵֽנוּ יְיָ צְבָאוֹת שְׁמוֹ קְדוֹשׁ יִשְׂרָאֵל: בָּרוּךְ אַתָּה יְיָ, גָּאַל יִשְׂרָאֵל:

True and certain, correct, enduring, straight, faithful, beloved, precious, pleasant, delightful, awesome, powerful, perfect, acceptable, good and beautiful is this assertion for us forever. True is the God of the world, our King, the Rock of Jacob, Shield of our salvation. Through all generations He endures and His Name endures and His throne is established, and His Kingship and His faithfulness is forever established. His words are living and enduring, faithful and precious for all time. As they were for our fathers so may they be upon us, upon our children and upon our generations, and upon all generations of the seed of Israel Your servants.

"Upon the first and upon the later generations, this assertion is good and enduring forever, true and faithful, an immutable law. True, you are Hashem, our God and the God of our fathers, our King and the King of our fathers, our Redeemer and the Redeemer of our fathers, our Maker, the Rock of our salvation, our Deliverer and our Rescuer, this has forever been Your Name. There is no God but You!

You have always been the help of our fathers, a Shield and a Savior to their children after them through every generation. In the heights of the universe is Your dwelling, and Your justice and righteousness reach to the ends of the earth. Happy is the one who obeys Your commandments and Your Torah while Your words are put upon his heart. True, You are the Lord of Your people and a mighty King to fight their cause. True, You are the first and You are the last and besides You we have no king, redeemer or savior. From Egypt You redeemed us, Hashem our God, and from the house of bondage You rescued us. All their firstborn You killed, and Your firstborn You redeemed. And You split the Red Sea and drowned the wicked, but Your dear ones You brought across. And the water covered their enemies, not one of them was left. For this, the beloved praised You and extolled God, and offered psalms, songs and praise, blessings and thanksgiving to the King, the living and eternal God. He is high and exalted, great and awesome. He humbles the arrogant and raises up the lowly, frees the captives and liberates the oppressed, helps the poor and answers His people when they cry out to Him. Praises to the God Most High, the blessed One Who is blessed. Moses and the children of Israel sang a song unto You with great joy. All of them said:

"Who is like You Hashem among the powers of the world; Who is like You, glorious in holiness, fearful of praises, doing wonders?"

With a new song the redeemed people praised Your Name on the shore of the sea. In unison they all thanked and acknowledged Your Kingship and said: "Hashem will reign forever and ever."

Rock of Israel, arise in help of Israel, liberate as You promised Judah and Israel. Our Redeemer, Hashem of hosts is His Name. Blessed are You Hashem, Who redeemed Israel.

The blessing moves on, serving as the transition from affirming the truth of the *Shema*—God is One with all—to the message of this blessing affirming God is active in the world, watching over and redeeming those He created. And so it describes some of the things He does: "True, you are Hashem, our God and the God of our fathers, our King and the King of our fathers, our Redeemer and the Redeemer of our fathers, our Maker the Rock of our salvation, our Deliverer and our Rescuer, this has ever been Your Name. There is no God but You!"

In describing God as the ultimate Redeemer, this blessing uses the Exodus from Egypt as an illustration because it is the paradigm example of redemption. The Jews became a people in Egypt. They came to Egypt as 70 souls and left with a population of two to three million. The whole experience of slavery with its horrors and cruelty forged upon them a common fate. It was the first time they, as a people, were in trouble and God came to their rescue. It set the paradigm for the future of Jewish history and this is why this blessing uses the Exodus to illustrate God as our Redeemer.

The Talmud[283] comments on such usage of the name of God, *Eh'yeh Asher Eh'yeh* (I Will Be What I Will Be), with God telling the Jewish people, "I was with them in that subjugation [Egypt] and I will be with them in the subjugation of other kingdoms." If God redeemed our people in Egypt, hopefully, He will do this again in our time.

And so the blessing emphasizes that God "has always been the help of our fathers," as if to indicate this will continue. The blessing seems to hint to only one condition: "Happy is the one who obeys Your commandments." Happy is he because, perhaps, it is he who will be redeemed.

The blessing then quotes two famous verses from the Song of the Sea sung by Moses and the Children of Israel after they crossed onto dry land, escaping Pharaoh and the pursuing Egyptians. The first: *Mi chamocha ba-eylim Hashem; mi kamocha nedar bakodesh; norah t'hilot, osey feleh* (Who is like You Hashem among the powers of the world; Who is like You, glorious in holiness, too awesome for praises, doing wonders)? This verse expands on the theme of a previous verse in this blessing: *Umibaladecha eyn lanu Go-eyl Umoshia* (Besides You we have no King who redeems and saves).

For more on the very powerful *Mi chamocha* verse, see Chapter 12, "Too Awesome For Praises."

What follows next is a second verse from the Song of the Sea: *Hashem yimloch l'olam va-ed* (Hashem will reign forever and ever)—God will always be there to redeem His people.

The blessing concludes: *Tzur Yisrael, kuma b'ezrat Yisrael, ufdey chinumecha Yehuda v'Yisrael. Go-aleynu Hashem Tz'va-ot Shmo, k'dosh Yisrael. Baruch Ata Hashem, Ga-al Yisrael* (Rock of Israel, arise in help of Israel, liberate as You promised Judah and Israel. Our Redeemer, Hashem of hosts is His Name. Blessed are You Hashem, Who redeemed Israel). While the first blessing before the *Shema, Birkat Yotzeyr,* made reference to the past with the creation of the world, this blessing after the *Shema, Birkat Geula,* ends with a plea for God to help us, liberate us and redeem us in the future.

Just as the *Shema* was immediately followed, without interruption, by the first word of this blessing, *emet* (truth), so, to affirm the truth of the *Shema,* the Talmud[284] requires this Blessing of Redemption to also be immediately followed by the *Amidah* without interruption. Before we approach a recitation of the *Ami-*

dah where we ask God to be involved in our lives—to help us by changing our lives for the better—we recall in this blessing the miraculous Redemption from Egypt where God most clearly had involved Himself in the lives of His people.

The Hebrew word for Egypt is *Mitzrayim*. As we learned at the end of Chapter 10, "*Tzitzit*," it contains the root word *tzar* (narrow). In the plural form, when used as a noun, *tzarot* usually means "troubles." Thus *Mitzrayim* can mean "narrow places" or "troubled places." God redeemed us from the land of *Mitzrayim*, the land of Egypt—the land of troubles. When we begin the *Amidah* that follows, in which we are more specific in our requests to God for help, we show our faith in God that He will redeem us soon from our own *Mitzrayim,* our own troubles and narrow places.

HASHKIVEYNU   *Hashkiveynu Hashem Eloheynu l'shalom* (Cause us, Hashem our God, to lie down in peace). We learned from the Talmud that the structure of Jewish liturgy requires two blessings after the *Shema* in the evening. However, as we have learned, the Talmud also requires that we immediately follow the first blessing after the *Shema*, the Blessing of Redemption, with the *Amidah*. If so, there would be no room for the second blessing, *Hashkiveynu*. The Talmud[285] solves this problem by labeling both the Blessing of Redemption and the *Hashkiveynu,* taken together, as *geula arichta* (one long Redemption blessing). The *Hashkiveynu* blessing is then considered as an extension of the *Birkat Geula* (the Blessing of Redemption).

Rabbeynu Yona[286] explains that the *Hashkiveynu* blessing has an historical dimension in that it was instituted to correspond to the prayer said by the Jews during the last of the plagues of Egypt—the death of the firstborn—that the plague should not reach their homes. Since this was a prayer for redemption during the redemption of Egypt, it is easy to see the Talmud's point that this is an extension of the Blessing of Redemption that focuses on the redemption from Egypt:

הַשְׁכִּיבֵנוּ יי אֱלֹהֵינוּ לְשָׁלוֹם, וְהַעֲמִידֵנוּ מַלְכֵּנוּ לְחַיִּים, וּפְרוֹשׂ
עָלֵינוּ סֻכַּת שְׁלוֹמֶךָ, וְתַקְּנֵנוּ בְּעֵצָה טוֹבָה מִלְּפָנֶיךָ, וְהוֹשִׁיעֵנוּ
לְמַעַן שְׁמֶךָ, וְהָגֵן בַּעֲדֵנוּ: וְהָסֵר מֵעָלֵינוּ אוֹיֵב דֶּבֶר וְחֶרֶב וְרָעָב
וְיָגוֹן, וְהָסֵר שָׂטָן מִלְּפָנֵינוּ וּמֵאַחֲרֵינוּ, וּבְצֵל כְּנָפֶיךָ תַּסְתִּירֵנוּ, כִּי
אֵל שׁוֹמְרֵנוּ וּמַצִּילֵנוּ אָתָּה, כִּי אֵל מֶלֶךְ חַנּוּן וְרַחוּם אָתָּה, וּשְׁמוֹר
צֵאתֵנוּ וּבוֹאֵנוּ לְחַיִּים וּלְשָׁלוֹם מֵעַתָּה וְעַד עוֹלָם: בָּרוּךְ אַתָּה יי
שׁוֹמֵר עַמּוֹ יִשְׂרָאֵל לָעַד:

Lay us down, Hashem our God, in peace, and raise us up, our King, to life. And spread upon us Your Sukkah of peace. And direct us before You with good advice. And save us for the sake of Your Name. And shield us and remove from us every enemy, plague, sword, hunger and grief. And remove Satan from before us and from behind us. And shelter us in the shadow of Your wings for You are a God that guards over us and rescues us. For You God are a gracious merciful King. O guard our going out and our coming in for life and peace from now and forever. Blessed are You Hashem, Who guards Your people Israel forever.

Peace and protection are the main themes of *Hashkiveynu*. Just as the Children of Israel felt so vulnerable on that last night in Egypt hearing the screams of death all around them, so when we lie down to sleep, we also feel a sense of vulnerability.

The Talmud[287] teaches that sleep is one-sixtieth of death. This is why when we awake, it is customary to wash our hands as is customary when leaving a cemetery. When we sleep, body and soul are somewhat separated as in death in that while the body rests, the soul is active and our dreams can contain messages from our souls. Sometimes a dream can be very disturbing and here our tradition recommends we fast upon awakening. The *Haskiveynu* prayer is then a prayer to guard us from the hazards of the night: "Shield us, remove from us every enemy, plague, sword, hunger and grief. And remove the spiritual impediment[288] from before us and behind us…Blessed are You Hashem, Who guards Your people Israel forever."[289]

Let me conclude the discussion of the blessings of the *Shema* with an observation: These blessings are patterned after the three paragraphs of the *Shema* as well. The first blessing before the *Shema*, *Birkat Yotzeyr*, emphasizes God as the Creator of all. It parallels the first paragraph of the *Shema* with the theme of the unity and greatness of God. The second blessing before the *Shema*, *Birkat Ahava,* deals with the special loving relationship between God and the Jewish people in the giving and accepting of the Torah. This parallels the second paragraph of the *Shema*: reward and punishment for keeping or not keeping the Torah. Finally, the blessing after the *Shema*, *Birkat Geula,* stresses the importance of the redemption from Egypt as does the final words of the third paragraph of the *Shema*.

WHY STRUCTURE MATTERS   I would like to add a last, crucial point. The structure of Jewish prayer sets the pattern of an elaborate dance with God:

- The opening Morning Blessings;

- The Psalms of *Pesuke D'zimra;*

- The *Barchu* call to prayer;

- The two blessings before the *Shema: Birkat Yotzeyr* and *Birkat Ahava (Ahavat Olam* for Sefardim);

- The *Shema;*

- The blessing after the *Shema: Birkat Geulah* (which consists of two blessings in the evening prayer);

- The *Amidah;*

- *Tachanum* and the *Ashrey* section after the *Amidah* (in the morning); and

- The *Aleynu* (and Psalm of the Day in the morning).

Indeed, this is nothing short of an elegant and moving dance with God.

Kabbalah teaches this is a dance through the four worlds of Action, Formation, Creation and Emanation.[290] Another approach sees this dance from the outer courtyards of the Holy Temple to the Holy of Holies and back.[291] Still others look upon this as climbing the ladder of Jacob's dream to God and back.

No matter how you look at it, this is a dance that can lift us up to amazing heights, so high our souls will soar as we feel intimately connected to God all day—each and every day.

There is currently a television show called "Dancing with the Stars." It takes a few celebrities—not proficient dancers—and they compete week after week until they become wonderful dancers. How do they do it? They practice often and hard every day. If you want to be able to dance with God, you cannot leave it for the once in a while you happen to find yourself in the mood or find yourself in a synagogue. You have to make this your spiritual practice and do this with *kavanah,* with meaning, focus and intension often—every day! You will be astonished at the difference this will make in your life.

The Amen Response

I f you were asked what the most familiar word in Jewish liturgy is, what would you say? *Shema, Baruch, Yisrael, Eloheynu, Hashem?*
My choice would be the word *Amen.* This is one of the first words a child learns when learning blessings because it is the way a Jew responds to hearing a blessing. In fact, *Amen* is so popular even non-Jews use this word in their prayers.

In his farewell address to the Jewish people before they were to enter the Promised Land, Moses instructs them to erect an altar, after they cross the Jordan River, for public worship in their new land; then they should have a dramatic ceremony with the Levite elders standing around the Holy Ark in the valley with half the people on Mt. Gerizim and half on Mt. Eyval. The Levite elders would first turn to Mt. Gerizim and pronounce the blessings that will come for following God's commandments…and the multitudes on the slopes would answer, "*Amen!*" Then they would turn to Mt. Eyval and pronounce the curses for disobeying God's commandments, and the multitudes would answer, "*Amen!*"[292]

Imagine how solemn and imposing this ceremony must have been.

What does the word *Amen* mean? Let me show you something surprising about this well-known Hebrew word whose actual meaning is known by very few. The Talmud[293] teaches (as further explained in The *Amidah* Supplement, Part 1: *Gevurot*) that—אָמֵן/*Amen*—is an abbreviation of the phrase אֵל מֶלֶךְ נֶאֱמָן/

Eyl Melech Ne-eman (God, King, faithful), as in God is a faithful King.

Each of these words represents one of the three core Jewish beliefs.[294] So when we say, "*Amen,*" we are not only saying we believe, but we are also proclaiming what we believe: *Eyl*—there is a God; *Melech*—God is our King and Ruler Who gave us the rules to live our lives through the Torah; and *Neh-ehman*—God is faithful. Even if we do not see the evidence now, God is faithful to eventually straighten out whatever evils are in this world. Some commentaries maintain *Amen* is derived from the word *emuna* (faith), while another[295] holds that the word *emet* (truth), is derived from the same root. Either way, *Amen* is an expression of trust and faith, responding to what was heard: "It is true, so be it!"

> I once heard a story of a great Rebbe whose blessings were known to have miraculous effects. Once he made a *shiva* call and the son of the deceased asked him why his father had to suffer so. Did the Rebbe not pray for him? After all, he was a faithful follower and supporter. The Rebbe responded that he visited his ill father many times and blessed him that he should feel better, but his father never said, "*Amen,*" to any of his blessings. His father never accepted the blessings and so he never received them.

Amen is clearly the proper response to a blessing, so much so that the Talmud[296] insists that reciting *Amen* after a blessing is so important it should be recited with great fervor. It even goes as far as to say, "He who responds '*Amen*' with all his might, all evil decrees against him are torn up."

Let me ask you now: Which is more important, saying a blessing or saying *Amen* to a blessing? You guessed it. *Amen* is more important, because with the response we now have two or more people praising God.[297] In fact, according to Rebbe Nachman,[298] within the word *Amen* there are encoded two of the main names of God. The *gematria* of *Amen* is 91 (*alef* + *mem* + *nun*/1 +

40 + 50 = 91) and this is also the sum of the *gematria* of Hashem (ה-ו-ה-י/*yud + hey + vav + hey*/10 + 5 + 6 + 5 = 26) and *Adonai* (אדני /*alef + dalet + nun + yud*/ 1 + 4 + 50 + 10 = 65).

So important is the *Amen* response that the sages teach us: "He who prolongs the saying of *Amen* will be granted the gift of long life."[299] "He who recites *Amen* with his entire strength will be granted immortal life."[300] The Talmud[301] also teaches there are certain types of *Amen* responses we should not recite: "an orphaned *Amen,* a hurried Amen, or a split *Amen.*"

What is an orphaned *Amen*? The rabbis looked upon a blessing as a sort of parent to the *Amen* response. When one says *Amen* without hearing the full blessing before, the *Amen* is looked upon as an orphan. In other words, one should not blindly mouth an *Amen* agreeing to something without hearing and understanding it first. Think of the people who wear their patriotism on their sleeves but do not show up to vote, or those who proclaim love for their parents but do not even show up to recite a *Kaddish* or observe a *yahrtzeit* for them, or those who talk of the State of Israel as a blessing for all Jews but do nothing to help her, or those who feel there is a need for synagogues and religious schools but do not lift a finger of support. What are they saying if not an orphaned *Amen*? They are not attached to the blessing.

What is a rushed *Amen*? This refers to someone who recites his prayer in a hurry just to fulfill his obligation and be done with it. When the famed Yiddish author Shalom Aleichem came to America in the early 20th century he remarked, "America is a peculiar country. It is a land where everyone rushes and grabs. One grabs a *barchu* or a *Kaddish,* and one grabs a walk or a schnapps."

How true! We are truly the "instant generation." Most of us are always in a rush. We build the fastest cars and planes. We have no time to cook, so we have microwave and convection ovens, instant coffee, frozen dinners and take-out meals at every supermarket. We do not have the time to get from place to place, so we carry an instant office with us on our laptop computers, tablets and smart phones. This is the reason, I think, why people sometimes say to the rabbi—even for a wedding ceremony—"Please Rabbi, make it short." If you do not believe me, think about the times you have seen someone looking at their watch during services when he or she should have been looking into the *Siddur*. If you rush through your prayers to God, why should God pay attention to them? Consider the Talmudic[302] adage: "One should not throw a blessing from his mouth." Our prayers to God are opportunities not to be squandered. They should be recited with respect and not as an unwanted chore. The truth is there is no blessing in a life based on a rushed *Amen*.

And finally, what is a split or partial *Amen*? This is when one does not say the entire word, but only a part of it. There are many phases in life where the split *Amen* plagues us—especially in our relationships when we do not see the whole person, but the side of the person that affects us the most. In the last generation many wives were looked upon by their husbands as cooks and housekeepers, and husbands were often looked upon by their wives as shlepers and garbage disposers. Sadly, these kinds of relationships still exist. There should be a real sharing of responsibilities. Even our greatest sages helped share the burden of housekeeping.

Today many dads try to help as much as they can with the kids and around the house, but they are often met by a wife who is so exhausted she finds it hard to appreciate their help. Then there is the husband who looks at his wife of 25 years and feels she is not the same beautiful woman he thought he married. Of course she is not the same. Neither is he! But 25 years of care, love and being best friends are too often easily forgotten, and the only ones who benefit are the divorce lawyers. Each spouse must be the *chaveyr*, the lover, the friend and companion. Anything less is a split *Amen*.

A Chassidic Rebbe was in a concentration camp with a number of his disciples when their turn came to be cast into the poison showers and the ovens. The Rebbe addressed his Chasidim and urged them not to yield to hysteria, but to die with dignity *al Kiddush Hashem* (for the Sanctification of God's Name). He then recited the special blessing, "Blessed is God, King of the Universe, Who has sanctified us by His commandments and commanded us to sanctify God's Name." To which the disciples responded with all their hearts and with all their might and with all their souls, "*Amen, Amen, Amen!*"[303]

So when we hear a *beracha*, no matter how short or long or how it is recited, let us respond in that spirit with a deeply felt and moving *Amen* that goes to the core of our faith and beliefs—that *Eyl*— there is a God; *Melech*—He is our King Who gave us the Torah, and *Ne-ehman*—He is faithful to straighten things out. Let us respond with an *Amen*, which, in the words of the Talmud, will give us the gift of long life and let us be granted immortal life.

CHAPTER 23

Is It Kosher to Pray?

Let me ask a question that might surprise you—a question you probably would never think to ask. What right do we have to pray? Yes, you read the question correctly. What right do we have to pray?

Now you are probably asking yourself, "Has this author gone off the deep end? Of course, we have a right to pray; we go to the synagogue, do we not?"

Think about it. Prayers of thanksgiving are always in order. Prayers of praise, if offered within acceptable guidelines, are certainly welcome. As we learned in Chapter 12, "Too Awesome for Praises," prayers of praise must either be quotes from the Bible or describing God's actions. Most of our heartfelt prayers, however, are prayers of petition like, "God, please help me!"

What are we saying to God when we ask for help? Are we saying, "God, make me well because when You made me sick, You might have made a mistake. Perhaps You did not realize that I am supposed to be well, so please hear my prayer and bring me healing." Is this what we are saying? If it is God's will we should be sick, how dare we pray and expect to change God's will?

It is the same question when we pray for almost anything. If God decreed I should be poor, what right do I have to pray for financial success? If God decreed I should suffer injustice, what right do I have to pray for justice?

Rabbi Joseph Ber Soloveitchik,[304] in an incredibly beautiful thought, points out that most of the great sages throughout the ages have taught us we do not pray in order to change God's mind. So why do we pray? If God decreed we should be ill for whatever reason, and then if we pray with the right intensity and fervor, and in the process, examine our lives and deeds to such an extent we change ourselves, then we become different people. God may have decreed Chaim should become ill, but through the experience of really deep prayer, it is possible he is no longer the same Chaim, and so, perhaps now he deserves *chayim* (life), blessing and health.

Prayer is not an attempt to change God, teaches Soloveichik. Prayer is a process of changing ourselves, and only through changing ourselves would it make sense you could dare attempt to alter the decree that existed for you previously.

Rabbi Meir Aldabi (14th century)[305] thus taught: "The entire concept of prayer is not meant to change God's will. Prayer is a door for the soul ... elevating a person from defilement to purity, bringing him closer to God. God, however, does not change in any manner."

It is fascinating that in Hebrew the word "to pray" is *l'hit-paleyl*. This is a reflexive form from the root verb פלל (judging), and so it literally means, "to stand in self-judgment." The same root can also mean "to attach" or "to become joined," indicating when we pray we attach or bond ourselves to God. While praying we become joined with God and judge ourselves; and in judging ourselves, we can change and become better human beings, more deserving of God's mercy.

PRAYING FOR OTHERS   My dear wife Cheryl once showed me a column in the newspaper[306] that began: "I used to think the fondest words in the whole world were, 'I love you,' but not anymore. Now the most special words of all are, 'I'll pray for you.'" I think there is something to this. Prayer, the author points out, is a gift: "You don't need to know what size a person wears or what his favorite color is...the poorest person in the world can give this gift to anyone...There are always people in need of the gift of prayer…people facing cancer, others having surgery, others struggling with the agonies of old age." As we will learn in the next chapter, when you pray for someone else God may answer your prayer first.

We are allowed to pray for ourselves because the very act of prayer may change us and then we are not the same person for whom our dire situation was decreed. But there is a special problem when we pray for others.[307] When a friend is seriously ill, you may come to the synagogue to have a special *Mishebey-rach* healing prayer recited for him/her, and you may include a special prayer in your own personal prayers. Now let us ask the same question we asked about a person praying for himself. If a person is sick, obviously God knows and may have decreed it. Who are we to interfere? What difference will our words make concerning the status of someone else? Will the person we are praying for become a different person just because we are praying for him/her? How can our prayers help someone else to change?

God told Abraham He plans to destroy the cities of Sodom and Gomorra. What does Abraham do? He argues with God. What a *chutzpa!* How dare he argue with God! The Torah here is teaching us we have a right to ask, to demand, and yes, even to argue with God. What an incredible idea!

Let us now ask, for whom was Abraham pleading? The righteous of Sodom and Gomorra or the wicked? If it was for both, then how could he challenge God by asking, "Would you still destroy it rather than spare the place for the sake of the 50 righteous people within it?"[308] God tells Abraham He is going to kill the wicked, but Abraham is asking for something far more. He pleads, "Perhaps there are 50 righteous people *b'toch ha-ir* (in the city—involved in the life of the city and its people) …Won't You save the city for the sake of the 50 righteous who are there?" What is Abraham asking for? He is asking God to save the wicked because of the righteous—and this is magnificent!

This is all summed up in Abraham's immortal challenge to God: *Hashofeyt kol haaretz lo yaaseh mishpat* (will the Judge of the entire world not do justice)?[309] But is it not justice to kill the wicked and save the righteous? This is exactly what God had said He was going to do—kill all the wicked people. Abraham then challenges God saying, "You can't do that. If You are going to be just, You have got to save the wicked for the sake of the righteous." Why?

Here comes the fundamental principle explaining the reason it is permissible to pray for someone else. The Torah[310] teaches God's justice must be total justice: *ki kol d'rachav mishpat* (for all His ways are just). God's justice is different than that dispensed by human courts. This is beautifully illustrated in a passage in the Talmud.[311] In delineating descendants of Aaron and Moses in the beginning of the book of Numbers,[312] the Torah mentions the death of Aaron's two sons, Nadav and Avihu, and adds, *uvanim lo hayu lahem* (and they did not have children)." The Talmud comments, *Hahayu lahem banim, lo meytu* (If they would have had children, they would not have died).

But if they had committed a sin worthy of death, why would the fact they had children make any difference in their punishment? It is because if someone is put to death, his family also suffers. Even though Nadav and Avihu may have deserved the death penalty, the Talmud teaches it would have been unjust for their children in such a case to become orphans.

If one commits a terrible crime he can be jailed for a year, for ten years; he can even be put to death. Who suffers? Of course he suffers, but this is not the end of the story. Who else pays the price? His wife, his children, his family. We could well ask, "But it is not fair; they didn't do anything wrong." What is the only answer you can give to this? The human justice system can only look at the crime. It cannot take into account that innocent children will suffer, will not have a father, a wage earner, a provider. We can never know all the ramifications of pronouncing a sentence upon someone, and therefore a human justice system cannot dispense total justice.

But God knows everything, and so God can dispense total

justice. As mentioned, the Torah teaches *ki kol d'rachav mishpat* (for all His [God's] ways are just). God has to take into account what a punishment will mean, not only for the sinner, but for all the people who are deeply connected to that person.

This is a fascinating concept. Now we can see the answer to the second problem of prayer—praying for someone else. What happens when we pray for someone seriously ill? What are we really saying to God? We are saying, "Even if the person may, for whatever reason, deserve his present situation, we want you to know, God, it hurts us also. So put us on the scale of justice, too, as You judge. How do we demonstrate it hurts us? We are coming to shul, offering a prayer, and giving charity on his or her behalf." Rabbi David Feinstein advises us, "We should try to form as many connections as possible" in our lives, for "there might come a time when we could be spared from a punishment that had been decreed because others would suffer unfairly."[313]

There are some who go to a Rebbe or another holy man and ask for a *b'rachah,* a blessing to help someone who is ill. How can this be effective? How can his prayers be more effective than anyone else's? What difference will it make? One either deserves to be ill or one does not. But if the Rebbe hears someone is ailing, and like most Rebbes, he is very sensitive, it hurts him as well, and so God must also put this holy person on the scale when He judges, and a holy person carries a lot of weight.

Do you see what Abraham was saying? Even though God was only going to kill the wicked, the righteous may still have had strong feelings for them. It would have hurt the righteous to lose their homes, their neighborhood, their livelihood, their friends. And so Abraham challenged God: "You can't destroy an entire city if there are 50, 45, 40, 30, 20, 10 righteous people. God, you can't destroy the cities because the righteous would be hurt, would be in pain, would grieve, and would suffer." The principle here is that sometimes a person could be saved, not on his own merit, but because of someone else's.[314]

Judaism makes God appear so super-fair in His dispensing

of total justice, it would seem almost impossible for suffering or death or tragedy to exist in the world. However, there is tragedy and the righteous do suffer and good people do feel pain. God has a right to say, "I know you are in pain, but trust Me nevertheless; I, God, know this must be."

A Caveat   Is it possible people can suffer for no possible reason, for nothing they have done in this lifetime? Yes. It could be for deeds done in a previous lifetime; this suffering might be a *tikun,* a path to repair the damage done to one's soul in that lifetime.

The Talmud[315] also indicates that suffering can occur because a person is in the wrong place at the wrong time. For proof it offers King Solomon's statement:[316] *Yeysh mispeh b'lo mishpat* (There are those that are swept away unjustly).

The Zohar[317] asks why Noah had to be put in an ark and not on an island to weather the storm and the flood, and it answers: *Ka-asher yiteyn r'hsut l'mashchit l'hashchit* (When permission is given to the destroyer to destroy, anyone who gets in his way might be destroyed).

When God was ready to bring the tenth plague upon Egypt, He commanded the Children of Israel to stay in their homes with a special sign of blood placed on the doorposts to keep the angel of death away. Why? So that the angel of death would not kill them together with the firstborn of Egypt—despite the fact they did not deserve death!

It is the consensus of Jewish tradition, however, that if one suffers—not on their own account—God has to somehow make it up to them either in this world or the next, or in another lifetime.

Unkosher prayer   It is not kosher to pray for anything you want. "What?" you might ask. "Does God not care about the yearnings of our hearts?" Yes, but some prayers are not appropriate—like asking God to do harm to others unless, perhaps, if someone is trying to destroy you. Yet even this may have limits, and so the Talmud[318] teaches us not to pray for the death of sinners, but rather that they not sin.

What if someone has done you great harm and embarrassment? Can you not pray he/she should suffer a similar fate? You should try to refrain from being vengeful. Instead pray for justice and leave it to God to decide the proper course of action. Even this, the Talmud[319] warns, should be done with caution.

Another kind of unkosher prayer, teaches the Talmud,[320] is to pray to change something that has already happened. A student, therefore, should not pray for a good grade on a test while his teacher is handing back the graded tests. The Talmud gives two compelling examples of when one might feel strongly motivated to pray, but should not. The first is that a husband must not pray for his pregnant wife to give birth to a male. This is a *tefilat shav,* a "prayer in vain," it teaches, because the sex of the child is already determined. The second example is that if someone heard the sound of crying coming from the direction of his home, he must not pray that it should not be coming from his home because it already is what it is!

Sometimes tragedy strikes because of another's free will and not because of God's intention. If someone was killed or suffered because of someone else's free will—because someone shoots a gun into a crowd, for example, and someone's life was cut short before his/her time—then God has to make it up to that soul. Most of what happens to us in life is ultimately God's decision and, as believing Jews, we have to say God's decisions sometimes may seem cruel and harsh, but God must have a reason. We must, however, do as much as we possibly can of the inner work necessary to change ourselves for the better in order to compel God to reconsider and answer our prayers.

Let us never lose sight that the ultimate purpose of prayer is not so much to change God's will, but to change ourselves. Let us remember the teaching of Rabbi Aldabi: "Prayer is not meant to change God's will. Prayer is a door for the soul...elevating a person from defilement to purity, bringing him closer to God."

CHAPTER 24

The Power of Prayer

We have learned about the power of prayer for connecting with God. We have seen, in our discussion of the *Shema*, how we can rise through five levels of the Israel within us to our higher selves, and how this corresponds to five meanings of *Yisrael*: one who struggles with God, one who struggles on behalf of God, one who becomes a champion of God, one who becomes straight with God, and one who sees God everywhere in the world. We have come to know we are all one with God; and in studying the *Amidah*, we experienced how to feel the presence of God as our *Mageyn*, our Shield and Protector.

In the middle section of the daily *Amidah*, we petition God for the things we want in life—knowledge, forgiveness, redemption, health, a good livelihood, justice, peace, and more. How effective are these prayers of petition? Can they really bring about a change in our circumstances? How many times have we prayed for something to occur and it did not happen? Can our prayers really make a difference other than helping to bring us closer to God?

Our sages tell us Moses pleaded and prayed numerous times to God to allow him to enter the Promised Land. He did not ask to lead the people into the land, just to experience it—to reach the goal of his life's work, especially after 40 long years as leader of the Jewish people and then he could die content. But it was not to be.

The sages tell us he prayed 515 times, corresponding to the *gematria,* the numerology of the word וָאֶתְחַנַּן/*Va-etchanan* (And I

[Moses] prayed). This *gematria* is *vav, alef, taf, chet, nun, nun*/6 +1 + 400 + 8 + 50 + 50 = 515. It is not surprising that 515 is also the *gematria* of תְּפִלָּה/*tefila* (prayer), which is *taf, fey, lamed, hey*/400 + 80 + 30 + 5 = 515.[321] Nonetheless, God still refused to allow Moses to enter. In fact, Moses tells us God said to him, "Enough! Do not speak to Me any more about this!"[322]

HaRav Reuven Katz, the father of my Rebbe, Rav Michael Katz, z"l, in his classic work *Dudaei Reuven*,[323] asks: "Why was it necessary for God to command Moses not to pray anymore? Just as he did not heed the first 515 requests so, too, God could have simply continued to refuse all future requests."

HaRav Katz answers that the Torah here teaches us a major principle concerning the efficacy of prayer. God forbade Moses to continue because if he had prayed just one more time, God would have had to relent. Such is the power of prayer! Since it was better for the people to have Joshua as their new leader taking them into the land without Moses' presence diminishing his leadership, God's answer was, "No!"

According to the Talmud,[324] the prophet Isaiah had warned King Hezekiah he would soon die. The king dismissed him saying, "I have learned from the house of my father's father (King David) that even if a sharp sword rests upon a person's neck, he should not stop praying to God for mercy!" Hezekiah then prayed with all his heart and God granted him 15 more years to live. It seems prayer is stronger than prophecy.

Jewish prayer can be very powerful, so never give up hope! The *Midrash*[325] comments on a verse in Isaiah[326] comparing Israel to a worm: "A worm can fell the mightiest cedars, but only with its mouth. It is a soft creature, but it can fell the hardest tree. Israel likewise can make use of prayer."

Do your prayers seem to be landing on deaf ears, giving you the feeling when you are praying that you are talking to a wall? Could it be because your prayers are perfunctory? You may recite the proper words at the proper time, but with how much feeling? Do you really mean the words while you are saying them? King

David teaches in the *Ashrey* prayer (Psalm 145): *Karov Hashem l'chol korav* (God is near to all who call upon Him) *l'chol asher yikra-uhu v'emet* (to all who call upon Him in truth). God can be close to us, but we must make the call—not just by reciting the proper words, but "in truth," by pouring out our hearts.

But what if you prayed again and again with all your heart and soul and nothing happened? How many of us have prayed that someone who was ill might live and then he or she died?

> There is a story of a little girl who cried the familiar lament: "I prayed that my grandmother should get all better and she died. How could God be so cruel?"
>
> Wisely her mother responded: "There are few deaths, thank God, where there is no one to pray for the one who is dying. Do you suppose that the gift of prayer was given to us in order that one may never die? Do you think God intended that we live on in growing infirmity, till at last we would pray for death to save ourselves from despair? Only God knows how to answer. God knows when to say, 'No.'"[327]

"I see," the skeptic might say. "If she gets better it is God helping her, and if she dies it is God saying, 'No.' How convenient!"

And I would say to the skeptic, "Yes, to a certain extent this is correct. Our sincere prayers from the depths of our hearts do have a profound influence upon God's decrees, but sometimes it is time for someone to die, even though we may feel he/she has died before his/her time. God does not always give us what we ask for. He gives us what we need! Sometimes God's answer must be, 'No!'"

Saadia Gaon (10th century) comments on Moses' prayer and tells us there are seven reasons why prayer is not accepted.[328] The first is if one prays, as did Moses, after God's decree is sealed—after God's plan is already in place. The second is if prayer is not given from the heart. The third is if one does not want to hear the words of the Torah. The fourth is because one ignores the cry of the poor. If you ignore the cry of God's children who need you He will ignore your cries. And the fifth, sixth and seventh are if one is sinful without remorse. Yes, we are all sinners, but if we are not sorry for our sins and we continue to ignore what God asks of us, then God will ignore what we ask of Him. As the prophet Micah[329] says of such people, "They cry out to God, but He will not answer them."

Finally, a prayer may seem to go unanswered because silence may actually be the answer. A person, in the depth of his being, knows the part he/she must play in bringing about change, even though this may be difficult, dangerous or scary. It may mean the uncovering of a strength or an ability you never realized you had. The answer may be that for your prayer to be answered, you now need to depend, not only upon God, but upon yourself as well.

GETTING TO YES   Okay, now we understand how God sometimes must answer our prayers by saying, "No." But how do we get to the state of "Yes!"—the state where God answers our prayers by giving us what we prayed for?

King David tells us the secret in the next verse of the *Ashrey* prayer: *R'tzon y'reyav yaaseh* (He will do the will of those who are in awe of Him), *v'et shav'atam yishma v'yoshi-eym* (and He will hear their cries and will save them). Be in awe of God—especially in your prayers. Align your intention with His—resolve in your prayers to do God's will—and He will align His intentions with yours—He will resolve to do your will. As it says in the *Pirke Avot*,[330] "Make your will like God's will, so that God will make your will like His will."

As we learned in Chapter 23, "Is It Kosher to Pray," deep prayer has the power to change us, to transform us so much that even if God decreed we should be ill, because of our prayers we might no longer be the same person for whom that illness was prescribed, and we can then begin to heal. The Talmud[331] advises that when we become ill we should search our lives to see if we ought to change our ways and ask forgiveness. This needs to be part of the process of deep prayer. Also, when illness or misfortune strikes, we need to ask God to help us understand the lesson we need to learn from what life has thrown at us. Once we learn the lesson, there is no further need for the distress. And so the Talmud[332] teaches: "Whoever prolongs his prayer (with meaning, focus, attention and all of the above), his prayer will not be left unanswered."

DO NOT BECOME ATTACHED TO THE OUTCOME   Having said all this, we should be mindful of one more crucial element to getting what we ask for: we must not become too attached to the outcome. Once we pray to God and ask for what we want, we must, as the 12-step recovery slogan puts it, "Let go and let God." How many of us know of a couple who could not conceive a child and after many years of doctors and treatments finally decided to adopt? Then, not too long after the adoption, the woman became pregnant without any treatments. They simply let go and let God. This is a great spiritual truth: Do what you can to help your situation, pray to God for help with all your heart, and then just let it go, give it to God to work out—you have done your part. Sometimes God sends us on a detour or two towards our goals because He has other important things in mind for us to do along the way.

> Once my flight was delayed for two hours. This meant I would be late for an important appointment, and I was upset. I sat down next to the gate beside a young man with spiked green hair and a ring through his nose. He saw my *kipa* and, guessing I was a rabbi, he began to ask me questions. It seemed to me that he was estranged from his Jewish family, and after an hour of conversation, I was able to convince him to give his mother a call. Yes, I may have made the trip with one purpose in mind, but God had His own agenda, and if we just let go and let God, we can have the privilege of being a part of it.

How do you know where you are supposed to be? How do you know why you are where you are? How do you know, while you are so busy fixating on where you think you ought to be, that you are not missing out on the things calling out to you right where you are? I was not thinking about God or holiness or Divine purpose during that two-hour delay. I was upset at being late, but God brought me to sit next to that young man because it was where I was needed.

According to Kabbalah, a divine spark is hidden within everything, and we find ourselves in situations not by accident, but in order to redeem the holy sparks that are present there. Every situation wants to positively change us; but, unfortunately, we are usually more focused on changing the situation. We hurry life along to get to "the point," as if we know where and what the point really is.

It may sound cliché, but the journey is the point—the opportunity to hear the call and to respond. The master key to a spiritual life is to be where you are, to really be in the moment and in the place you find yourself in, and not to be so possessed and focused on what you want to happen that you do not see the Divine sparks calling out to you on the way. So just let go and let God!

Letting go and letting God is a liberating and beautiful experience. Understanding that although we do not know why this or that is happening to us, or how we are going to get out of the situation we are in, or how we are going to get better, or how we are going to stop drinking or drugging or smoking … God knows.

Forget about worry! I know this is difficult—especially for Jews! But understand it is not up to you to come up with all the answers; you just have to let God in and listen for the solutions He will provide. If you worry about how you will do it, or how you will have the strength to manage, you have got things completely backwards! You *do not* have the strength or the knowledge, and by worrying about how you will do it, you will have missed the point. You don't have the strength or knowledge, but God does!

Understanding this feels great. It does not mean you are not going to have to work hard at solving your problems, just that you do not have to fill yourself with worry. Our pain, most of the time, comes from unfulfilled expectations. So do not expect—do not be attached to the outcome. Sometimes God has something else in mind for us, so accept what God has in store for you. Put your trust in Him, listen to His message and feel His strength as he shows you the path: let go and let God.

Immediately, benefits will be felt and become visible and tangible, inside and out. You will feel renewed strength, faith and courage because God's Presence will have become increasingly active active within you. Your prayers will be more effective and your understanding of the Presence of God within you will be clearer. As you let go and trust God, everything is transformed— yes, everything—into a blessing. God continuously makes dark places light, rough places smooth, crooked places straight and empty places full. He does this for everything—including you! You just have to let go and let God.

> Once a man was asked, "What did you gain by regularly praying to God?"
>
> The man replied, "Nothing ... but let me tell you what I lost: anger, ego, greed, depression, insecurity, and fear of death."

Sometimes, the answer to our prayers is not gaining, but losing.

PRAYING FOR OTHERS   As we learned in Chapter 23, another path to having your prayers answered is to pray for someone else. As the Talmud[333] teaches: "One who prays for his neighbor and needs the same thing is answered first." Rabba bar Mari learns this from Job, whose fortune was changed only after he prayed for his friends.[334] Rava learns this from Abraham, who prayed for Avimelech and his wife who had become barren, and then suddenly Sarah, who had been barren for so many years, became pregnant.[335]

There is a great story[336] about a ship wrecked during a
storm at sea that beautifully makes the point. Only two of
the men on board were able to swim to a small, desert-like
island. The two survivors, not knowing what else to do,
decided to pray to God for help. However, to find out whose
prayer was more powerful, they agreed to divide the territo-
ry between them and stay on opposite sides of the island.

The first thing they prayed for was food. The next
morning, the first man saw a fruit-bearing tree on his side
of the land, and he was able to eat its fruit. The other man's
parcel of land remained barren.

After a week, the first man was lonely and he decided
to pray for a wife. The next day, another ship was wrecked,
and the only survivor was a woman who swam to his
side of the land. On the other side of the island, there was
nothing. Soon the first man prayed for a house, clothes, and
more food. The next day, like magic, all of these were given
to him. However, the second man still had nothing.

Finally, the first man prayed for a ship, so that he and
his wife could leave the island. In the morning, he found a
ship docked at his side of the island. The first man boarded
the ship with his wife and decided to leave the second man
on the island. He considered the other man unworthy to
receive God's blessings, since none of his prayers had been
answered.

As the ship was about to leave, the first man heard a
voice from heaven booming, "Why are you leaving your
companion on the island?"

"My blessings are mine alone, since I was the one who
prayed for them," the first man answered. "His prayers were
all unanswered and so he does not deserve anything."

"You are mistaken!" the voice rebuked him. "He had
only one prayer, which I answered. If not for that, you
would not have received any of my blessings."

"Tell me," the first man asked the voice, "What did he

pray for that I should owe him anything?"
"He prayed that all your prayers be answered!"

Praying for someone else can be an extremely powerful path for connecting with God. When God sees you mercifully take precious time out of your prayer experience to pray for one of His creatures, His mercy towards you is enhanced. So before you pray, I suggest you make a list of people you know are in need of God's help. If they are ill, recite their names (Hebrew is preferable, but God knows their English names, too) in the *Refa-eynu Hashem* (God heal us) blessing of the *Amidah*. There is a special insertion in most prayer books for this prayer where you can add the names of those you want to ask to be healed. If you are unable to find this in your prayer book, just add your own prayer from your heart with their names. Here is the *Refa-eynu Hashem* prayer of the *Amidah* with one version of that insertion:

רְפָאֵנוּ יי וְנֵרָפֵא. הוֹשִׁיעֵנוּ וְנִוָּשֵׁעָה כִּי תְהִלָּתֵנוּ אָתָּה. וְהַעֲלֵה רְפוּאָה שְׁלֵמָה לְכָל מַכּוֹתֵינוּ.

Heal us Hashem, and we will be healed. Save us and we will be saved for You are the One we praise. And raise up a complete healing for all our ailments.

[Add the following prayer with names for those you know who are ill.]

יְהִי רָצוֹן מִלְפָנֶיךָ יי אֱלֹהֵי וֵאלֹהֵי אֲבוֹתַי. שֶׁתִּשְׁלַח מְהֵרָה רְפוּאָה שְׁלֵמָה מִן הַשָּׁמַיִם. רְפוּאַת הַנֶּפֶשׁ וּרְפוּאַת הַגּוּף לְחוֹלֶה ...... בֶּן/בַּת ...... בְּתוֹךְ שְׁאָר חוֹלֵי יִשְׂרָאֵל:

May it be Your will, Hashem my God and God of my fathers, that You send quickly a complete healing from Heaven, a healing of soul and a healing of body to . . .

son/daughter of ... [mother's name] among the other
ones in Israel who are ill.

כִּי אֵל מֶלֶךְ רוֹפֵא נֶאֱמָן וְרַחֲמָן אָתָּה. בָּרוּךְ אַתָּה יי, רוֹפֵא חוֹלֵי
עַמּוֹ יִשְׂרָאֵל:

For You are God, a King who is a faithful and merciful
Healer. Blessed are You, Hashem, who heals the sick
among His people Israel.

In other situations—beside illness—where people you know need
help, add their names in the *Shema Koleynu* (Hear our prayers),
blessing at the end of the middle petition section of the *Amidah*.
You can make a list as done in the exercise at the end of the *Amidah* Supplement Part 3, Section: *Shema Koleynu: Hear Our Voice*,
and have this in front of you for reference. Pour out your heart
to God on their behalf as you then pour out your heart to God
on your own behalf.[337] You will find special insertions for personal prayers to be added to the *Shema Koleynu* in many prayer
books, but any prayers from your heart are fine, inserted before
the last verse preceding the signature blessing—*Ki Eyl shomeya
t'filat amcha Yisarel b'rachamim* "(For you are God who hears
the prayers of your people Israel with mercy." I cannot stress
how crucial and powerful is this path to "Yes," to getting God to
answer your prayers and to achieving greater closeness with God.
Pray for someone else, as the Talmud suggests, and God might
answer your prayers first!

Here is the *Shema Koleynu* prayer with a version of a prayer
for sustenance to be inserted as stated above:

שְׁמַע קוֹלֵנוּ יי אֱלֹהֵינוּ חוּס וְרַחֵם עָלֵינוּ. וְקַבֵּל בְּרַחֲמִים וּבְרָצוֹן
אֶת תְּפִלָּתֵנוּ. כִּי אֵל שׁוֹמֵעַ תְּפִלּוֹת וְתַחֲנוּנִים אָתָּה. וּמִלְּפָנֶיךָ
מַלְכֵּנוּ רֵיקָם אַל תְּשִׁיבֵנוּ:

Hear our voice, Hashem our God, be compassionate and have mercy upon us, and accept with mercy and favor our prayers. For You are God Who hears prayers and supplications. And before You, our King, do not allow us to go away empty handed.

[Add the following prayer for your livelihood and sustenance and insert any personal prayers]

אַתָּה הוּא יי הָאֱלֹהִים, הַזָּן וּמְפַרְנֵס וּמְכַלְכֵּל מְקַרְנֵי רְאֵמִים עַד בֵּיצֵי כִנִּים. הַטְרִיפֵנִי לֶחֶם חֻקִּי, וְהַמְצֵא לִי וּלְכָל בְּנֵי בֵיתִי...
מְזוֹנוֹתַי...קוֹדֶם שֶׁאֶצְטָרֵךְ לָהֶם, בְּנַחַת וְלֹא בְצַעַר, בְּהֶתֵּר וְלֹא בְאִסּוּר, בְּכָבוֹד וְלֹא בְבִזָּיוֹן, לְחַיִּים וּלְשָׁלוֹם, מִשֶּׁפַע בְּרָכָה וְהַצְלָחָה, וּמִשֶּׁפַע בְּרָכָה עֶלְיוֹנָה, כְּדֵי שֶׁאוּכַל לַעֲשׂוֹת רְצוֹנֶךָ וְלַעֲסוֹק בְּתוֹרָתֶךָ וּלְקַיֵּם מִצְוֹתֶךָ. וְאַל תַּצְרִיכֵנִי לִידֵי מַתְּנַת בָּשָׂר וָדָם. וִיקֻיַּם בִּי מִקְרָא שֶׁכָּתוּב: פּוֹתֵחַ אֶת יָדֶךָ וּמַשְׂבִּיעַ לְכָל חַי רָצוֹן. וְכָתוּב: הַשְׁלֵךְ עַל יי יְהָבְךָ וְהוּא יְכַלְכְּלֶךָ.

You are Hashem, the God Who feeds and supports and sustains everyone—from the horns of the wild ox to the eggs of lice. Grant me and all the members of my home … (add others if you want) food…and (add other things you want to pray for), before I have a need for it. With rest and not with aggravation, in a permissible way and not in a forbidden way, with honor and not disgrace, for life and for peace, from the heavenly flow of blessing and success, and from the heavenly flow of the spring on high, so that I can do Your will and toil in Your Torah, and fulfill Your commandments. Do not allow me to become dependent on the gifts of other people. And let there be established in me the verse: "You open Your hand and satisfy the desire of every living thing."[338] And the verse: "Send your burdens to Hashem and He will support you!"[339]

כִּי אַתָּה שׁוֹמֵעַ תְּפִלַּת עַמְּךָ יִשְׂרָאֵל בְּרַחֲמִים. בָּרוּךְ אַתָּה יי,
שׁוֹמֵעַ תְּפִלָּה:

For you hear the prayer of Your people Israel with mercy. Blessed are You Hashem, Who hears prayer.

A BLESSING ON YOUR HEAD   Another way our tradition tells us we can pray for someone outside the customary three times a day *Amidah* prayer experience, is to give someone a *b'racha* (a blessing). It was not too long ago that Jews would bless each other as part of their daily routines. If someone was kind enough to do you a favor, what was the appropriate response? "May Hashem bless you." Just as when someone sneezes today, we still say, "Bless you!" In today's modern and overly rationalistic world, it practically never occurs to us that we can affect a change in the natural order of things with a *b'racha,* a blessing to someone. Judaism says this is within our power. God told Abraham: "You shall be a blessing."[340] The Midrash[341] elaborates and tells us God said to Abraham: "Blessings are given to your hand. Until now, they were in My hand. I blessed Adam and Noah. From this time on you will bless whomever you wish."

God, in this verse, is in effect telling us that as part of the Divine partnership with human beings, He will consider our blessings as He manages this world just as He considers our prayers. And there are special times when our power to bless is enhanced, like a bride giving a blessing to others at her *bedeking,*[342] or a *Kohen* (priest) blessing the congregation, or a blessing coming from a righteous person. Giving someone a *b'racha* is more than a hopeful wish. It is a prayer calling upon God's help. If the *b'racha* is sincere and made with proper focus and attention, it can be most powerful for both the giver and the recipient.

Life experience has shown, however, that sometimes, even if we live a good life, a righteous life, a holy life…even if we align our intentions with God's intentions…even if we pray sincerely every day for others…even if we ask for forgiveness with a full heart…

even if we search hard to find the lessons in our misfortunes… some prayers do not seem to be answered. When this happens, Jewish tradition implores us, NEVER GIVE UP! Do not let your prayers become unused packages in heaven that were never sent because people stopped praying as in the Chapter 15 story. The Talmud[343] implores us: "If you pray and are not answered, pray again!" As we learned from the story of King Hezekiah, "Even if the sword is on your neck, do not stop praying for mercy."[344]

Rebbe Nachman taught: "Many years may pass, and it may seem that you are accomplishing nothing with your prayers. Do not give up, for every word makes an impression. It is written, 'Water wears away stone.'[345] It may seem that water dripping on stone will never make an impression, but after many years, it can actually make a hole in the stone." And so our prayers![346]

DO NOT BE AFRAID TO ASK! One of the strongest impediments to prayer, I have found for many, is a reluctance to ask God for what we need and want. Sometimes this is because we are hesitant to bother God; sometimes it is because we do not feel worthy; and sometimes we feel God should know what we need and what we want, so why ask? If He is not giving us these things, then God has His reasons.

Rabbi Benjamin Blech[347] tells the story of how, when he was a young child, he could not understand how Moses could be, as the Torah[348] describes him, a man who was, "heavy of speech and heavy of tongue." How could Moses, the man destined to be the greatest leader of the Jewish people, have a speech defect? Would not his stuttering make him unsuitable? So he asked his teacher, "Since God can do anything, why didn't He heal Moses?"

After sharing with him how the classical commentators address the question, his teacher told him the answer he preferred and urged him to always keep it in mind—especially when life presents difficult problems that might need

God's help. Rabbi Blech writes that his teacher said to him: "Yes, Moses would have been far better off had he had the gift of eloquence in addition to all of his other virtues. His stuttering was a disability, and of course God could have easily removed this stigma. So why didn't He? Because Moses never asked! In all his humility, Moses didn't feel worthy of making the request, and God wanted to show us, by way of His dealings with the greatest Jew in history, that the prerequisite for His answering our prayers is for us to verbalize them."

"Never be afraid to ask anything of God," his teacher concluded. "If you're withholding a request because you think it's too much to ask for, that's an insult to the Almighty, almost as if you're implying it's too hard for Him to accomplish. If God wants to say no, that's up to Him. Your role is to make clear you believe in His power to accomplish anything, no matter how difficult."

So do not be afraid to ask! God has created the world in such a fashion that we would pray to Him for our needs. We need rain to water our crops and so the world is set up so that we look to Heaven for rain. Rebbe Nachman advises us to pray for everything: "Make it a habit to pray for all your needs, large and small. Your main prayers should be for fundamentals, that God help you in your devotion, and that you be worthy of coming close to Him. Still, you should also pray even for trivial things."[349] Does this mean it is permissible to pray for your favorite sports team to win? Absolutely! It is even acceptable to pray that your garden blossom.

However, when we pray for our needs we should not ask for riches, honors and physical pleasures alone. No, we should ask God to give us what we ask—health, prosperity, good relationships—so we may better serve Him.[350] Give God a good reason in your prayers to give you what you ask.

As far as not feeling worthy enough for prayer, Yosef Albo

teaches:[351] "One may have doubts as to whether he is worthy of having his prayers accepted. Even though one should not be righteous in his own eyes, one should not use this as an excuse to refrain from praying to God for his needs. One who refrains for this reason does so because he believes that good is only granted by God as a reward for one's deeds, and never as an act of love and mercy on the part of God. This opinion is not correct. It is explicitly written, '[We do not present our supplication before You] because of our righteousness, but because of Your great compassion.'"[352]

So when you pray, go ahead and think big, Ask God—the All Merciful—to fulfill your dreams and answer your prayers.

LET'S MAKE A DEAL! What do you do if—even after being told God wants you to pray (see Yosef Albo above)—you still think you are the worst sinner or, at least, not righteous enough that God should even consider your prayer? Well, this is a great way to begin! Who feels worthy of God answering his prayers? Just humbly tell God you do not feel worthy and as you pray add, "If in your infinite Mercy You will grant me what I ask, I will be forever grateful."

In fact, you can even offer God a bribe! Do not be shocked. It is a time-honored Jewish custom to bribe God. See The *Amidah* Supplement, Part 3, Section "*Din*, Justice," for more on how to properly offer God a bribe. A classic example of this is the *Mishebeyrach* prayer for the sick that is said when the Torah is read. In it we make a pledge to charity and ask: "In reward for this, may the Holy One Blessed Be He, be filled with compassion for him/her [that we pray for] to restore his/her health." Please note the gift or pledge to charity is not conditional upon God answering your prayers in a timely manner.

And the gift need not be just money. It can be time and/or effort for a worthy cause. It can be pledging to perform a *mitzvah* with greater energy and focus—from making your Shabbat more meaningful to visiting the sick. It can be a *kabbalah*, accepting

upon yourself something new to increase your closeness to God—
like reviewing the Torah portion for the week to come every week
by reading an *aliya* a day or regularly attending a Torah class
or coming to the synagogue more often to pray. Whatever it is,
when you seriously need God's help, it is a great idea to make a
deal with God by doing something you feel is significant to draw
closer to Him.

PRAYER CAN BE PROPHETIC   The Talmud has many stories of
rabbis who were able to make ac-
curate predictions based upon whether their prayers were fluent
or not. If the prayer was "fluent in their mouths," they knew their
prayer was accepted. If they stumbled on their words, they knew
it was not.[353]

> It sounds unbelievable, but I can relate to this because it
> has happened to me several times. The first time was about
> 30 years ago. I was saying a *Mishebeyrach* prayer for the
> sick for a dear congregant recovering from surgery when
> suddenly I stumbled badly and could not remember the
> words of the prayer or even his Jewish name. This was
> surprising since I knew the prayer by heart, and I knew his
> Jewish name well because I had been praying for him for
> some time. Suddenly, a sinking feeling welled up in my gut.
> Later it was revealed that at the same moment I stumbled in
> prayer, he had died. This same scenario has repeated itself
> several times over the years in similar and different ways.

I do not think I am unique in this regard. I think this sort of thing
happens to us all. We need only to pay attention when we pray.
We may just be surprised by the messages we receive.

CHAPTER 25

May We Not Stumble

Yes, the prayers of our hearts ascend to Heaven and can be a force for positive change in the world, but it should be understood that the holy words themselves of the Jewish sacred prayer traditions have incredible power to literally transform our lives.

Let me conclude this book by illustrating this fundamental concept with an amazing story by S. Y. Agnon, Nobel laureate, titled: *V'lo Nikasheyl* (May We Not Stumble).[354] In it, he writes about the power of the words of Jewish prayer traditions. Agnon, who died in 1970, was one of the great classic Israeli writers. He wrote mostly about conflicts between traditional Jewish life and the modern world. Although most of his works were fiction, the power of this story lies in the fact that not only is it true, Agnon himself was a participant.

By way of introduction, it is important to note that the structure of Jewish prayer was first formulized by the Men of the Great Assembly in the 5th century BCE, but there was little attempt to standardized an actual text until after the destruction of the Second Temple in the year 70 CE, Thereafter, constant revisions and minor changes were made by various communities until the advent of the printed *Siddur* in the 16th century. With the expulsion of the Jews from their land by the Romans in the 2nd century, there developed two basic traditions: Ashkenazic or German and Sephardic or Spanish. Sometimes these traditions overlapped, as when several Ashkenazic Chassidic communities adopted the tradition of the famous mystic, Rabbi Isaac Luria (Ari), which is very similar to the Sephardic text. All in all, Jewish prayer traditions present a rich tapestry of devotion to God. Agnon's true story is an example of how powerful the traditions of prayer are. Agnon writes in classic literary Hebrew. I tried to maintain the flavor of that literary tradition in my translation.

V'LO NIKASHEYL

MAY WE NOT STUMBLE!

S.Y. Agnon

A person should never change the *nusach* (the formula of the text) of the prayers of his fathers because the prayers of Israel ascend to the gates of Heaven… [I know because] I did change the *nusach* of the prayers that I recite when I pray…

How did this happen? Originally I prayed with my father, may his memory be blessed, in a small synagogue of Kloyz Chasidim. These Chasidim prayed with the Sephardic [Ari] *nusach*, and so I also prayed with this Sephardic custom. When I had grown somewhat, I went to learn Torah in an old *Beit Midrash* (House of Study) that prayed in the formula of the Ashkenazic German Jews which they had received from their fathers and their fathers' fathers from the days the first Jewish exiles reached Germany. They were so scrupulous not to add to it nor subtract from it nor change a thing—not even a word!

I thought, "Is it possible that I, the smallest of students, should depart from this tradition?" So I … prayed using their *Siddur* (prayer book) … with the exception of the *Birkat Hamazon* (The Blessing After Meals). That I did not change from the *nusach* of my father, may his memory be for a blessing. As he was accustomed to say in the prayer, *Racheym* (Be merciful [the third blessing in the *Birkat Hamazon*]), the words *shelo neyvosh v'lo nikaleym v'lo nikasheyl* (that we not feel inner shame nor be humiliated and do not stumble), so I did the same, even though most of the *Siddurim* (prayer books) did not mention the supplication, *v'lo nikasheyl* (and do not stumble) …

Years later, after growing up, I was fortunate to be able to make *aliya* (literally "ascent," but meaning to move to Israel) to the Land of Israel … Once we entertained a guest, Riva, a beautiful girl, the daughter of well-to-do people, the daughter of great Ashkenazic rabbinic leaders that served many holy communities in the Diaspora. When she heard me recite, *"v'lo nikasheyl* (and do not stumble)" in the grace after meals, she asked, "What is the source of this supplication?"

I told her, "This is what I learned in my father's home."

She said, "How can you say, 'This is what I learned,' when this supplication is not even mentioned in the *Siddur* (prayer book)?"

"Of course it is mentioned!" I said, and I took a *Siddur* to show her but I couldn't find this supplication in it. I took another *Siddur* but I [also] didn't find it … Since I am fluent in many different prayer traditions, I have collected many *Siddurim*. I stood and searched every one of the *Siddurim*, but I didn't find in the grace after meals in any of them the mention of these two words, *v'lo nikasheyl* (and do not stumble).

Riva then said, "I told you that these words are not at all part of this prayer." And when she said this, it deeply hurt me like [the hurt of] a man who says to his friend, "This coin has become worthless."

After a time … she returned to Germany to complete her studies ....

After some time, my father died, may his memory be

for a blessing, and … it struck me that for many years I had
been praying with many different traditions and when I
would be called to lead the prayers [in honor of my father],
I might become confused in my prayer, and so I resolved to
go and buy a *Siddur* (prayer book) [like the one used in the
synagogue I now attend and review it].

I entered a bookstore. I just happened to pick up a grace
after meals pamphlet. It was the same one that was hung in
my father's home above our table—probably on a rack or
shelf with a number of such pamphlets, as is often the custom. I glanced and saw written in the prayer *Racheym* were
the words "*v'lo nikasheyl* (and do not stumble)." I bought
the pamphlet and left rejoicing …

It occurred to me that I should send this pamphlet to
Riva, in order to show her that these words weren't just in
my imagination [that my father's tradition was legitimate]
… Right then I took an envelope and wrote her name …
and address … and I dipped the end of the pen in red ink
and wrote on the bottom the words, "*v'lo nikasheyl* (and do
not stumble). If you read you will see."

After some time she wrote me a letter of thanks … she
also wrote that she was determined to make *aliya* and with
her was her fiancé to whom she would soon be married in
Jerusalem ….

They did not make a fancy wedding. They just went
to the house of the rabbi of their neighborhood and he
arranged the wedding. Later they gathered ten men [the required forum for a Jewish wedding meal], with me among
them, and entered an inn for the wedding meal. After we
ate and drank they honored me to say the *Sheva Brachot*
[the Seven Blessings of marriage said at the wedding meal]
… I recited the grace after meals and when I reached the
prayer *Racheym,* I said, as is my custom, the words "*v'lo
nikasheyl* (and may we not stumble)." I could feel the bride
was staring at me, even though my eyes were focused on

the words of the blessings ….

Later as I began to leave … the bride left to accompany me. I told her, "You should return. It is dishonorable for a bride to accompany others as they leave."

She said, "Does my teacher fear that demons will attack me when I return?"

I replied, "God forbid! It is not so. Nevertheless we must be fearful [of your honor]."

She said, "I am not afraid. I have special protection."

"What is it?" I asked. She took out a little book inlaid with precious stones and pearls. I glanced and saw that it was the pamphlet of the grace after meals booklet that I had sent to her.

I said, "The booklet is worth pennies and you wrapped it in gold?"

"This book deserves to have such a beautiful cover," she said, as she lowered her head in shame, "because it caused a miracle for me."

What miracle did it do for her? A non-Jewish man wooed her to marry him and they set a date. When the time approached, he came to her apartment and took her hand in his to go with him. Suddenly, there was a knock on the door and a package was delivered to her. She opened it and looked at it and out came the two words, *V'LO NI-KASHEYL* (MAY WE NOT STUMBLE!), spread out before her in red ink. The message entered her heart and resonated within her: *V'lo Nikasheyl* (May we not stumble)!

She sent the gentile away and returned to her father. There she rediscovered a Jewish friend, with whom in her youth she was very close, and their love returned. She went with him on *Aliya* to Israel and married him according to the laws of Moses and Israel. This woman said to me, "Every day we bless you, for with the merit of your gift I was able to remain a Jew and I was worthy to make *Aliya* to the Land of Israel …."

> How many great men, how many words of the wise
> said: "A person should always be careful with the customs
> of his fathers?" If because of two words from our prayers
> a soul in Israel was saved and remained a Jew, how many
> souls in Israel would be saved from apostasy and ruin, if
> all of Israel would only be careful with the customs of their
> fathers?

Why should we keep the sacred traditions of our fathers? It is because those traditions provide us with a unique, fulfilling, marvelous, exhilarating, and best possible opportunity for a truly deep relationship with God. Besides, as I pointed out in the beginning of this book, a Jew has to *daven*, a Jew has to pray! *Davening*, Jewish prayer, is in his *kishkes*, his guts, his spiritual DNA. It is a hunger of the soul, an outpouring of longing for God, a yearning to dance with his Creator. The sacred traditions of the Jewish prayer service are the chief path we have been given to feel God's *Shechina*, His Presence—and connect with Him in this world. I pray that I, God's humble servant, have been helpful to you along this path so that you can come closer to God in your spiritual journey.

How It Works

The *Amidah* is our most important prayer; but it is long, so long we might get lost among its many blessings. This is why it is essential to understand the structure of the *Amidah* to avoid losing the state of connection felt in its first blessing. In fact, through understanding and utilizing the thematic changes of the *Amidah*'s structure, one can intensify feelings of closeness and attachment to God.

Why 18? The *Amidah* is also called the *Shemoneh Esrey* (The Eighteen) because originally there were 18 blessings. After the destruction of the Second Temple in 70 CE, according to many sources, heretical sects—including early Christians—tried to sway the hearts and minds of Jews. To counter this, the *Nasi,* the leader of the Jewish people—Rabban Gamliel II—added a prayer asking God to rid the Jewish people of such heretics.[355]

The method he used focused on the synagogue because the synagogue has always been a place where Jews come not only to pray, but to meet and greet each other and exchange information.

During the Clinton administration, there was a story making the rounds in which the President, one Saturday morning at a meeting of his cabinet, asked: "Why is it that the Jews always seem to know what is going on before anyone else? No matter how much we seek to keep things hush-hush, no matter how we try to plug all the leaks, they always seem to know what's happening. Tell me, how do they do it?"

Hesitating at first, a member of his cabinet responded: "Mr. President, I am not Jewish myself, but I have a lot of Jewish friends. I think I know how they do it. You see, when a Jew wants to find out the inside story, he comes to the synagogue and turns to his neighbor and says: 'So, *nu*?' Then he learns everything he wants to know."

As the story goes, President Clinton asked, "That's all there is to it? They just say, 'So, *nu*?' and then the news spills out? Well. I'm going to try it and find out for myself."

With that, the President assembles a motorcade and heads for the closest shul. Without warning, the entourage pulls up to the synagogue just as the Torah reading is beginning. Quietly, unobtrusively, the President enters the synagogue, sits down beside a little old Jew and then, in his best Yiddish intonation, asks: "So, *nu*?"

The old Jew replies: "I hear the President is coming here to pray with us this morning!"

The tale is a bit far-fetched. Still, there is a kernel of truth in that the synagogue has always been where Jews gather and find out what is happening. In Talmudic times, the followers of heretical sects would come to the synagogues trying to sway hearts, as well as to gather information that could be used against the Jews.

So Rabban Gamliel II added a nineteenth blessing—*Birkat Haminim*, a "Blessing to protect us from the Heretics"—to discourage them from coming and to impress upon the Jews the real dangers these heretics represented. Anyone leading the service who refused to recite this prayer, or any worshipper who did not respond "Amen" to its recitation, immediately identified himself as one of the heretics. We still refer to the *Amidah* as *Shemoneh Esrey* (Eighteen) because it is our hope that eventually this kind of heresy will disappear and there will be no further need to recite this additional blessing.

If the daily *Amidah* has nineteen blessings, why were there 18 in the first place? The Talmud[357] teaches this relates to the 18 times God's Name is found in Psalm 29 and in the *Shema*, and to the 18 vertebrae of the spine. Now that we have 19 blessings, the Talmud points out there is an additional reference to God's Name in Psalm 29 (אֵל, besides the 18 times the name י-ה-ו-ה appears), and in the *Shema* the word *Echad* (One)," refers to God, and there is a tiny vertebra at the bottom of the spine that was not included in the original count.

From my perspective, I like the fact that 18 is the *gematria* of the word, *chai* (life), signifying that the life of the Jew is tied into our connecting with God through prayer. According to Arye Kaplan,[357] one can look at the entire *Amidah* as the vehicle through which a person perfects his life. In the *Amidah* one develops a relationship with God as he asks Him to provide everything needed for his life to maintain that relationship.

The Talmud[358] divides the *Amidah* into three distinct sections: the first three blessings, the middle 12 (now 13), and the last three. Rabbi Chanina said: "In the first three blessings, one is like a servant who praises his master before making a request. In the middle section, he is like a servant who seeks a portion from his master. In the last three he is like a servant who has received a portion from his master, goes and leaves him [after expressing his thanks]." Hence the first section is referred to as *Shevach* (Praise), the second as *Bakasha* (Petition), and the third as *Hoda-ah* (Thanks).

For each blessing, I have presented an analysis that hopefully will enhance its understanding and theme, while offering the reader something to think about and focus on when reciting the *Amidah*. We must always give special focus, as we have learned, to the first blessing, because this helps us create an elevated connection to God that sets the tone for the rest of the *Amidah*.

For the 18 blessings that follow, I recommend choosing one each day for special focus as you recite the *Amidah*. You can go in order or choose any one, it matters not, but before you begin to pray, it would be helpful for you to review the commentary that follows on the blessing you choose. After several cycles of this practice, you will find yourself giving special focus to those passages that touch the needs and yearnings of your heart and soul at that moment.

THE FIRST THREE, *SHEVACH*   God is Amazing! We learned the first blessing, *Avot*, in detail in Chapters 14-16. Quickly summarizing, this first blessing connects us with God as being the God of our ancestors and encourages us to emulate the Godly qualities they manifested: Abraham manifested the quality of *Gedula* (greatness) expressed as *Chesed* (loving kindness); Isaac manifested *Gevura* (inner strength); and Jacob manifested *Yirah* (awe—the intense state of wonder, joy and fear all at once). As we recite this blessing, we connect with the four increasing steps of intimacy towards God as our King, Helper, Savior and Shield while feeling the power of God's protecting Shield.

בָּרוּךְ אַתָּה יי אֱלֹהֵינוּ וֵאלֹהֵי אֲבוֹתֵינוּ. אֱלֹהֵי אַבְרָהָם. אֱלֹהֵי
יִצְחָק. וֵאלֹהֵי יַעֲקֹב. הָאֵל הַגָּדוֹל הַגִּבּוֹר וְהַנּוֹרָא אֵל עֶלְיוֹן. גּוֹמֵל
חֲסָדִים טוֹבִים. וְקוֹנֵה הַכֹּל. וְזוֹכֵר חַסְדֵי אָבוֹת. וּמֵבִיא גוֹאֵל
לִבְנֵי בְנֵיהֶם לְמַעַן שְׁמוֹ בְּאַהֲבָה. מֶלֶךְ עוֹזֵר וּמוֹשִׁיעַ וּמָגֵן: בָּרוּךְ
אַתָּה יי, מָגֵן אַבְרָהָם:

Blessed are You Hashem, our God and God of our Fathers; the God of Abraham, the God of Isaac and the God of Jacob; the great, the mighty and the awesome God, God the most High; Who does beneficial acts of kindness, and is the owner of all things; who remembers the kindness of the Fathers, and will bring a redeemer to their children's children for the sake of His Name, with love. He is King, Helper, Savior and Shield. Blessed are You Hashem, the Shield of Abraham."

GEVUROT   The next blessing is called *Gevurot* because it speaks of God's "strengths," strengths only God can have—like being the One Who controls the wind and rain, Who sustains us, supports those who fall, heals the sick, frees the captives, keeps faith with those who sleep in the dust, and—perhaps the greatest of all—the One who revives the dead.

אַתָּה גִּבּוֹר לְעוֹלָם אֲדֹנָי. מְחַיֵּה מֵתִים אַתָּה רַב לְהוֹשִׁיעַ: (בחורף:
מַשִּׁיב הָרוּחַ וּמוֹרִיד הַגֶּשֶׁם:) מְכַלְכֵּל חַיִּים בְּחֶסֶד. מְחַיֵּה מֵתִים
בְּרַחֲמִים רַבִּים. סוֹמֵךְ נוֹפְלִים. וְרוֹפֵא חוֹלִים וּמַתִּיר אֲסוּרִים.
וּמְקַיֵּם אֱמוּנָתוֹ לִישֵׁנֵי עָפָר. מִי כָמוֹךְ בַּעַל גְּבוּרוֹת וּמִי דוֹמֶה לָּךְ.
מֶלֶךְ מֵמִית וּמְחַיֵּה וּמַצְמִיחַ יְשׁוּעָה: וְנֶאֱמָן אַתָּה לְהַחֲיוֹת מֵתִים:
בָּרוּךְ אַתָּה יי, מְחַיֵּה הַמֵּתִים:

"You, God, are forever mighty. You revive the dead. You are powerful to save. (In the winter say: You cause the wind to blow and the rain to fall.) You sustain the living with kindness and revive the dead with great mercy. You support all who fall and heal the sick. You set the captives free and keep faith with those who sleep in the dust. Who is like You, Lord of power? Who resembles You? You are the King Who brings death and restores life and causes salvation to flower. You are faithful to revive the dead. Blessed are You Hashem, Who revives the dead."

The first blessing of the *Amidah* touches on the meaning of life, indicating that we can develop our souls—as did our Fathers—by having a relationship with God. But no matter how meaningful our lives are, if it all would end with death, its meaning would only be temporary. This second blessing of the *Amidah* demonstrates life's meaning is not temporary, but permanent—life does not end with death!

Notice that Revival of the Dead (Resurrection) is mentioned three times in this blessing. Why is it so important as to warrant such emphasis? It is because belief in the Revival of the Dead is the foundation upon which all other core Jewish beliefs stand. Without it, belief withers and falls away. This may sound very strange, especially since there are so many Jews today who do not have a strong belief in the Revival of the Dead. In fact, how often do you hear Jews talking about Resurrection? For some, this may seem like a foreign belief; others simply may not have given it much thought. So how can this be the foundational Jewish belief?

To begin with, on one level, Revival of the Dead is not necessarily a future occurrence. It can happen here in this world.

God has the power to revive the "living dead." Who are the "living dead?" These are people who have given up on life because their lives have not gone well or because they just feel their lives are worthless and they are worthless. They have fallen so far that they figuratively, if not literally, "sleep in the dust." They may have heard, but have not accepted, the idea that they too are an image of God! To quote that great philosopher Snoopy: "God don't make no junk!"

In fact, the kinds of people helped by God in this blessing experience a form of revival; i.e., those who fall, who are ill, who are captive, and who are so low they sleep in the dust. God has the power to revive them by infusing them with renewed hope and purpose.[359] There are times in our lives when we all feel so very low. If we will then pour out our hearts in prayer to God, if our souls will yearn to attach to Him as the Source of life's energy, God will then release the reservoir of holy potential lying dormant and blocked within us. We can thus literally experience a personal resurrection! We have all seen people change their lives by renewing their attachment to God.

The deeper meaning of the concept of the Revival of the Dead is the understanding that God is always fair—God must be fair, even if we cannot see it at times. Let me explain with a special *Mishnah* from the only chapter in the six orders of the Mishnah, the first writing of the Oral Torah, which discusses what a Jew should believe.[360] Chapter 10 in the tractate *Sanhedrin* begins:

Kol Yisrael yeysh lahem cheylek laOlam Haba (All Israel have a share in the World to Come). The Mishnah goes on to tell us we can lose our reserved place in *Olam Haba* (the World to Come), if we do not have three core beliefs.

Before we discuss these beliefs, let us first ask, what is *Olam Haba* (the World to Come)?

Olam Haba really means three different things, sometimes referring to one or all three. We will review these in the order in which they occur.

Olam Haba refers to the World of Souls where the soul goes when a person dies. A human being is a combination of body and soul. The body, according to the Torah, comes from the dust of the earth and is therefore material, hence mortal: "From dust you come and to dust you will return."[361] The Torah also tells us how God gave life to this "dust of the earth" to create a human being: *vayipach b'apav nishmat chayim* (and God blew into the human's nostrils the soul of life).[362] God blew into Adam of His Spirit, a holy *neshama,* an eternal soul which is the Image of God in us. The obvious conclusion is that if God is immortal, then we who have some of His Spirit within us must be immortal as well. *Olam Haba* (the World to Come), is the World of Souls.

Olam Haba also denotes the world of *Mashiach* (the Messiah). This can be translated as "the Coming World" of Messianic times on earth. When will the Messiah come and change this world for the better? We will deal with this question further in our discussion of the 15th blessing of the *Amidah*: *Malchut Beyt David* (The Kingship of David), in The *Amidah* Supplement, Part 3: Help My People. For now, we must understand why belief in a Messianic era in history is crucial to having faith in God.

God created the world with something special in mind for human beings: *Gan Eden* (the "Garden of Eden," paradise). This paradise contained the perfect conditions to maximize the relationship between God and human beings; but the human beings, Adam and Eve, sinned and were thrown out of paradise. What happened to *Gan Eden,* to this paradise? According to Torah,

God did not destroy it. He put an angel in front to guard it so that we do not return until we are ready. The very fact that God did not destroy *Gan Eden* means that eventually (hopefully) we each will go back and complete the circle of history—going back to the kind of world God originally intended.

There is a problem, however. When the Messiah comes, this will be wonderful for the generation welcoming him. Hopefully, this will be our generation, but what about our grandparents or their parents who are no longer around? They will never know the glory, the joy, the indescribable bliss of human life on earth in the time of the Messiah. Why should they not live to experience this? They might be aware of it from the World of the Souls, yes, but still they will not be able to experience it.

The third meaning of *Olam Haba* solves the problem: *T'chi-yat Hameytim* (Revival of the Dead or Resurrection). The righteous among the dead will be resurrected and come back to earth to live in the Messianic Era. There are all kinds of questions you can ask, such as: If you have been reincarnated[363] several times and therefore, have lived more than one life, which one of you comes back, which body will you have? If your wife died and you remarry, do you come back with wife number one or number two? What about having two mothers-in-law—will that be paradise on earth? What happens with someone who was blind or deaf or who suffered another physical impairment—does he come back healed? Will we still have to observe all the *mitzvot* (commandments of God)?

Some of these questions have been answered by our sages. Defects, for example, will no longer exist. Some people will not merit resurrection, as we have learned, but whoever does will come back whole. At what age do we come back? One opinion is we come back in the full vigor and vitality of youth, while another opinion is we come back at the age in which we died, but we will not be infirm. The Zohar[364] teaches that every deserving body will be resurrected, no matter how many times it was reincarnated. Each body will have a *nitzotz*, a spark of its original soul. If one's first wife died and he remarried, he might have both wives. It is a bit more problematic if one's husband died and she remarried. For the answers to all these questions, we will have to wait until the Messiah comes with the answers.

Olam Haba can mean three different things, depending upon the context of how it is used. What is the meaning of "All Jews have a share in the world to come" in the context of our Mishnah? It means all three: the world of the souls; the Messianic Era; and Revival of the Dead. It means that our souls have a share of eternity, rather than extinction.

Our Mishnah reads: *Kol Yisrael yeysh lahem cheylek laOlam Haba* (All Israel have a share in the World to Come). Note the Mishnah does not say, "All Israel *will* have a share." It says, "All Israel *have* a share." But the Mishnah continues: *V'eylu sh'eyn lahem cheylek laOlam Haba* (And these are the ones who have no share in the World to Come).—In other words, these are the ones who end up not getting there.

The Mishnah then lists three categories: *Ha-omeyr eyn t'chiyat hameytim min haTorah* (Those who say Revival of the Dead is not from the Torah); *eyn Torah min hashamayim* (the Torah is not from Heaven); *v'apikores* (and one who rejects God). What is absolutely startling is that these three categories do not include people who commit terrible crimes. Those who have committed some of the most grievous sins—even capital offenses—can still end up in the World to Come if they truly regret and repent sins. The three categories of people who do not get in are people who suffer a lack of faith.

The first category describing those who do not get to the "World to Come" is: *ha-omeyr eyn t'chiyat hameytim min haTorah* (those who say Revival of the Dead is not from the Torah). It is very strange this should appear at all—let alone as the first category—especially since there are many people who struggle with this belief. On the simplest level, why should the person who does not believe in *Olam Haba* be denied entrance to *Olam Haba*? Simple! If you do not believe in *Olam Haba* you do not get it! Let us continue with the Mishnah and complete the other two categories, and then we will return to this question.

The second category in the Mishnah describing those who do not merit going to *Olam Haba* pertains to those who say *V'eyn Torah min hashamayim* (the Torah is not from Heaven), i.e., not from God. Wow! The Mishnah has just excluded a lot of people. Just think of the divisions we have in the Jewish world today and what these represent theologically. Reform, Reconstructionist and today's Conservative Judaism would have a serious problem with this Mishnah. Mostly, they subscribe to variations of the 19th century Julius Wellhausen School of Biblical criticism that maintains that the Torah is a document produced over many centuries from several sources.[365] In other words, from this perspective, the Torah is not necessarily the direct Word of God!

Maimonides takes the strict approach of the Mishnah: If you do not accept these three beliefs—which he expands to 13— then you do not get into the World to Come. Yosef Albo (1380- 1435),[366] on the other hand, teaches: If by virtue of your education and thinking, you come to the conclusion such a belief is not what is demanded by God in the Torah, then you are making an intellectual error, and are, therefore, not excluded. One can make a case that most non-religious Jews today fit into this category.

The third category, the Mishnah teaches, is *V'apikores*. What is an *apikores*? It comes from the Greek philosopher Epicurus, the founder of Epicureanism, the philosophy that teaches—put very simply—"Eat, drink and be merry for tomorrow you may die." Epicurus, to the sages of the Talmud, became the paradigm for a heretic, but in the context of the Mishnah it has a special usage: one who denies the belief in God. The ultimate *apikores* is one who rejects God.

So, according to this Mishnah there are three beliefs a Jew must have. The first is that there is a God Who created the world and cares about His Creation. And because He cares, because He loves us, because He wants the optimal relationship with us, God gave us the Torah as His guide for how to be in this relationship—and this becomes the second principle. Belief in Torah implies that this world is run by law and order. There are rules to the world, and we ought to be good and not evil because God wants us to be good. Belief in Torah also implies God will see to it that people are responsible for their actions. If we believe in the Torah, then the good guys should have it good and bad guys should have it bad, but when we look at the world we realize, "It ain't necessarily so!"

The greatest religious problem everyone has to face is the dilemma philosophers call "theodicy," or in Hebrew, *Tzadik v'ra lo, rasha v'tov lo* (The righteous suffer while the wicked prosper). There are good people who live such hard lives and there are bad people who are living it up. This can only lead one to doubt the Torah is true, or that God gave us the Torah, or that there really is a God in the world. For in the Torah, God seems to promise reward and punishment for one's actions. If we do not solve the problem of *Tzadik v'ra lo*, of why bad things happen to good people, then we will not continue to accept the first two principles of faith and our faith will wither and fall.

There is only one solution to this problem. Justice is not always immediately apparent. Sometimes we must wait to see justice. When you are suffering, if you are told the suffering is for a reason, and at the end there is a prize making all your suffering worthwhile, you would have a much easier time bearing the pain. You might be in pain, but there is a reason. The problem is that we only see a part of the race. We rarely see the finish line. Why does God choose to defer rewards? Why does God give wicked people good things? There are reasons.[367] If you believe in God and in the justice promised by His Torah and you see there is not always justice in this world, then there is only one way you can continue your faith, and this is to add a third belief to your belief in God and His Torah: *T'chiyat Hameytim* (Revival of the Dead).

Maimonides, in his *Thirteen Principles*, deals with this struggle of faith on both a global and a personal level. On a global level, his twelfth principle as summarized in the *Yigdal*[368] prayer teaches: "God will send us a Messiah to redeem those longing for His final salvation." The world may not yet seem to be what it should be. Good nations, like the State of Israel, may seem to be treated unfairly by the world. But when the Messiah comes, everything will change and true justice will prevail.

For the individual, why is it life often seems so unfair? Why do so many good people suffer? The answer is seen in Maimonides' thirteenth principle: "God will revive the dead in His abundant kindness; blessed forever is His praised Name." The principle of Revival of the Dead indicates that what happens to us after our few years of life here on this earth is fairer in quantity, in quality, in every dimension of fairness, than what is happening to us here on earth now. So belief in *Techiyat haMeytim*, Revival of the Dead, is a belief in the fairness of God and is, therefore, crucial in order to make our belief in God and His Torah credible.

Most people believe in God, for without God there is nothing. We can understand why we should believe in Torah, because the source of our relationship with God is His Torah. But it is not so easy to understand why Revival of the Dead—why this one belief—is so crucial in order to maintain one's faith. The answer is that Revival of the Dead means more than just Resurrection of the Dead. It means whatever inequities and evils we see on this earth will eventually be straightened out. Its message for us is: Do not judge life by the short time span your *neshama*, your holy soul, is living in the apartment known as your body. Often the fairness of God plays out beyond this lifetime.

When bad things happen to good people without good reason, God has to make it up to them! It may be in another reincarnated lifetime; it may be a reward in the World of the Souls; it may be in Messianic times; but God has to make it up to that soul, and this is what belief in the Revival of the Dead includes! It is the ultimate fairness of God.

We learned in Chapter 22: The Amen response, *Amen*—אָמֵן—is an abbreviation of the phrase *Eyl Melech Ne-eman*—אֵל מֶלֶךְ נֶאֱמָן—"God, King, Faithful," or "God is a faithful King." The

Hebrew word for God is אֵל, *Eyl*. If God had just created the world and left it alone, He never would have become our Ruler Who gives us laws. What is the term for a king or ruler in Hebrew? מֶלֶךְ/*Melech*. A king knows what is going on in his kingdom and issues edicts and rules. The fact God revealed Himself and gave us the Torah—teaching us how to best live our lives by following His laws—makes Him our King.

However, life often seems unfair. We all see instances where the righteous seem to suffer and the wicked prosper. We all experience times in our own lives when we are at a loss to understand what we did to deserve our terrible fate. How can we believe in a God Who allows this to happen? God must also be fair!

The third category of faith is the concept of ultimate fairness—in the afterlife if not here on earth. What Hebrew word could we use to say God faithfully, eventually, rectifies the wrongs on this earth? נֶאֱמָן/*Neh-ehman* (Faithful). God is *neh-ehman*, faithful to keep His word. God tells us again and again in His Torah, "If you will be good, I will be good to you. If you will be bad, bad things will happen to you." Know that God must be fair and even if we do not see this fairness in our lifetimes, eventually it will be straightened out.

These three categories of faith of the Mishnah are subsumed under three words recited before the *Shema Yisrael* (if praying in private) stating our belief in God. When we say we believe, we are expressing our אֱמוּנָה/*emuna*, our "faith." The shortened form of the word *emuna* is אָמֵן/*Amen*. Every time we say *Amen* we are saying, "We believe." Where did the word *Amen* come from? As we learned in Chapter 22, "The Amen Response," the Talmud[369] tells us that the word *Amen*—אָמֵן—is an acronym of the three words representing the three categories of faith: אֵל מֶלֶךְ נֶאֱמָן, *Eyl Melech Neh-ehman*. If you take the first letters of these three words, this spells אָמֵן/*Amen*. So when we say *Amen*, we are not only saying we believe, but we are also proclaiming what we believe: אֵל/*Eyl*, there is a God; מֶלֶךְ/*Melech*, God, our Ruler, gave us the Torah; and נֶאֱמָן/*Neh-ehman*, if we do not see this now, we have faith that whatever evils we experience in this world eventually will be straightened out—a belief in the fairness of God.

God does fix things here on earth, but the court of last resort for understanding why bad things happen to good people is *Olam Haba*—more specifically, the last stage of *Olam Haba, T'chiyat Hameytim*, Revival of the Dead.

So as we recite this second blessing of the *Amidah*, which expounds on the *Gevurot*, the powers of God, let us keep in mind that God is so powerful He can lift us up—no matter how low we have fallen. And even more, He will be perfectly fair with us no matter what.

KEDUSHAT HASHEM   The third blessing in this first section is called *Kedushat Hashem* (The Holiness of God's Name). When the *Amidah* is recited silently, this blessing is very short:

אַתָּה קָדוֹשׁ וְשִׁמְךָ קָדוֹשׁ וּקְדוֹשִׁים בְּכָל יוֹם יְהַלְלוּךָ סֶּלָה: בָּרוּךְ
אַתָּה יי, הָאֵל הַקָּדוֹשׁ:

You are holy and Your name is holy, and holy ones praise you every day *Sela!* Blessed are You, Hashem, Holy God.

God is *HaKadosh Baruch Hu* (The Holy One, Blessed be He). When we say God is holy, however, what do we mean? The word for "holy" in Hebrew, *Kadosh*, indicates separateness. In the Torah,[370] God commands us: *Kedoshim t'hiyu* (Be Holy)! Rashi explains the verse: "Be removed from (sexual) immorality." A holy person, therefore, is one who by his actions separates and raises himself above those who are immoral. When we say God is holy, this indicates God is separate from human beings who, by nature, commit sins. Unlike human beings, God is perfect and always good.

In the next few words of God's command in the Torah to be

holy, God challenges us: "Be holy because I, Hashem your God, am holy!" In other words, proclaiming God as holy challenges us to emulate him and try to be holy ourselves. Implied in this verse is the thought that because we were created in His image, we have the capacity—and even the obligation—to be holy as well. How do we define holiness? The answer points to a major Torah principle: *Ma hu af ata* (Just as He (God) does, so must you do).[371] In Latin this is called *imitatio Dei* (imitating the Deity). The Talmud,[372] by illustration, teaches that just as God shows His compassion by clothing the naked (Adam and Eve); visiting the sick (Abraham); comforting the mourners (Isaac), and burying the dead (Moses), so must we!

In Judaism, to be holy is not to be a recluse ascetic, cut off from the world and real life. To be truly holy, one must be involved in life, helping others and thereby helping to perfect the world. To be truly holy, we must not only do Godly things, we must bring God into everything we do. For example, a Jew does not just eat; he first blesses God as the source of his food, thereby bringing down the flow of holiness into the food from Above. As we eat the food, we then fill ourselves with holiness. Being holy is an attitude demonstrating that God is our partner in life in everything, and the more we include Him in our lives, the more we will become what we were meant to be.

So when we recite this *Kedushat HaShem* blessing, we should focus on God's holiness and our yearning to emulate this holiness in our actions.

In the public repetition of the *Amidah*, we recite the longer form of this blessing called, the *Kedusha*, with the verses of praise of God's holiness from the angels recorded by the prophets. On the Sabbath and holidays, the *Kedusha* is more elaborate with longer passages introducing the holy verses of the angels in the *Musaf Amidah*, additional verses from the angels are added.

Here is the weekday text of the *Kedusha*:

נְקַדֵּשׁ אֶת שִׁמְךָ בָּעוֹלָם. כְּשֵׁם שֶׁמַּקְדִּישִׁים אוֹתוֹ בִּשְׁמֵי מָרוֹם.
כַּכָּתוּב עַל יַד נְבִיאֶךָ: וְקָרָא זֶה אֶל זֶה וְאָמַר:

קָדוֹשׁ. קָדוֹשׁ. קָדוֹשׁ יי צְבָאוֹת. מְלֹא כָל הָאָרֶץ כְּבוֹדוֹ:

לְעֻמָּתָם בָּרוּךְ יֹאמֵרוּ:

בָּרוּךְ כְּבוֹד יי מִמְּקוֹמוֹ:

וּבְדִבְרֵי קָדְשְׁךָ כָּתוּב לֵאמֹר:

יִמְלֹךְ יי לְעוֹלָם. אֱלֹהַיִךְ צִיּוֹן לְדֹר וָדֹר. הַלְלוּיָהּ:

We will sanctify Your Name in the world, just as they (angels) sanctify it in the *Heavens* above, as it is written by Your prophet: They call to one another and say:

"Holy, Holy, Holy is God, Master of Legions, the world is filled with His glory."

Those opposite them say:

"Blessed is the glory of God from His place."

And in Your holy writings it is written:

"God will rule forever, Your God, Zion, from generation to generation."

From generation to generation we will declare Your greatness. To all eternity we will sanctify Your holiness. And Your praise, our God, will not depart from our mouth forever. For You, God, are a great and holy King. Blessed are You Hashem, the holy God.

There are three main verses from the angels, recorded by Isaiah (6:3), Ezekiel (3:12) and King David (Psalm 146:10), indicated above with an italic font. See Chapter 20, "The Biggest Blessing," for more detail in understanding the first two verses. In short, in this first verse of angelic praise from Isaiah, the *Serafim* angels sing out: *Kadosh, Kasdosh, Kadosh, Hashem Tz'va-ot, m'lo chol haaretz k'vodo* (Holy, Holy, Holy is God, Master of Legions, the whole world is filled with His glory).

What does, *M'lo chol haaretz k'vodo* (the whole world is filled with His glory) teach us? That wherever you might look, you can see God revealed in the world because the whole world testifies to God's glory. When we say the threefold repetition of *Kadosh* (holy), it is customary to lift yourself up on your toes each time, emulating the movements of the angels and thereby expressing your desire to elevate yourself and come closer to the holiness of God.

The second verse is from Ezekiel: *Baruch k'vod Hashem mimekomo* (Blessed is the glory of God from His place). This is recited by the *Ofanim* and *Chayot Hakodesh* angels opposing the *Serafim* angels of Isaiah, saying, in effect, "No, sometimes in life the pain is so great that we cannot see the glory of God everywhere. Our world is sometimes a world where God hides His face and we cannot see Him. Nevertheless we praise God saying, 'Blessed be the glory of God from His place!' wherever that is."

In the third verse King David proclaims: *Yimloch Hashem l'olam, Elohayich Tziyon, l'dor vador Haleluya!* (God will rule forever, your God, Zion, from generation to generation, praised be God). In other words, no matter where God is, it is God Who makes the rules. God—and only God—is in control. Even if you cannot see God at all, He is here and He is in charge. He will rule forever, until the end of days, the days of the Messiah and the Messianic Age when all questions will be answered—even the ultimate question of the fairness of life: "Why do the righteous suffer and the wicked prosper?"

We will then experience the justice, the compassion and the utter holiness of God.

Let Me Have It!

Now comes the time to ask for the desire of our hearts. We praised God in the first section of the *Amidah* as God Who had an amazing relationship with our forefathers, Who is the most holy and the most powerful—so powerful He can even bring the dead to life.

In the *Shema*, as we have learned, when we read the holy verses from God's Torah, we listen as God speaks, in effect, to us.

Now, in the middle section of the *Amidah*, called *Bakasha* (Petition), it is our turn to speak to God—to literally pour out our hearts to Him!

But not on Shabbat or holidays! The spirit of holy days is reserved for drawing closer to God through praise rather than through petition, as it says in Psalm 119:164, "Seven times in the day I will praise You." The Midrash[373] understands seven times of praise to refer to the first three and last three blessings of the *Amidah* in praise to God and to the unique middle section on Shabbat—the seventh day—of only one blessing praising God for giving us these special holy days as a special path to him. Also, says the Midrash,[374] if one prays on Shabbat for things he needs and does not yet have, or even healing someone who is ill, he will become troubled. Shabbat was given to us for holiness, delight and rest, and not for worry.

But let us turn now to the *Bakasha* (Petition) section of the *Amidah* recited the rest of the week.

"Who am I to ask anything of God? Why should God listen

to me?" you might ask yourself. The Torah tells you who you are. You are an image of God, and God wants to hear your prayers. How do we know? As stated in Chapter 9, "Keeping Me on Track," our sages asked why God brought the Jewish people from Egypt, a land where the Nile River watered the crops whether there was rain or not, to the land of Canaan—a land where most of the necessary water comes from rain. Our sages answered: so that the Jewish people would look to Heaven for their sustenance and pray for rain. In other words, God has created the world in such a fashion that we would pray to Him for our needs.

"But who am I?" you still might ask. Listen to this story.

> In the synagogue of the renowned Rav Yisrael of Salant—founder of the nineteenth century Mussar movement—there was a poor ignorant tailor who stood praying the *Amidah* longer than Rav Yisrael, rocking to and fro with great ecstatic fervor. When Rav Yisrael asked how the man, who could barely read Hebrew and hardly understood even the plain meaning of the words, could pray with such *kavana* (focus and intention), this is the response he gave:
>
> "I'm the most stupid, poorest member of this congregation. The *shamash* doesn't even know my Hebrew name and my father's name to call me up for an honor to the Torah. No one has time or patience to listen to me. I once even conducted an experiment. I stood in the marketplace early one Thursday morning and cornered Reb Shmuel, the banker, asking, 'Do you have time to listen to me?' He at least didn't pass me by, but he hastily referred me to his secretary, who would never dream of giving me an appointment. I even accosted you, the great Rav Yisrael, with my request for time to listen to me, and although you smiled at me more warmly than the others, you had to rush off to lecture your students.
>
> "Apparently, no one important has time to listen to me, the lowest of congregants," he continued, "not Reb Shmuel

the banker, not Reb Dovid the judge, and not Rav Yisrael of Salant. But I have news for you, great Rabbi. When I take a *Siddur* (prayer book) in my hand, the same *Siddur* taken by the banker, the judge, and you the rabbi, and when I wrap myself in a *tallis* (prayer shawl), the same *tallis* taken by the banker, the judge, and the rabbi, and I stand in prayer before God…God has time to listen to me. And if I stand at my prayers longer than you, great Rabbi of Salant, God has more time to listen to me than to listen to you! Now do you understand my fervor?"

Karov Hashem l'chol korav (God is near to all who call upon Him), the Psalmist teaches us.[375] *L'chol asher yikra-uhu v'emet* (to all who call upon Him in truth). In other words, God has time to listen to us all for as long as we need.

What are our needs? What should we pray for?

EXERCISE   When I teach about the *Amidah* and come to the *Bakasha* (Petition), middle section, I often utilize the following exercise with my students. It is an exercise I think would be useful for everyone to do from time to time. So let us do it now.

> Imagine you were granted an exclusive audience with God Himself and you could ask for anything you want—not one request, two or three, but as many as you want. In preparation for what will most certainly be the most amazing experience of your life, take a piece of paper and make a list of the things you want to ask for. Take a moment to review and study your list.
>
> Here is your once in a lifetime chance to know God will listen to all your requests. What are you going to ask for? For wealth? For health? For peace? Your first thought might be that your list will be endless. However, the reality is that most people's lists are very short—most struggling to come

up with even ten requests, let alone 13 as in this *Bakasha* (Petition) section of the *Amidah*.

Well, three times a day, you are granted an exclusive audience with God Himself—just like the poor tailor in the story. Three times a day, as you recite the *Amidah*, God gives you His full attention for as long as you need and He is eager to hear your requests.

The surprising thing about this middle section of the *Amidah* is that its 13 requests probably encompass most, if not all, of your requests, plus some important ones you may not have thought of. The sages[376] encourage us to add our own personal prayers, corresponding to the theme of the particular blessing we are reciting. As we recite the blessing for healing, for example, we can insert a prayer for God to heal ourselves or those close to us who are ill, mentioning their names; or in the prayer for sustenance we might add a prayer for our own prosperity. See the section, "Praying for Others" in Chapter 23, "Is it Kosher to Pray," for a more thorough discussion of personalizing your prayers.

Let me add one more thought about this petition section of the *Amidah* illustrated by the following story[377]:

Two friends were discussing some of the more difficult issues of life. One said, "Sometimes I would like to ask God why He allows poverty, famine, and injustice, when He could do something about it."

The other replied, "Well, why don't you ask Him?"

The response came quickly: "Because I am afraid that God might ask me the same question."

Understood in all these requests is the thought that as you ask God to give you understanding or health or prosperity or peace, you commit yourself to bringing, in your own way, understanding, health, prosperity and peace to the world.

Let us now take a close look at these 13 petitions. I have

tried to enhance and expand the understanding of the text of each blessing and thereby give the reader something to think about while reciting them. This chapter will discuss the first six petition blessings, which focuses on the needs of our lives now. The next chapter will discuss the next six which focuses upon our future and the future of the Jewish people, plus a general prayer for God to hear our prayers.

Bina (knowledge, insight and insight)   I suspect not many of us have "insight and knowledge" on our list of requests, but if you think about it, both are essential in order for us to grow and develop our minds as well as our souls. In this blessing we thank God for giving us a mind and the ability to think. We pray for God to help us to increase our "knowledge, insight and intellect." For those of us who experience a "recall" problem as we age or as we deal with the great stresses life can bring, this is a fitting time to pray for that as well.

אַתָּה חוֹנֵן לְאָדָם דַּעַת. וּמְלַמֵּד לֶאֱנוֹשׁ בִּינָה: חָנֵּנוּ מֵאִתְּךָ דֵּעָה
בִּינָה וְהַשְׂכֵּל בָּרוּךְ אַתָּה יי, חוֹנֵן הַדָּעַת:

> "You grace man with knowledge, and teach insight to mortals. Grace us from Yourself with knowledge, insight and intellect. Blessed are You, Hashem, Who graces us with knowledge."

The word *da-at* means "knowledge," and it encompasses the ability to think. This is the first of all the requests because knowledge, understanding and intellect help us use our time on earth wisely, and with proper understanding we now can ask for what is truly important.

On a deeper level, *da-at* in the Torah also refers to the intimate connection between a man and a woman, as in: "Adam knew Eve, his wife, and she conceived and gave birth to Cain."[378] Asking

God for *da-at*, therefore, is also an appeal for help to strengthen our intimate connections to each other and especially to Him, before Whom we are praying.

TESHUVA (RETURN)   It is intriguing that the second and third petition blessings amount to a request for forgiveness and not a request for God to give something or to do something special for you. It is a plea to remove a very heavy burden. Guilt is a powerful emotion that can be very destructive. God, however, does not want us to walk through life with the heavy burden of guilt on our shoulders. Like a loving parent, God does not want to punish either. As we will see in The *Amidah* Supplement, Part 3: "Din, Justice" God does not punish, He fixes.

Difficult times, which are perceived as punishments in life, are *nisyonot* (trials or tests) motivating us to change. God wants us to do *teshuva*, to "return" to who we were meant to be. As Isaiah teaches:[379] "May the wicked forsake his way, and the sinful one his thoughts and return to Hashem and He will be merciful, and to our God Who is abundantly forgiving." God says,[380] "I do not desire the death of the wicked, but that the wicked turn from his evil ways and live."

הֲשִׁיבֵנוּ אָבִינוּ לְתוֹרָתֶךָ. וְקָרְבֵנוּ מַלְכֵּנוּ לַעֲבוֹדָתֶךָ וְהַחֲזִירֵנוּ בִּתְשׁוּבָה שְׁלֵמָה לְפָנֶיךָ. בָּרוּךְ אַתָּה יי, הָרוֹצֶה בִּתְשׁוּבָה:

"Return us, our Father to Your Torah. And bring us closer, our King, to Your service; and bring us back before You with complete repentance. Blessed are You, Hashem, Who desires repentance."

Before we ask for forgiveness for our sins, we ask God for permission to ask. You might think this is an odd request, but think of a person who comes before a judge after committing a minor crime. He begs for leniency and the judge lets him go. After a while he is brought back before the same judge after committing the same crime. Again he begs for mercy, telling the judge he has children and a family to support, and again the judge lets him go, but this time with a severe warning. Now if the man is caught committing the same crime a third time, the judge most likely will throw the book at him and put him in jail! We come before God, the Supreme Judge, asking for forgiveness again and again for the same sins. By what right do we have even to ask? It is only because, as the blessing concludes; "Blessed are You, Hashem, Who desires repentance." So we bless God for being so merciful and compassionate that He listens to our repentance.

In addition, we ask God for help in the process. Repentance is hard work. For example, Maimonides[381] tells us that the first step is to recognize you did something wrong. Most of us believe we are basically good people. Most of us have become masters at rationalizing our behavior, so much so that it is difficult for us even to recognize that much of what we are doing is wrong; and so we implore God, "Return us," "bring us closer," and "bring us back," for we cannot do this without His help.

SELICHA (PARDON ME)   There are several steps in repenting for our sins, but the first step, as we said above, is perhaps the most difficult: *Hakarat hacheyt* (recognizing we have sinned). What is so difficult about this? We know if we have cheated on our spouses or if we were dishonest with others. We know if we ate things we should not have eaten. The real problem is that as masters of rationalization we can rationalize away almost any sin. We become like the Flip Wilson character, Geraldine, explaining to God and to ourselves, "The devil made me do it!" In this blessing, we recognize and confess we have sinned:

סְלַח לָנוּ אָבִינוּ כִּי חָטָאנוּ. מְחַל לָנוּ מַלְכֵּנוּ כִּי פָשָׁעְנוּ. כִּי מוֹחֵל
וְסוֹלֵחַ אָתָּה. בָּרוּךְ אַתָּה יי, חַנּוּן הַמַּרְבֶּה לִסְלֹחַ:

"Forgive us, our Father, for we have erred with sin. Pardon us, our King, for we have willfully sinned. For You pardon and forgive. Blessed are You, Hashem, Who is gracious and abundantly forgiving."

Sometimes we try hard to forget, burying what we have done in our subconscious.

> There is the story of a man who is stopped for speeding on the highway and gets very angry at the policeman. "Number one, I want to tell you I was not speeding, and number two, I have never told a lie. I don't lie and I don't speed. Here, my wife is sitting right next to me, and she knows I never lie and I wasn't speeding. Why don't you ask her?"
>
> The policeman has the evidence in his radar gun, but is fascinated by this tale. He leans into the car and he says to the lady, "Was your husband speeding?"
>
> And she replies, "He is right. He never lies and he wasn't speeding. We have been married for more than 25 years, and one thing I learned that is absolutely clear, never contradict him when he is drunk!"

The husband wanted to forget his transgressions and wanted everyone else to forget them too.

The ability to forget the past can be a blessing. If we had to live our lives burdened with the weight of past grief and disappointments, if we could not banish from our minds our accumulated failures, fears and frustrations, if the wounds we suffer on life's battlefields were always raw and stinging, life would be continuously miserable, and we would not be able go on.

But we must never forget who and what we are, and this includes owning up to what we have done wrong and remembering it so we can learn from our past and change for the better. Besides, no matter how hard we try to forget, we should always remember God sees everything we do, and with God there is always a permanent record. Journalist, Bob Greene, in his book *Cheeseburgers*,[382] writes the following about our "Permanent Record":

234 DANCING WITH GOD

"There are thousands of theories about what's gone wrong with the world, but I think it comes down to one simple thing: The death of the Permanent Record.

"You remember the Permanent Record. When you were in elementary school, junior high school, and high school, you were constantly being told that if you screwed up, news of that screw up would be sent down to the principal's office and would be placed in your Permanent Record.

"Nothing more needed to be said. No one had ever seen a Permanent Record; that didn't matter. We knew they were there. We all imagined a steel filing cabinet, crammed full of Permanent Records, one for each kid in the school. I think we always assumed that when we graduated our Permanent Record was sent on to college with us, and then when we got out of college our Permanent Record was sent to our employer, probably with a duplicate copy sent to the U.S. Government…

"As Americans began to realize that there was no Permanent Record, and probably never had been, they deduced for themselves that any kind of behavior was permissible … It has been so long since we have believed in the Permanent Record that the very mention of it today probably brings a nostalgic smile to our faces. We feel naïve for ever having believed that a Permanent Record was really down there in the principal's office anyway.

"And who really knows if our smiles may freeze on some distant day, the day it is our turn to check out of this earthly world, and we are confronted with a heavenly presence greeting us at the gates of our new eternal home, a heavenly presence sitting there casually leafing through a dusty, battered volume of our Permanent Record as we come jauntily into view."

Yes, God keeps a permanent record of our deeds; however, we are not doomed for our transgressions as long as we do *teshuva. Te-*

shuva or "repentance," according to Maimonides, is accomplished with three basic steps—recognition, remorse and commitment not to sin again. These can be expanded to five: recognition, remorse, confession, reconciliation (with restitution where possible), and resolving not to sin again. This is very much like a 12-step program for those with addictions in that it is structured and achievable. Working the steps is not easy, but it is doable.

We have covered the first step, *hakarat hacheyt,* or recognition. The second step is *charata* (remorse). It does not help to ask for forgiveness from God if we do not genuinely feel sorry for what we have done.

The next step, *vidui* or confession, begins the outward process of *teshuva* by articulating aloud our sins. Saying what we have done wrong helps us own up by making it real, and it can also help lift the burden of guilt we carry on our shoulders.

The fourth step is *peyra-on* (reconciliation or restitution). The Talmud[383] teaches: "For sins between man and God, Yom Kippur atones. But for the sins between man and his fellow man, Yom Kippur does not atone until he appeases his fellow man."

We can recognize our sins, regret any harm these may have caused and confess our sins before God. Nevertheless, our *teshuva* is not complete until we confront the one whom we have hurt, make restitution where possible and ask for forgiveness. *Teshuva* requires us to bare ourselves and our souls before the one whom we have hurt and before God. This is perhaps the moment of our greatest vulnerability, but asking for forgiveness directly is the step that must be taken to bring about wholeness and resolution. By taking the brave step of apologizing, we give that person the opportunity to forgive us.

The final step is *azivat hacheyt* (resolving not to sin again). Maimonides teaches that the ultimate *teshuva* happens when we are faced with the same temptations again and reject our past sinful behavior. We know our sinful behavior was inappropriate. We probably knew this as we were doing it. Yet we continued to act the same way. *Teshuva* requires renouncing the behavior that leads us astray from our true essence. We need to change, to get back to our real selves! So when we hear disparaging remarks about someone, we should walk away, or better yet, ask the person gossiping to stop. When we feel anger welling up inside, let us turn away and find a way to stem the anger. When we think we are so clever and are about to offer a sharp verbal sting, let us keep it to ourselves. This all requires determination and effort, but the potential for personal growth is so great it can transform us.

So when you begin this prayer and say, *Slach lanu Avinu ki chatanu* (Forgive us, our Father, for we have sinned), take a moment to review your actions. Pick out one or two things you have done that you are not so proud of and go through the five steps—as much as possible while in prayer: recognition, remorse, confession, reconciliation/restitution, and resolving not to sin again. The steps you could not complete in prayer, like restitution, resolve to do as soon as possible. This five-step process works because it is structured and deliberate. This will help you rediscover your true essence of wholeness and holiness.

Do not be dissuaded into thinking you have sinned too much and distanced yourself so far from God to ever be in God's favor again—as the Ethics of the Fathers[384] teaches: "Don't consider yourself a wicked person." Remember, in this blessing we refer to God as "our Father," and a father never gives up on his child—always hoping he will return to him. According to the Talmud,[385] the heavenly Gates of Tears are never closed.

> In fact, repentance can be a powerful path to God, as revealed by the Ropshitzer Rebbe.[386] A man came to Naftali Ropshitz (Chassidic master 1760-1827) and questioned him about the following passage in the Talmud:[387] *Eyn adam nokeyf etzba-o milmata ela im keyn machrizin alav milmala* (No man bruises his finger here on earth unless it was decreed against him in heaven). The man asked, "I can understand that if a person lifts his hand to do something good, then Heaven will give him the go-ahead. But if a person lifts

his hand to do something bad, how could it be possible that Heaven would decree that he should be allowed to do it?"

The Ropshitzer Rebbe said, "Yes, if a person is going to do something good, heaven decrees to go ahead and do it. But if a person is going to do something bad, then the decree is that a new path is about to be made to come closer to God."

The man looked puzzled, and so the Rebbe explained that when a person moves away from God, God follows him where ever he goes, so that just in case he wants to come back to God, all he has to do is make an about-face to find Him. In a sense, every time a person moves away from God, then that person creates a new path to return to God. All he has to do is to turn around and come back.

One more thought about forgiveness. Why is Yom Kippur, the Day of Atonement, the holiest day of the year, referred to in the Torah[388] as *Yom HaKippurim*, using the plural form—*Kippurim*—for the word atonement instead of the singular *Kippur*? It is because there is more than one direction forgiveness needs to travel. Yes, we must ask each other—everyone we know—to forgive us if we have offended them, but we need to tell them we forgive them as well. This may seem formulaic, but there is magic to asking, "Forgive me," and to saying, "I forgive you." We never know how we may have hurt someone, and such a recitation in itself may be so healing.

Similarly, as we ask God to forgive us for the sins we knowingly committed and for those we unknowingly committed, we also must forgive God! Most of us, at one time or another, have held a vestige of resentment towards God for what we perceive as unjust pain that life threw at us. So forgive God and tell Him that though you may not understand, you trust He loves you and has your best interests in mind.

And most important of all, forgive yourself!

We often come down hard on ourselves for not doing better.

We promised ourselves we would lose those ten pounds, or stop smoking, or learn more, or make up with our sister, friend and others. No matter what you may have done, forgive yourself. Resolve each time you recite this prayer of forgiveness to do better by doing one more step towards forgiveness. Each small success will push you to go further and further.

G'ULA (REDEMPTION)   See how we suffer: The Passover Haggadah teaches a major principle of Jewish history: *B'chol dor vador omdim aleynu l'chaloteynu* (In every generation someone arises to destroy us). Whether it is a pharaoh, or Amalek, or Haman, or a Caesar, or a Crusade, or an Inquisition, or Chmelnitsky, or a Czar, or Hitler, or an Ayatollah, this happens in every generation. While it seems as though there is no rest for the Jewish people from the threats of those who wish to destroy them, history will bear out that their enemies have disappeared while the Jewish people are still here bearing testimony to God's greatness. God has redeemed us again and again for His Name's sake.

Why did the sages make the blessing for redemption the seventh one in the *Amidah*? The Talmud[389] records Rava as saying, "Since [the Jewish people] are destined to be redeemed in the seventh [year of a Sabbatical Year cycle], they made it the seventh blessing."

רְאֵה בְעָנְיֵנוּ. וְרִיבָה רִיבֵנוּ. וּגְאָלֵנוּ מְהֵרָה לְמַעַן שְׁמֶךָ. כִּי גוֹאֵל חָזָק אָתָּה. בָּרוּךְ אַתָּה יי, גּוֹאֵל יִשְׂרָאֵל:

"See how we suffer, so fight our fight, and redeem us quickly for the sake of Your Name. For You are a mighty Redeemer. Blessed are You, Hashem, Redeemer of Israel."

On a personal level, in this blessing we ask God to see our individual suffering.[390] Life is always challenging us and sometimes the challenges we face seem too much to bear. In almost every family there are strained relationships. Some people feel trapped in a loveless marriage. Some are estranged from their children, parents or siblings. Some face the challenge of disease and illness, while others are crushed by financial and/or legal burdens or the loss of a livelihood. Still others are caught in the seemingly neverending cycle of addiction.

No one escapes the challenges of life. These provide great opportunity for personal growth, but sometimes it just seems so hard!

This blessing does not ask God to eliminate our personal challenges. Life without challenge would have little meaning. Rather, this blessing asks God to acknowledge our challenges, our struggles and help us fight our personal battles so that we can get some relief from the stresses and strains that they bring, enabling us to better confront them. Recalling the exercise from Chapter 4, *"Avoda,"* as we recite this blessing we should be crying out from inside of us, "Hashem help me! Hashem help me! Hashem help me and the Jewish people confront the challenges that face us. Redeem us!"

The *G'ula* (Redemption) blessing comes before the blessing for healing because most ailments have an emotional component. Disease is really "dis-ease," so we ask God to redeem us from the emotional stress and to grant us a healing of the spirit before we ask for bodily health.

R'FA-EYNU (HEAL US) Did you ever stop to ask: Why is there illness in the world? Each of us will either suffer a major illness or have a loved one who does; and at least in our hearts, we wonder why anyone has to suffer this way. According to the Midrash,[391] there was no sickness in the world until Father Jacob asked God for illness. What??? Why would anyone in their right mind ask to be sick? Before Jacob, suggests the Midrash, when it was one's time to leave this world, one simply sneezed and expired. This perhaps explains the universal custom of saying, "God bless you," when we hear someone sneeze.

So why does illness exist in the world? Father Jacob did not want the suffering sickness often brings, he just wanted to have some warning before he died, says the Midrash, so that he would have time to put his affairs in order.

Is there any other reason why God might bring illness upon someone? There are several approaches from our tradition. Here are just a few.

One approach tells us that sometimes God will bring an illness upon us to give us a good kick in the pants when we are ignoring Him or not showing appreciation for all He has given us in this world. Kabbalah might suggest that sometimes one suffers illness as a correction for one's soul for something one has done in a previous lifetime. Sometimes illness occurs because there is a crucial lesson that can only be learned through illness and recovery. An illness might be a *kapara*, an "atonement," a lesser substitute for something worse that might have happened. Illness can bring families and whole communities closer together. There are more reasons given, and any one or more can apply in any given situation.[392]

Ultimately, no one ever really knows why one becomes ill. Sometimes it is just, as the sages call it, *derech ha-olam* (the way of the world) or *derech hateva* (the way of nature). We may call it "dumb luck." There are illnesses out in the world, and we may just be in the wrong place at the wrong time and catch one—like the SARS epidemic a few years ago, or the swine flu that brought illness to so many people just because they were on an airplane with someone else who was sick. But for whatever reason illness occurs, the Talmud[393] suggests we use our illnesses as opportunities to review our lives and the direction we are going in order to make corrections and better ourselves.

רְפָאֵנוּ יי וְנֵרָפֵא. הוֹשִׁיעֵנוּ וְנִוָּשֵׁעָה כִּי תְהִלָּתֵנוּ אָתָּה. וְהַעֲלֵה רְפוּאָה שְׁלֵמָה לְכָל מַכּוֹתֵינוּ. כִּי אֵל מֶלֶךְ רוֹפֵא נֶאֱמָן וְרַחֲמָן אָתָּה. בָּרוּךְ אַתָּה יי, רוֹפֵא חוֹלֵי עַמּוֹ יִשְׂרָאֵל:

"Heal us Hashem, and we will be healed. Save us and we will be saved for You are the One we praise. And raise up a complete healing for all our ailments. For You are God, a King who is a faithful and merciful Healer. Blessed are You, Hashem, who heals the sick among His people Israel."

"Heal us Hashem and we will be healed." There is an old story about a very prominent doctor who dies and goes to heaven. Before entering heaven he encounters a long line waiting to get in. The doctor, unaccustomed to waiting in line, goes right to the front of the line and says, "I demand to be let in immediately."

Gently the gatekeeper explains, "Although you were a great doctor and did many great deeds, here you will just have to wait in line like everyone else."

After a little while, the doctor sees what looks like another doctor—with a doctor's coat and stethoscope—go right up to the front of the line and go right in. Incensed, the doctor again goes to the front of the line and demands an explanation. "Oh that's God," the gatekeeper informs him. "He just loves to play doctor!"

Yes, God loves to play doctor, to heal. God is the ultimate doctor. But does this mean we should rely only on our prayers to God for healing and not go to the doctor? Not at all! The Talmud[394] makes it clear from the doubling of the word for healing in the Torah,[395] *v'rapo y'rapey* (and heal him he shall be healed), that "permission was granted by God for a doctor to heal." Yes, healing comes from God, but healing can also come from a doctor. We believe doctors are agents of God in that God is an active participant in every healing procedure.[396] In a sense, God is holding the doctor's hands and guiding him as he heals. So we do both. We go to the doctor and we pray.

Since illness will not be eliminated in our lifetime unless, hopefully, the Messiah comes, it is crucial we understand that ultimate healing comes only from God. So we beg God to heal us—even from festering maladies that have not yet manifested.

"Save us and we will be saved." It has been suggested this can refer to negative side effects of the cure and so we pray not only for healing, but to save us from the adverse effects of that healing.

"For You are the One we praise." If we give any thought to the magnificent intricacy of the human body God created, we cannot help but praise God. The greatest scientists of all time cannot come close to creating anything as wonderful as the human eye, let alone the brain. Yet if but one part of the body is not functioning well, we begin to suffer and it becomes more difficult to praise God. Psalm 115 teaches us, "The dead cannot praise You, God, nor anyone who descends into silence. But we praise Hashem." We praise You, Hashem, even though we may be ill. And we implore You, God, to give us complete health so we can praise You better—with our full strength.

"For You are...a faithful and merciful Healer" It is crucial to acknowledge God as the ultimate Healer. No healing can occur unless He wills it to be so. Why? Because only then do you open yourself up to receive His complete healing. This is part of a major, powerful spiritual principle: surrender. If after doing everything you can to facilitate healing, you surrender yourself to God, trusting in His goodness, then you allow His healing to enter—healing for your body and healing for your shattered soul. You see, if you hold back and do not surrender, you are saying by your actions you do not believe God has the power to heal you, and so if you do not believe it, it may not happen!

This blessing for healing offers us one of the most intense opportunities for connection with God—both with our prayers for our healing and especially with our prayers asking God to heal others. See Chapter 24, "The Power of Prayer," for how to take full advantage of this special opportunity for connection.

One more thought. As we learned in the previous chapter, *Ma hu af Ata* (Just as God does, so must you do), if you want God to bring you healing, do all you can to be His helper in bringing healing to the world. Support medical research, help your neighbor who is ill, volunteer at a local hospital, visit the sick—in short, find a way to be a healer.

BIRKAT HASHANIM (Bless us with prosperity, literally, "Blessing of the years"): Who would refuse a blessing of prosperity? Who doesn't want to be rich? Having more than you need, however, does not mean you will be able to enjoy it. In this middle section of the *Amidah*, we have asked God for insight, knowledge and forgiveness; we have asked Him to see the problems and challenges we confront and to redeem us; and we asked for healing. Only with the peace of mind and knowledge of those blessings can we begin to really enjoy the bountiful blessings God has blessed us with.

בָּרֵךְ עָלֵינוּ יי אֱלֹהֵינוּ אֶת הַשָּׁנָה הַזֹּאת וְאֶת כָּל מִינֵי תְבוּאָתָהּ לְטוֹבָה. וְתֵן בְּרָכָה (טַל וּמָטָר לִבְרָכָה) עַל פְּנֵי הָאֲדָמָה וְשַׂבְּעֵנוּ מִטּוּבֶךָ. וּבָרֵךְ שְׁנָתֵנוּ כַּשָּׁנִים הַטּוֹבוֹת. בָּרוּךְ אַתָּה יי, מְבָרֵךְ הַשָּׁנִים:

"Bless for us, Hashem our God, this year and all the kinds of produce for good. And bring blessing (dew and rain—said in the winter from December 4th or 5th until Passover) upon the face of the earth, and satisfy us with Your goodness, and bless our year to be like the good years: Blessed are you, Hashem, Who blesses the years."

There are those who think that since everything comes from God, they might as well sit back and wait for God to shower them with what they need. After all, the Talmud[397] tells us a person's sustenance for the year is decreed on Rosh Hashanah.

However, sitting back and waiting for God to do something reminds me of the story of two friends who meet for coffee to catch up. Harry tells his friend Sam, "Congratulate me because my daughter just got engaged."

Sam says, "*Mazal tov*, what is the future groom like?"

"He is going to be a great scholar and he studies Torah all day," answers Harry.

And then Sam asks, "But how is he going to support your daughter?"

Harry says, "Well, I asked him the same thing. First I said, 'How will you be able to rent an apartment?' And he answered, 'God will provide.' Then I asked him, 'How will you be able to feed the family?' Again the answer, 'God will provide.' How will you be able to buy health insurance?' Again the answer, 'God will provide.'"

"So what do you like about him?" asked Sam.

Harry replied, "I love how he calls me God!"

This blessing does not ask God to help you win the lottery or to be showered with a windfall of wealth. Yes, God will provide, provided we do the necessary work as well. We ask God to bless our "produce"—what we produce—so that it will be for our good.

"Bless us Hashem … this year." The blessing emphasizes "this year" in order to tell us we need to live in the present, if not in the moment. We must enjoy the blessings God showers upon us and not just store these away for a rainy day. Yes, it is important to plan for the future and have some savings, but it is God Who blesses us with what we have, and it is insulting—showing a lack of faith—to hoard it away and not use much of it. The Talmud[398] teaches: "Hurry up and eat! Hurry up and drink, since the world from which we must depart is like a wedding feast [where the food is here one day and gone the next]!" This is why, teaches the Talmud,[399] God gave the Jews in the wilderness only one day's supply of the miracle food manna each day. In this way, the Jews would have no sense of security other than God.

Many who suffered the economic crash in the fall of 2008 told me they wished they had taken that trip to Israel or given a large gift to charity before they lost most of what they had. So if God blesses you with plenty, then enjoy it and spread it around to help others, and have faith God will then bless you with more.

"And bring blessing upon the face of the earth." This blessing of prosperity is not just personal, but also universal. We ask God to bless the whole world with prosperity as well for we are all part of the global community. The prosperity of one part of the world might well affect the prosperity of the whole world—as we have seen in recent years. Where we see suffering in the world, it is our job to use what God has given us to help. So as we ask God to bless us and the world, we commit ourselves to do what we can to help the world prosper.

"Satisfy us with Your goodness." "If I were a rich man" is not the tone of this prayer. We ask God to "satisfy" us. In other words, give us what we need. God does not always give us what we ask for, but He does give us what we need!

The last commandment in the Ten Commandments is "Thou shalt not covet." What is so wrong with wanting what someone else has? More specifically, the prohibition is against wanting the physical and material things of someone else—his house, his wife, his fortune. Coveting someone's knowledge or spiritual level is not necessarily a bad thing. It can spur one on to greater heights. However, coveting someone's physical and material possessions sends the message to God that you do not agree with His management of the world, that He should have given that person's material things to you. Do not ask God for what someone else has. Ask him to give you what you need for a full and meaningful life, and if you want more than you think He has allotted for you on Rosh Hashanah, give Him a good reason to bless you with more. Tell Him about the worthy things you plan to do with your extra portion.

Help My People

We ask God to help us and to give us what we need in the first six blessings of the middle section of the *Amidah*. In the next six blessings we ask God to do the same, only not for us as individuals, but for us as His people.

It has been pointed out[400] that each individual petition in the first six blessings corresponds directly to a petition for the Jewish people in the next six. These 12 petitions then conclude with the *Shema Koleynu* prayer asking God to "hear our voice" and answer our prayers.

Understanding the structure of this middle section is essential in order to appreciate the changes in focus from personal to national needs. One cannot be a complete Jew in isolation—living and observing Torah and Jewish life by him- or herself. Jews; and by extension, all human beings need each other to find their path to God.

The Jewish people are an organic unit whose fate is inexorably intertwined. If Jews in Ethiopia are starving and persecuted, the Jewish people will mount a campaign—as they did with Operation Moses in 1984—to free them. Incidentally, this was the first time in history blacks were taken out of Africa to freedom and not to slavery. When Jews were caught between fighting combatants, as happened in Kosovo in 1998 between Christians and Moslems, the State of Israel brought them out to safety. *Kol Yisrael areyvim zeh lazeh* (The fate of all Israel is tied together, one to the other).[401]

Kibutz Galiyot (Bring our people home): The first blessing on behalf of the Jewish people is, understandably, a call for Jewish unity—to gather all Jews together, even those who have been lost.

תְּקַע בְּשׁוֹפָר גָּדוֹל לְחֵרוּתֵנוּ. וְשָׂא נֵס לְקַבֵּץ גָּלֻיּוֹתֵינוּ. וְקַבְּצֵנוּ
יַחַד מֵאַרְבַּע כַּנְפוֹת הָאָרֶץ. בָּרוּךְ אַתָּה יי, מְקַבֵּץ נִדְחֵי עַמּוֹ
יִשְׂרָאֵל:

"Sound the great *shofar* for our freedom. Raise the banner to gather our exiles. And gather us together from the four corners of the earth. Blessed are You, Hashem, Who gathers together the dispersed of His people Israel."

"Sound the great *shofar*." Just what is the "great *shofar*?" The "great *shofar*" is a reference to a verse in Isaiah[402] where the prophet proclaims: "It shall be on that day that the great *shofar* will be blown and those who are lost in the land of Assyria and those who were dispersed into the land of Egypt will come and bow to God on the holy mountain in Jerusalem."

In other words, Isaiah was predicting the day would come when the Jewish people would be exiled, which happened after the destruction of the first Temple. They would then be returned to their land and worship God in their rebuilt Temple. This is exactly what happened. The second Temple was built as prophesied some 70 years later. When we ask that the great *shofar* be sounded, we are asking that it be sounded for today's Jews who are exiled—especially those who suffer persecution and discrimination.

The blessing is also a call for God to help lost Jews to be returned to the fold. In the year 722 BCE, the Assyrian Empire conquered the northern kingdom of Israel and scattered its inhabitants, who subsequently came to be known as "the Ten Lost Tribes." The Talmud teaches that one day the Ten Lost Tribes will be returned to Israel.[403]

Significant research has been conducted in our time to identify these lost tribes in different areas of the world. Whether or not it is true that the Tribe of Dan is really in Ethiopia, as claimed, it does seem rather convincing from observing the customs of the Falasha Mora people that there were lost Jewish souls there; also with the Bene Ephraim in southern India and the Bnai Menashe in northern India, and others.

The Spanish Inquisition of 1492 and its forced conversions of Jews, followed by similar inquisitions in Portugal and their colonies in the New World, have created an underground subculture of families, who even today in Spain, Mexico, New Mexico and elsewhere, secretly practice Jewish customs—often not knowing why. These are possibly lost Jews as well.

Tragically, there are many lost Jewish souls in the world today. It is estimated that two thousand years ago there were seven to eight million Jews in the world.[404] Even allowing for the loss of population due to war, pogroms, persecution, and other catastrophic circumstances, the Jewish population today should be in the hundreds of millions! Yet the Jewish population today is estimated at only fourteen million![405]

The return of the Jewish people to their land in our time has sparked latent Jewish souls everywhere. "Sound the great *shofar*," we pray, for nothing stirs the Jewish soul like the *shofar*. Gather them up, return them to their land, and make it so that they can worship with us at our rebuilt Temple.

"Raise the banner to gather our exiles. And gather us together..." A banner is something more tangible than the sound of the *shofar*. It is something one can see. In other words, we pray God will make it clear to all Jewish souls that we need to be together, united, as one People of Israel. This is our destiny. There are great differences among Jews: Ashkenazic, Sephardic, Orthodox, Traditional, Conservative, Reform, Reconstructionist, and others. We must put our differences aside and unite.

The word *neys* (banner), also means "miracle." The prayer then becomes, "Raise a miracle to gather our exiles." Do whatever it takes, God—even a miracle!

"Blessed are You, God, Who gathers together the dispersed of His people Israel." "The dispersed" in Hebrew is *nidchey*, which literally means, "pushed out." The Jewish people were pushed out of their land by the Romans in the first through the third centuries. They wandered for millennia over the face of the Middle East, Africa, Asia Minor and Europe looking for a place to rest. They were again and again pushed out from here to there, and so we pray that God will gather those of His people who were "pushed out" and bring them home to the Land of Israel.

We have seen this happen in our day. Besides the tens of thousands of Ethiopians airlifted to Israel, almost a million Jews have come to Israel from the former Soviet Union. May Hashem gather up all our lost Jews—lost because of how the world has treated them and/or lost because they have drifted far from God and their people.

DIN (JUSTICE)   Justice has always been a fundamental principle in Judaism,[406] as God says about Abraham, the father of Judaism: "He commands his children and his household after him that they keep the way of God to do *tzedaka* and *mishpat* (justice)."[407] The word *tzedaka*, often translated as "charity," comes from the word *tzedek*, which means "right." It is the right thing to give charity. But *tzedek* also means "justice," indicating that justice in this verse—as well as in the signature of this blessing—is doubly important. As if to emphasize the point, the Torah later commands us: *Tzedek tzedek tirdof* (Justice, justice shall you pursue).[408]

Yet sadly, although Jews have always held justice in the highest esteem, there have been others, over the millennia, who did not always feel justice applied equally to Jews. Jewish history is filled with unjust accusations and persecutions. Even today, the world judges the Jewish state by a different standard. Almost everything it does to defend itself from threats to its existence and acts of terror is called unjust and inhumane. This blessing is a plea to God to restore justice to the world and to remove the sorrow and groaning that results from injustice.

הָשִׁיבָה שׁוֹפְטֵינוּ כְּבָרִאשׁוֹנָה וְיוֹעֲצֵינוּ כְּבַתְּחִלָּה. וְהָסֵר מִמֶּנּוּ יָגוֹן וַאֲנָחָה. וּמְלֹךְ עָלֵינוּ אַתָּה יי לְבַדְּךָ בְּחֶסֶד וּבְרַחֲמִים. וְצַדְּקֵנוּ בַּמִּשְׁפָּט. בָּרוּךְ אַתָּה יי, מֶלֶךְ אוֹהֵב צְדָקָה וּמִשְׁפָּט:

> "Restore our judges as it originally was and our advisors as it was in the beginning. Remove from us sorrow and groaning. Rule over us, God, by Yourself, with kindness and mercy and righteousness and justice. Blessed are You, Hashem, a King who loves righteousness and justice."

The Torah tells us one way to enforce justice: "Judges and police officers shall you appoint in all your cities."[409] The Kotzker Rebbe takes special note that the word "you" in the verse in Hebrew is in the singular, and he explains this teaches us that each of us should judge and police himself, keeping himself on the right track.

What about judging others? After all, imitatio Dei (imitating God), as we have learned in The *Amidah* Supplement, Part 1, is a major principle in Judaism. So if God judges and punishes people, would it be okay for us to do the same? Let us take this a bit further: the Torah says that God takes revenge.[410] Would it then be okay for us to do so as well? However, the Torah specifically commands us: "You shall not take revenge and you shall not bear a grudge."[411] Many times in the Bible it seems God behaves as if He is angry. Why can we not behave with anger? God does!

Clearly God never meant for us to imitate Him in this way, and so the sages[412] teach that the *mitzvah* of imitating God is given to urge us to do acts of *chesed*, of love and kindness—not to judge others, nor take revenge, nor act with anger. So do not judge others. It is not your place, your position or your role in the world to behave as a judge. If you are a judge in a court, a teacher or a parent, then it is part of your job. But otherwise, who asked you? You may not like what someone does, but why judge?⁴¹³

> There's an old Jewish joke about two litigants who came
> before a rabbi to ask who is right. One comes into his study
> to present his argument, and after listening the rabbi says,
> "You know, you're right!"
>   After the first one leaves the other comes in and pres-
> ents his side, and the rabbi thinks a little and says, "You
> know, you're right!"
>   After he leaves, his *gabai*, who is sitting and listening to
> all this, asks politely, "Excuse me for asking honored Rabbi,
> but how can they both be right?"
>   So the rabbi thinks for a moment and says to him, "You
> know, you're also right!"

That is the joke, but it is not a joke. Why should we not think:
"You're right and you're right. Why can't they both be right? That's
also right!" No two people live in the same world. You see the
world through your eyes and your neighbor sees it through his.
Why look askance at someone else? Why let someone else's behavior eat you up?

   This is especially important in family relationships. If close
family members who live out of town decline an invitation to a
Bar Mitzvah, do not get angry at them. You do not know their
business. Perhaps they cannot afford to come right now and are
too embarrassed to tell you. When your children marry and you
feel your child's in-laws are not as generous to the couple as you
are, do you want to walk around aggravated and angry? Do you
want to make your life tough? Judge them, get angry! Do you
want to be happy? Do not judge them. Who knows what is going
on in their lives? Choose to be happy by avoiding judging others.

   Do not be a punisher. There are too many people who feel
if someone wronged them, there must be consequences. Do you
want to be aggravated and angry? Start judging! And if judging
does not make you aggravated enough, when your spouse does

something to upset you—just to make sure both of you will be miserable—punish your spouse by withholding your affections and giving him/her the silent treatment for a few days instead of talking it out. Now you have shown him/her! But you have damaged your relationship. Only God punishes!

Once a man came to me with a not too unfamiliar dilemma. A person he was close to had betrayed his trust and had caused him great embarrassment and even humiliation in the community. After many months, the feelings were still strong. He felt uncomfortable asking God to do anything that might cause pain to a fellow Jew, and so he asked me if it was permissible to pray to God to punish this person. I told him it is not up to us to punish or even to ask for punishment. Only God can punish, but we can ask God for justice.[414] And so he prayed for justice—which did eventually come to pass!

Let me add an exquisite footnote from the *Nefesh Hachaim*,[415] a great mystical text: God never punishes! He only fixes! God repairs! It is true. When you get to the next world and you are confronted with your sins, you may blush or feel embarrassed; you may feel terrible, but it is not a punishment. It is what you did to yourself. God does not punish, He repairs!

When God confronts us with a challenge in our lives, it is for our own good so we can repair a flaw in our character or have the opportunity to grow to greater spiritual heights. Do not make the mistake the friends of Job made when they told him he must be a bad person, because otherwise, why would God allow him to suffer so much. God does not punish, He repairs!

When we become a judge and punisher, when we get angry at someone and raise our voice, or label others with names, are we repairing? Are we fixing? Not really. Criticizing the ones we love never accomplishes anything other than destroying relationships and self-esteem. If we do it anyway, thinking, "He/she deserves it!," that is punishing.

According to the sages, the injunction to imitate God should never be used to judge others. However, if you insist saying, "God judges so we can judge," then our tradition must remind you that God does not punish. God fixes! So first of all, do not judge people. Judging others guarantees misery. And secondly, do not punish because punishing people breaks and destroys. It never fixes.

A third lesson on judging: If you cannot resist judging someone because you are so hurt you cannot get past it, if you rationalize to yourself saying you are like God Who punishes, let me ask you: what about taking a bribe? Is a judge allowed to take a bribe? Of course not!

Does God take bribes? It might appear from the Torah[416] He does not. However, there is a great *Midrash*[417] on the third verse of the priestly blessing: *Yisa Hashem panav eylecha v'yaseym l'cha shalom,* "May God lift up His face to you and grant you peace." "Lift up the face" is an expression also meaning "to overlook." In other words, the blessing may be understood as: "May God overlook your sins and grant you peace." The *Midrash* has God saying: *Ani nosey panim,* "I will overlook." Thus, God takes bribes in the sense that if people do other good deeds, He will take this into account when judging them. And so within the totality of judgment, God does accept bribes!

> An old story tells of a businessman who dies and finds himself on the line where it is decided whether he gets into heaven or not. In front of him he sees a man being asked to tell about the good deeds he has done. He lists them along with how much he has given to charity over the years. After he finishes, the angel in charge tells him to proceed through the gates into heaven.
>
> When it is the businessman's turn, he clears his throat and says he did not have time for many good deeds, and had not given much to charity over the years. He then takes out his check book and says, "Just tell me how much it will cost and I will write you a check."
>
> The angel says to him, "Checks? We don't take checks. Up here we only take receipts." In heaven they take receipts.

It is not a joke. It is true!

Do you want to bribe God? Come up with receipts. Be overly generous. It is said, "You can't take it with you." That's true! So ask your family to bury you with your charitable receipts. Bribes are welcome in heaven!

If you have a dispute with long-time friends, or perhaps with someone you are indebted to, or with relatives, are you going to judge them? Are you going to punish them? What about the good memories? What about the wonderful things that have happened over the years between you? Are they not worthy as a bribe?

You know, God doesn't only accept bribes from the person being judged. If your father did acts of kindness for others, this is also an acceptable bribe in heaven. So if someone from the family who is close to you, who did so much for you, hurts you, accept that as bribe. A judge does not take bribes, but the Torah does not prohibit a litigant from taking a bribe from the other side.

How can you be angry at your husband or wife? After all, he/she married you. Remember how the other ones did not want you? So the next time you get upset at your spouse, remember how, when life was dark, when you needed help, he/she was there for you. Remember some of the wonderful things they did for you.

And if these three lessons have not been enough, there is a final, delicious lesson from the Baal Shem Tov, the founder of *Chassidut*.

> The Baal Shem Tov teaches that when you come up to heaven, there is a very unique way in which you will be judged. God will present you with a hypothetical situation similar to your life but occurring in the life of someone else. And so when your soul arrives, you will be asked: "The *Bet Din* of heaven is sitting in judgment and they need one more judge. Can you sit in?"
>
> You'll say, "Me, a judge?"
>
> "Yes you. You are a very important person."

They will pull you in to sit with the heavenly court and they will bring someone in front of you to judge. Now you can get out all your frustrations. They will say this person mistreated his wife. They will play a video of him (okay, the Baal Shem Tov did not have videos, but Kabbalah does tell us that after you die you will see a panorama of your life unfold before you much like a movie) screaming and raising his voice at his family. The wife and children are crying. You will judge and say, "This is terrible. Throw the book at him!"

And they will say, "Aha, *Ata ha-ish*, this was you!!!"

Now that you know the Baal Shem Tov's secret, when you go up to heaven and you are told they need a judge, and they then show you this terrible video, what will you say? "Well, the yelling was just for a minute. You have to understand, there were mitigating circumstances. He was upset because of something that happened to him. He later apologized and asked for forgiveness."

And then they will say, "*Ata ha-ish*, that was you."

And you will say, "Really? I'm so surprised!"

The *Beyt Halevi*,[418] a great 19th century sage, adds that you do not have to wait until you get to heaven and they pull you into a courtroom. *Kol hadan et chaveyro l'chaf zechut, danin oto l'chaf zechut* (All who judge their fellowman, giving them the benefit of the doubt, will in turn be judged with the benefit of the doubt). So when you see a car cut you off on the way to work, or an old woman driving 15 miles an hour in a 35 miles-per-hour zone, remember you will be in the heavenly courtroom someday judging.

Whom are you judging? The *Beyt Halevi* teaches that you are judging yourself. Whom are you judging when you criticize someone who speaks harshly? When you criticize your children for not listening to you or for not using good judgment, whom are you judging? You are judging yourself! You are projecting your previous bad behavior upon them. God is watching how you react. *Ata ha-ish*, it is you! What a lesson!

When we put others down, we instinctively feel we look better in the process. But we do not! When we get aggravated, when we are stressed and upset, we let our guard down and say things that, perhaps, would be better left unsaid. It is so worthwhile to catch yourself and tell yourself perhaps you do not know the whole story. If you must judge, judge *l'chaf zechut,* judge favorably. Remember, God is watching!

So when you recite this blessing and ask God to be the Judge of Judges and restore justice for the Jewish people, and for all, remember God is the only true Judge.

BIRKAT HAMINIM   (a blessing to protect us from the heretics):
As we have learned at the beginning of The *Amidah* Supplement, Part 1, in Talmudic times the followers of heretical sects would come to the synagogues trying to sway the hearts of their fellow Jews, as well as to gather information that could be used against them. So Rabban Gamliel II had this prayer added to discourage them from coming, and to impress upon Jews the real danger these heretics represented.

וְלַמַּלְשִׁינִים אַל תְּהִי תִקְוָה. וְכָל הָרִשְׁעָה כְּרֶגַע תֹּאבֵד. וְכָל אוֹיְבֵי
עַמְּךָ מְהֵרָה יִכָּרֵתוּ. וְהַזֵּדִים מְהֵרָה תְעַקֵּר וּתְשַׁבֵּר וּתְמַגֵּר וְתַכְנִיעַ
בִּמְהֵרָה בְיָמֵינוּ. בָּרוּךְ אַתָּה יְיָ, שׁוֹבֵר אוֹיְבִים וּמַכְנִיעַ זֵדִים:

"And for the slanderers, may they have no hope. And may all wickedness perish instantly. And all Your enemies, may they be speedily cut down. And may the willful sinners be speedily uprooted, broken, cast down and humbled speedily in our days. Blessed are You, Hashem, Who breaks enemies and humbles the willful sinners."

This blessing begins with the Hebrew letter *vav,* connecting it with the previous blessing in which we bless God as, "The King Who loves righteousness and justice." For righteousness and justice to flourish, we must eradicate evil and sometimes its perpetrators. This may seem, at first, to fly in the face of the advice of the sages not to judge your fellow man. This is certainly good advice in the realm of relationships. However, when we see real evil in the world, we must do what we can to eliminate it. This blessing calls upon God's enemies to be "uprooted, broken, cast down and humbled speedily in our day." Evil must never be tolerated. If you repay evil with mercy it will only bite you in the end and become stronger.

> We see this most clearly in the story of Cain and Abel in the Midrash.[419] The Midrash answers the question: Who was stronger—Cain or Abel? It was Cain who killed Abel, so it obviously seems Cain was the stronger one. Not so, says Rabbi Yochanan. He quotes the verse in the Torah:[420] "Cain spoke with his brother Abel; and it happened that when they were in the field, that Cain rose up against Abel his brother, and slew him." Two questions bothered our sages: What did Cain say to his brother and from where did he rise up to kill him?
>
> Rabbi Yochanan explains that Cain had started to fight with Abel, but as they fought on the ground it was Abel who was the stronger one, and Abel got on top of Cain, pinning him to the ground. Then, as the Torah tells us, "Cain spoke unto Abel his brother saying." What did he say? Rabbi Yochanan tells us: "We are the only sons in the world. What will you tell father if you kill me?" Then Rabbi Yochanan adds, "Abel was filled with compassion and released his hold, whereupon Cain rose up and killed him." And from this our sages warn: "Do not be kind to an evil man lest he repay you with evil."

Yes we must eradicate evil, but not necessarily the evil doers.

The Talmud[421] tells the story of some highwaymen in the neighborhood of Rabbi Meir who caused him a great deal of trouble. Rabbi Meir prayed they should die. His wife Beruria asked, "What is your reasoning that such a prayer is permissible?"

He responded: "Because it is written:[422] 'Let *chata-im*, 'sinners,' cease from the earth.'"

She challenged him: "Is it written *chotim*, 'sinners'? [No,] it is written *chata-im*, [which literally means] 'sins.' Furthermore, look at the end of the verse: 'and let the evil men be no more.' Since their sins will cease there will be no more evil men. Rather pray for them that they should repent and there will be no more evil men." He did pray for them and they repented.

This blessing does not pray for evil doers to die, but for all wickedness to perish and the evildoers to be humbled. As we say in the Yom Kippur liturgy, quoting the prophets: "May the evil one forsake his path…and return to God."[423] "Do I desire at all the death of the evil man? Thus says the Lord God: Repent and live!"[424]

Jews have had to confront the worst evil again and again as they were targeted for oppression, persecution, conversion and extermination. It has been this way for thousands of years and it continues to this very day. Jews, however, do not pray for the death of their enemies, only that their evil not succeed—that all efforts bent on destroying the Jewish people physically and/or spiritually be eliminated. The blessing is written in the present tense because it is still happening now. As we recite this blessing, we should have in mind one or two current threats to the Jewish people and pray that God will keep us safe so we can continue to do His will.

TZADIKIM (The righteous ones): Did you ever think of yourself as righteous? Probably not. Few if any ever do, and if you think you are such a righteous soul, you probably are not.

Truly righteous people are too humble to think of themselves in this way.

Did you ever desire to become righteous? Most people think being righteous is too hard to achieve, that it is reserved for a very few who have the time and means to study Torah and Talmud all day. But righteousness and Godliness are as much, or more, about righteous behavior than the study of Torah. All of us have the potential to become a *tzadik,* as we see from the prophet Isaiah,[425] who says: "Your nation will all be *tzadikim* (righteous)." From the Talmud[426] we learn that before a soul is born it is commanded by an angel to, "swear that you will be righteous and not wicked." This tells us every soul has the capacity to be righteous. Judaism teaches that even though we think we may never become righteous, we must always strive to achieve this and in doing so we perfect our souls, making God proud.

The Talmud[427] teaches that in each generation there are 36 righteous souls—not known to the great multitudes—and who themselves are unaware of the fact they are among those who by reason of their purity and tenderness sustain the entire world. As taught in the book of Proverbs,[428] *Tzadik y'sod olam* (the righteous one is the foundation of the world). You may not be one of the 36, but you just may be a righteous soul. As we pray for God to be compassionate towards the righteous, we should add a prayer for God to help us become righteous.

עַל הַצַּדִּיקִים וְעַל הַחֲסִידִים. וְעַל זִקְנֵי עַמְּךָ בֵּית יִשְׂרָאֵל. וְעַל פְּלֵיטַת סוֹפְרֵיהֶם. וְעַל גֵּרֵי הַצֶּדֶק. וְעָלֵינוּ. יֶהֱמוּ רַחֲמֶיךָ יְיָ אֱלֹהֵינוּ. וְתֵן שָׂכָר טוֹב לְכָל הַבּוֹטְחִים בְּשִׁמְךָ בֶּאֱמֶת. וְשִׂים חֶלְקֵנוּ עִמָּהֶם לְעוֹלָם וְלֹא נֵבוֹשׁ כִּי בְךָ בָּטָחְנוּ. בָּרוּךְ אַתָּה יְיָ, מִשְׁעָן וּמִבְטָח לַצַּדִּיקִים:

"May Your compassion be aroused, Hashem our God, on the righteous, the pious, the elders of Your people the house of Israel, the remnant of their scholars, the righteous converts and on us. And grant a good reward to all who truly trust in Your Name. And put our lot forever with them and we will not be ashamed because we trust in You. Blessed are You Hashem, Who is the support and trust of the righteous."

This is truly a special blessing. First, it is the thirteenth blessing of the *Amidah*. As we learned in our discussion on the *Shema*, 13 is a special number because it is the numeric value of the words, אֶחָד/*echad* (one) — *alef* + *chet* + *dalet*/ 1 + 8 + 4 = 13 and, אַהֲבָה/ *ahava* (love) — *alef* + *hey* + *vet* + *hey*/1 + 5 + 2 + 5 = 13. When we pursue righteousness, we feel more intensely our oneness with God and His love for us.

In this blessing we ask God to be compassionate with six categories of people:

"the righteous (*Tzadikim*), the pious (*Chasidim*), the elders of Your people the house of Israel, the remnant of their scholars, the righteous converts and on us."

Tzadikim, the "righteous", were discussed above. *Chasidim*, in this prayer, does not necessarily refer to the disciples of the Baal Shem Tov—members of modern day *Chassidic* dynasties— because the prayer predates the Baal Shem Tov. It translates to "those who are pious" to such an extent they go beyond the letter of law and tradition to serve God.

Who are the "elders of Your people?" They are the elderly among us. By their life experience, they have acquired, no doubt, a special wisdom that enriches all our lives. We pray especially for those among them who are ill and in need of God's help. This teaches us to have a special sensitivity and appreciation for our elderly. Also, the "elders of Your people" can refer to those who have accepted upon themselves the responsibilities of leadership in the Jewish community as an officer of a shul, a *baal tefilah* (one who leads the service), a *gabai* (a leader of the synagogue who stands in guard as the Torah is read), and all *kley kodesh* (those who lead and organize the Jewish communities and their worship services).

"The remnant of their scholars" refers to those who transmit "their Torah," *sofreyhem*, and the Torah of previous generations to us and to our children. This teaches us to have a special reverence and respect for our teachers.

> I remember hearing about a great Torah scholar who gave special honor to a particular teacher of small children. When asked why he gave this teacher such honor, the Torah scholar responded it was this teacher who had taught him how to read and nothing he had learned since would have been possible without this teaching.

It is remarkable how high Judaism holds the importance of teaching. In fact we have a mourning period—*sefira*—that commemorates the loss of teaching. In Judaism, a teacher is to be held with the same reverence as a parent.[429]

The next category is "righteous converts." God has a special affection for righteous converts. The Torah again and again implores us to love the convert,[430] while the Midrash teaches: "Dearer to God than all who stood at Mount Sinai is the convert. Had they not witnessed the lightning, thunder, the quaking mountain and the sounds of the shofar, they would not have accepted the Kingship of Heaven. But the convert, who did not see or hear any of these things, surrendered to God and accepted the yoke of the Kingship of Heaven. Is there anyone dearer [to God]?"[431] It is because righteous converts chose to follow God and His Torah that they are referred to today as "Jews by choice."

However, it is not always easy for a convert. People have their prejudices and sometimes the convert is the victim. How many times have you heard, "She'll always be a *shiktza* (derrogatory term for a non-Jewish woman)," or "Once a *goyisha kop* (gentile head), always a *goyisha kop*."

> What about all those jokes, like the old one about the convert standing in the *mikveh* to complete her conversion when the convert yells out to the rabbi, "Do I really have to

go under the water? I'm so afraid of putting my head under water."

The rabbi reassures the convert and again explains how important it is to have the holy waters of the *mikveh* completely envelop her. But the frightened convert is not sure she can go through with it and asks, "What will happen if I only go into the water up to my neck?"

The rabbi responds, "Most of you will be Jewish, but you will always have a *goyisha kop* (a non-Jewish head)!"

We may chuckle when we hear these jokes, but they are not really funny and belie the strong sense of commitment to Jewish life a righteous convert has. We ought to appreciate the amazing commitment a convert makes in terms of lifestyle, family and friends. When we pray for righteous converts in this prayer, we ought to be inspired by them to become a Jew by choice ourselves, increasing our love and commitment for God and Torah.

The final category is "us." As we call upon God to be compassionate to "the righteous, the pious, the elders of Your people the house of Israel, the remnant of their scholars, the righteous converts," we ask Him to be compassionate upon us as we try to emulate their amazing qualities and "put our lot forever with them and we will not be ashamed because we trust in You."

What does it mean to have trust in God? It does not mean we trust God will be our butler and do everything we ask. It means we trust God has our best interests in mind and will take care of us and whatever happens to us is for the best. We must trust that even sickness and tragedy are a good-not-yet-understood, as we learned in Chapter 6, "God's Name," concerning the name of God, *Elohim.* This state of trust makes for a much calmer and healthier life, as the prophet Jeremiah teaches: "Blessed is the person who trusts in God, then God will be his security."[432]

Binyan Yerushalayim   (Rebuilding Jerusalem): What is Jerusalem? For millennia, Jerusalem, for most Jews in the Diaspora, was a dream—a shiny "City of Peace" (its literal meaning) on a mountain top. Three times every day in the *Amidah*, Jews have faced toward Jerusalem and recited this blessing pleading with God to rebuild Jerusalem. Again in the prayers after every meal they have called upon God to rebuild Jerusalem. Jews end their holiest day, Yom Kippur, and the Seder on Passover with the fervent hope, *L'shana haba-a biYerushalayim*, "Next year in Jerusalem." At every Jewish wedding the groom breaks a glass in remembrance of the destruction of Jerusalem. On the ninth day of the Jewish month of Av every year, Jews cry over the destruction of Jerusalem.

When Jerusalem was captured by the Babylonians, who first exiled the Jewish people off their land in 586 BCE, the Jews vowed, "If I forget you, O Jerusalem, let my right hand become paralyzed. Let my tongue cleave to the roof of my mouth, if I remember you not; if I set not Jerusalem above my highest joy."[433]

The rabbis of the Talmud glorified Jerusalem, suggesting: "Ten measures of beauty descended to the world, nine were taken by Jerusalem."[434] "Whoever did not see Jerusalem in its days of glory never saw a beautiful city in his life."[435] Jerusalem became more than a location. It was a tangible hope, a promise that God had not forgotten them and would one day return the Jewish people to Jerusalem and restore its glory and its holy purpose of being a beacon of God's word and light to the world: *Ki miTziyon teytzey Torah udvar Hashem miYerushalayim* (for from Zion[436] will the Torah come forth and the word of God from Jerusalem).[437]

וְלִירוּשָׁלַיִם עִירְךָ בְּרַחֲמִים תָּשׁוּב. וְתִשְׁכֹּן בְּתוֹכָהּ כַּאֲשֶׁר דִּבַּרְתָּ. וּבְנֵה אוֹתָהּ בְּקָרוֹב בְּיָמֵינוּ בִּנְיַן עוֹלָם. וְכִסֵּא דָוִד מְהֵרָה לְתוֹכָהּ תָּכִין: בָּרוּךְ אַתָּה יי, בּוֹנֵה יְרוּשָׁלָיִם:

"And to Jerusalem Your city may You return with compassion. And dwell in it like You have spoken. And may

You rebuild it speedily in our days as an eternal structure. And may the throne of David be established with it. Blessed are You, Hashem, Who builds Jerusalem."

"And to Jerusalem Your city may You return with compassion." This prayer calls Jerusalem *Ircha* (Your city), meaning God's special city. Again and again the Torah tells us the Jewish people are to worship God, *bamakom asher yivchar Hashem* (at the place where God will choose).[438] Jerusalem is the city God chose to house His Holy Temple—the place mankind could most effectively connect with Him.

The centrality of Jerusalem as the supreme spiritual center of the world from which God's loving energy flows into the world is given support in an unlikely place—Pangaea. Pangaea is the name given to earth's original combined land mass by a symposium in 1926 discussing Alfred Wegener's classic work, *The Origin of Continents and Oceans*.[439] In short, Wegener proposed the now commonly accepted theory of continental drift: since the shape of the continents fit together so well, it is safe to assume all the continents at one time formed a single land mass—a supercontinent—that slowly broke away drifting to their current locations.

In the Creation story, the Torah also suggests that originally there was one land mass on the face of the earth. On the third day of Creation, God commanded all the waters to be "gathered to one place."[440] If all the waters were in one place, the rest of the earth must have then been covered by one great land mass. What was at the center of Pangaea—the single land mass of the world before it was broken up into continents? Jerusalem! Jerusalem is the center of our world.

King David, looking at this city he built that was so precious to him, remarked: *Yerushalayim Hab'nuya, k'ir shechubra la yachdav* (The built-up Jerusalem is like a city that united together).[441] I once heard Rabbi Benjamin Blech explain the power of this verse. He asked: "Why is there such a powerful bond between the Jew and Jerusalem?" Yes, it was the capital city of King David and his successors. Yes, it is the site of the Temple Mount and the Western Wall, remnants of the holy Temples. But there is even a deeper bond.

The Hebrew word יְדִיד/*yedid* (friend) is spelled *yud-dalet-yud-dalet*, a doubling of יָ-ד/*yud-dalet,* which is also a word—יָד/ *yad* (hand). What is true friendship? It is when I stretch out my hand to you and you to me—the doubling of hands, the doubling of *yud-dalet*, which forms the word *yedid* (friend). The *gematria*, the numerical value of the word *yedid* is 28 (*yud + dalet + yud + dalet*: 10 + 4 + 10 + 4 = 28), which is the same as the word כֹּחַ/ *Koach*, or "strength" (*kaf* + *chet*: 20 + 8 = 28). When friends come together—hand in hand—that is strength. On a deeper level, God says to us, "You want Me to extend My hand to you? You extend your hand to Me, then together we will meet." That is why 28 is such a powerful number. It is *Yedid*, the meeting of two hands.

King David describes Jerusalem "as a city that is united together." The power of Jerusalem is that it is a city that brings people together and also brings together people and God. Every major religion recognizes the holiness of Jerusalem as a place to come closer to God. This is why Jerusalem houses along with its unique synagogues the holiest of churches and mosques. יַחְדָו/ *Yachdav* (together) has a special spelling in this verse—it is missing a *yud* before the final letter *vav*—and this leaves it with a numerical value of guess how much? Twenty-eight!

Let us go even deeper. What is the date of Yom Yerushalayim, the day celebrating the modern reunification of Jerusalem in the Six-Day War of 1967? Long ago it was foretold Jerusalem would be reunited with the Jewish people in the Jewish month of Iyar—a month where remarkable things would take place. Yom Yerushalayim, the day of the reunification of Jerusalem, this meeting of God and man that is called by King David *Yachdav* (together), is—you guessed it—the twenty-eighth of Iyar. How beautiful!

Why has Jerusalem been fought over for so many thousands of years? Why have so many religions claimed it to be their own?

Because Jerusalem's spiritual power is evident to all who have been there. The Jewish hope is that just as Jerusalem is the physical center of our world, it will be restored as the spiritual center of the world for all mankind—*Ircha*— God's special city. This blessing insists, like the Babylonian exiles, that we not forget Jerusalem and that three times a day we pray for its restoration to be complete.

"An eternal structure…and may the throne of David be established with it." Please God, let there be no more destructions of Jerusalem. Restore it now and forever. And one more thing, restore as well the sovereignty of David over it. In the next blessing we will explain how it can be that David will rule once more in Jerusalem.

"Blessed are You, Hashem, Who builds Jerusalem." It is noteworthy that the blessing does not read "*Yivneh Yerushalayim* (Who will build Jerusalem)," but *Boneh Yerushalayim* (Who builds Jerusalem). The building of Jerusalem is a process that began with our prayers right after its destruction and continues to this day. Although the city has been largely rebuilt in our time, until the Holy Temple is restored, this remains an on-going process.

The Talmud[442] tells us that the last Temple was destroyed because of senseless hatred among Jews. As long as we fail to end the senseless hatreds and bickering among us, the Temple will not be rebuilt. We can help God rebuild Jerusalem by rejecting hate and learning to love our fellow human beings—by seeing in every person the image of God. As Isaiah[443] taught: "Zion will be redeemed with judgment and those who return with righteousness."

MALCHUT BEYT DAVID   (The Kingship of David): In our discussion of the second blessing of the *Amidah* (section *Gevurot*), we learned that *Olam Haba* (the World to Come) has three meanings: the World of Souls we all return to when we die; the Revival of the Dead at the end of time; and also the world of *Mashiach* (the Messiah). We left the question "When will the Messiah come?" for this blessing where we pray for his coming.

When will the Messiah come? The Midrash[444] tells us about a precondition for his arrival. This is referred to by the sages as *Chevley Mashiach* (the birthpangs of the Messiah). The Midrash explains with a parable about a father and son on a journey to a city. The son asks his father, "How will I know when we get close to the city?" The father responds, "I will give you this sign: when you see a cemetery, you will know that the city is near." The Midrash felt that it was clear from the prophets and other sources that a precondition for the return of the Jews to Israel would be a cemetery. It was not specified how many people would be in the cemetery, but there would be an event that would cause the death of countless Jews. Do the six million Jewish graves of the Holocaust in our time qualify? The Talmud[445] quotes a number of sages who prayed they may be spared the terrible experience of *Chevley Mashiach*, that God not allow them to live to see it. Could it be we have already experienced the birthpangs of the Messiah in our time?

We do not know how long the *Chevley Mashiach* (the birthpangs of the Messiah), will last. Some women have prolonged labor pains and it may take them several days before their baby is born. Just as labor pains are stinging contractions followed by periods of calm, so too will this period preceding the coming of the Messiah see periods of pain followed by calm or even great strides towards the Messianic era. In this spirit, with the establishment of the State of Israel in the aftermath of the Holocaust, and especially with the return of Jerusalem and other holy cites during the Six-Day War, many religious people who were formally anti-Zionists have joined the Chief Rabbinate in Israel in calling the modern State of Israel *Reyshit tz'michat g'ulateynu* (the beginning of the sprouting of our redemption). After all, we see that the borders of Israel have now been restored as described in the Torah.

But as we get closer to the Messianic era, we must keep in mind the story of Moses, the first Messiah. When Moses initially appeared before Pharaoh to redeem the Jewish people, Pharaoh not only did not listen to him, he made life even harsher by ordering the Jewish people to gather their own straw to make bricks—something that was previously provided for them. Moses in frustration then cried out to God, "Why have You sent me?" Just because there are setbacks and things may seem to get worse, it does not mean the Messiah is not at hand. It is just the contractions before the birth.

In the 20th century we have witnessed the fulfillment of many Biblical prophecies. Prior to the 20th century, the Land of Israel was a shadow of what it had formerly been, as conqueror after conqueror raped the land of its foliage and resources. Now, with the modern State of Israel, the land has been replenished, and ancient city after city has been rebuilt and repopulated with Jews, fulfilling the prophecy of Ezekiel: "Thus said the Lord God: 'When I have cleansed you of all your iniquities, I will people your settlements, and the ruined places shall be rebuilt; and the desolate land, after lying waste in the sight of every passerby, shall again be filled.'"[446]

In our own generation we have seen the dramatic fulfillment of Isaiah's prophecy: "I will bring your seed from the (Middle) East and will gather you out of the (European) West; I will say to the North (Russia), 'give back,' and to the South (Ethiopia), 'do not withhold.'"[447] The ingathering of the exiles—one of the most important set of Biblical Messianic promises—is in the process of being fulfilled right now before our eyes. See the tenth blessing, *Kibutz Galiyot* (above), for more about this.

Isaiah[448] predicted 2,700 years ago that someday there would be a radically new world in which "no more shall there be an infant or graybeard that does not live out his days; he who dies at a hundred years shall be reckoned a youth, and he who fails to reach a hundred shall be reckoned accursed." Before the mid-19th century, the annual death rate for humans fluctuated between 30 and 50 deaths per 1,000 individuals. The toll among the young was especially high. Almost one third of the children born died before their first birthday. Because childbirth was hazardous, mortality among pregnant women was also high. A century ago, the infant mortality rate was 25 to 30 percent. Now it is less than one percent in much of the world! Had this radical improvement occurred over a few years, it would have greatly impressed people, but since it happened gradually over several generations, the fulfillment of this part of Isaiah's prophecy has gone unnoticed and uncelebrated.

If the Jews of Ethiopia, two generations ago, had been told their children and grandchildren would someday fly to Israel on giant silver birds, they would have thought this would be a Messianic miracle. If Soviet Jews had been told a generation ago that the Communist regime would collapse, the Soviet Empire would disintegrate, and close to a million Soviet Jews would immigrate to Israel, they would have conceived this only as a Messianic dream. Is it not amazing how people adjust to living in a radically new world and forget the past so quickly?

This is all in the years leading up to the coming of the Messiah. But what will life be like in the Messianic era after the Messiah comes? The Bible teaches us that the prophet Elijah will come and prepare the Jewish people's hearts for redemption and rectify their conduct.[449] There will be a war between Gog and Magog.[450] Actually, the sages speak of three great wars to be fought.[451] Perhaps, we have already experienced at least the first two—WWI and WWII. After the third and final war, there will be no more war. The lion and the lamb will lie together. People will end their bickering and quarrels. *V'haya Hashem l'melech al kol haaretz* (God will be accepted as King by the entire world).[452]

When the dream of the universal acceptance of God is fulfilled, this will change the very nature of life on earth. It will be truly wonderful. Maimonides[453] adds, "There will be neither famine nor war, neither envy nor competition, for good things will flow in abundance…and the world will not pursue anything but to know God alone."

Remember the answer Kabbalah gives as to why God created the world? It was so He would have an opportunity to display His goodness. In the Messianic Era, people will know God and live in a constant state of appreciation for all He has done and does for us.

אֶת צֶמַח דָּוִד עַבְדְּךָ מְהֵרָה תַצְמִיחַ. וְקַרְנוֹ תָּרוּם בִּישׁוּעָתֶךָ. כִּי
לִישׁוּעָתְךָ קִוִּינוּ כָּל הַיּוֹם. בָּרוּךְ אַתָּה יי, מַצְמִיחַ קֶרֶן יְשׁוּעָה:

> "May the offshoot of Your servant David soon sprout, and may his ability to radiate his light be raised high through Your salvation, for we wait for Your salvation all day. Blessed are You, Hashem, who makes the ability to radiate the light of salvation to sprout forth."

Who will be the Messiah who will redeem the world? First of all, our tradition teaches us that the Messiah will be the reincarnation of the soul of Adam, the first human being, and King David as indicated by the first letters of the names Adam, David, *Mashiach* (Messiah)—*alef, dalet, mem*—which spell אָדָם (Adam).[454] He will be a descendant of King David, a human being born[455] to a mother and father.[456] He will also be a prophet, a warrior, judge, king and teacher of Torah. He will defeat the enemies of Israel, return the Jews to their land, and reconcile them with God as he rebuilds the Temple and brings to the world a period of spiritual and physical bliss where everyone will have a direct connection with God.

"May the offshoot of Your servant David soon sprout." There are several places in the Bible where the Messiah is referred to as *Tzemach David* (the offshoot of David). For example, Zechariah: "Behold the days are coming when I will raise unto David a righteous sprout; and he shall reign as king and prosper and he will administer justice and righteousness in the land."[457] It is the offshoot of that original soul, Adam, and of King David.

"…and may his ability to radiate his light be raised high through Your salvation." A more literal translation would be: "and raise the ray (*keren*) of salvation through Your salvation." The Hebrew word *keren* also means "horn," which is a metaphor for power. King David and his descendants have a special relationship with the horn because David was anointed to be king by the prophet Samuel from a horn flask.[458] When Moses descended from Mt. Sinai with the Ten Commandments, the Torah tells us that *Karan or p'ney Moshe* (The skin of the face of Moses radiated light).[459] We pray here that God, in His mercy, will help enhance the light of the Messiah to make him as effective as possible. You see, even the Messiah does not become a Messiah automatically. Just like any of us, he has to work hard to achieve the great potential inherent in his soul.

So when will the Messiah come? The Talmud[460] tells the story of Rabbi Yehoshua ben Levi, who met the Messiah disguised as a poor man at the gates of Rome. He recognized him from a description he was given by the prophet Elijah in a vision. He asked him, "When will you come, Master?"

The Messiah answered, "*Hayom*, today!"

Overcome with joy, Rabbi Yehoshua departed. The answer of the Messiah—"*Hayom! Hayom*! Today! Today!"— kept ringing in his ears. Today the *Mashiach* (Messiah) will appear. Today the exile will end. Today the persecutions will cease. Today Israel will be restored to its former glory. Eagerly he waited. His heart palpitated with expectation and excitement. But the minutes turned into hours, which turned into days. Doubt and frustration gnawed at the great sage's heart. He was disillusioned, humiliated and embittered.

After some time Rabbi Joshua once again encountered Elijah in a vision, and he protested that the Messiah had lied to him. Lovingly Elijah replied, "You misunderstood, my son. (*Hayom* means not only "today," but also "the day.") This is what he said to you: '*Hayom*, the day when you will hear his voice!'" The Redeemer meant he would come on the very day when the people are willing to listen to his voice.

The Messiah is ready to appear at any moment. It is the Messiah who yearns for salvation ... But do we want to be redeemed? The

Messiah keeps calling, "*Hayom, Hayom.*" His voice is, however a call in the wilderness.

There is a more contemporary story from the 18th century that makes a similar point. This was the time of the rise of Chassidism led by the Baal Shem Tov who taught that everyone can get close to God though prayer even though one is not a scholar. There was an opposing movement called the Mitnagdim (literally, "the opposition") led by the Vilna Gaon that insisted upon Torah learning as the chief path to God. There were other important differences concerning practice and philosophy, but that is not germane to the story. The story has it that God had decided the Jews of Eastern Europe had suffered enough for hundreds of years, and so He said: "Let me send the Messiah and bring the final redemption to my people."

To announce his coming, the Messiah was sent to a small Eastern European town where the Jews had suffered so much. But where should He make this announcement? He decided to go to the little *shtiebel* (small synagogue) where the Chasidim of the community would come to pray and worship. But then he realized that if he goes to announce his coming first to the Chasidim, then the Mitnagdim who live in that community would say: "If he first went to the Chasidim, then this cannot be the true Messiah."

The Messiah then thought to announce his coming to the Mitnagdim of the community, but then he realized if he did this, the Chasidim would say: "He went to the Mitnagdim to announce himself; he must be a false Messiah." So the Messiah had a dilemma. How did he resolve it? Simple—the Messiah did not come! Remember, the Second Temple was destroyed because of senseless hatred of one for the other. The Messiah is not going to come and rebuild the Temple until we rectify this sin and strengthen the love and respect that should flow from one to another.

"…for we wait for Your salvation all day." Maimonides thought waiting and yearning for the Messiah so important that he included it as the twelfth of his *Thirteen Principles of Faith*.[461] We have the power to bring the Messiah. One of the questions the Talmud[462] teaches us that we will be asked on our final exam when we appear before God after we die: "*Tzipita liy'shua*? (Did you yearn every day for the coming of the Messiah?)" God may have a specific date for the coming of the Messiah, but we have the power to bring him earlier, to bring him anytime.

The Talmud[463] reinforces this idea in a comment of a verse in Isaiah.[464] The verse tells us the Messiah will come: *B'ito achishena* (In its time, I will hasten it). If the Messiah will come in its time, when it is supposed to come, how can it be hastened? The Talmud solves the apparent contradiction by stating: "If they are worthy, I will hasten it; if not [he will come] at the due time." How can we be worthy? By showing love for each other, by yearning for the Messiah and the peace he will bring to the world every day, by repenting for our sins and by following God's factory-authorized manual for living a good life in this world—the Torah. In fact, the Talmud[465] says if Israel would only properly observe just one Sabbath, the Messiah would come immediately. The sages in their wisdom, therefore, built into the *Amidah* the concepts of redemption, the ingathering of exiles and Messiah, so that we would be reminded of these crucial concepts every day—several times—and yearn for their fulfillment.

"Blessed are You, Hashem, who makes the ability to radiate the light of salvation to sprout forth." O God, our world is in such trouble. There is war and terrorism and economic turmoil. People are confused, starving and hurting. Please God, don't wait; bring the Messiah now! As the Lubavitcher Chasidim chant: "We want *Mashiach* now!" It is in this signature blessing that we ask God to hasten the coming of the Messiah, and by doing so, we pledge to do whatever we can to be worthy. So when will the Messiah come? It is up to us!

Shema Koleynu (Hear Our Voice): This blessing is the last of the 13 petitions in this middle section of the *Amidah,* and it is perhaps the most important. For all the other blessings in this section, as we have learned, the sages encourage us to add our own personal prayers corresponding to the theme of the particular blessing. In this blessing, we can ask for anything we desire. This is a marvelous opportunity, and it should not be wasted.

> Exercise   Make a list of things and people you want to pray for, and think about how to formulate your prayer. If needed, when you are praying, just as one would look in the *Siddur,* you can look at the list to remind you of what and whom you have decided to pray for while you recite this blessing. See Chapter 24, "The Power of Prayer" (Section: Praying for Others) for more formal insertions of personal prayers in this blessing.

Caution: Do not rush through your personal prayers as some people often do while reciting the words of the *Siddur.* The Talmud[466] teaches, "One who prolongs his prayers will not be turned away empty-handed." So take the time to recite your prayers slowly and from the heart. This will have such a powerful impact not only in Heaven, because of your obvious sincerity, but also within you as you feel more connected to God Who hears your prayers.

שְׁמַע קוֹלֵנוּ יי אֱלֹהֵינוּ חוּס וְרַחֵם עָלֵינוּ. וְקַבֵּל בְּרַחֲמִים וּבְרָצוֹן אֶת תְּפִלָּתֵנוּ. כִּי אֵל שׁוֹמֵעַ תְּפִלּוֹת וְתַחֲנוּנִים אָתָּה. וּמִלְּפָנֶיךָ מַלְכֵּנוּ רֵיקָם אַל תְּשִׁיבֵנוּ: כִּי אַתָּה שׁוֹמֵעַ תְּפִלַּת עַמְּךָ יִשְׂרָאֵל בְּרַחֲמִים. בָּרוּךְ אַתָּה יי, שׁוֹמֵעַ תְּפִלָּה:

"Hear our voice, Hashem our God, be compassionate and have mercy upon us, and accept with mercy and favor our prayers. For You are God Who hears prayers and supplications. And before You, our King, do not allow us to go away empty handed. For You hear the prayer of Your people Israel with mercy. Blessed are You, Hashem, Who hears prayer."

There is an old joke about a man who comes to Jerusalem and prays his heart out at the *Kotel* (the Western Wall). Suddenly he hears the voice of God speaking to him, telling him how proud he is of all the good things he has done in his life. God then tells him He will grant him one request. The man thinks for a few moments about all the things he and his family could use, and then asks, quite unselfishly, "Please make peace between the Israelis and the Palestinians."

The voice responds, "You're talking to a wall!"

Sometimes we may feel when we are praying that we are talking to a wall, because we have prayed and prayed over a long period of time for something or someone and nothing has happened. Judaism says to us when we feel this way: Do not despair and do not give up. God hears our prayers. It could be God's answer is "No," or that the time is not right yet for what we ask, but do not lose hope. Ask God—if what you ask for is not to be—to please show you the proper path. Too often, we spend our time thinking about why God does not answer our prayers. A loved one passes away after a long illness. Why did God not answer our prayers for her recovery? We want our children to be happy and successful. When things do not turn out the way we expect, we cannot help but wonder why? God listens to our prayers and yes, He answers them—but not always in the way we expect.

There is the story of a Jewish grandmother and her grandson at the beach. He is playing in the water while she is standing on the shore not wanting to get her feet wet. All of a sudden, a huge wave appears from nowhere and crashes directly onto the spot where the boy is playing. The water recedes and the boy is gone, swept away.

The grandmother desperately wades into the water, but she can't find him. So she holds her hands to the sky, screams and cries: "God, how could You? Haven't I been a wonderful grandmother? Haven't I been a wonderful mother? Haven't I kept a kosher home? Haven't I been active in Jewish causes and given generously to charity? Haven't I lit candles every Shabbat and Yom Tov? Haven't I tried my very best to live a life that You would be proud of?"

She goes on and on until a voice booms from the sky, "All right already!" Suddenly, another huge wave appears out of nowhere and crashes on the beach. As the water recedes, the boy is sitting in the sand smiling and splashing around as if nothing had ever happened. The voice booms again. "I have returned your grandson. Are you satisfied?"

She looks at her grandson, and then pointing to the heavens, she says, "He had a hat!"

Yes, God listens to our prayers and answers them—but not always in the way we expect. An important principle to understand is that God does not necessarily give us what we ask for. He does, however, give us what we need.

As hard and as difficult as the situation in the Middle East is for Israel, for example, we should not give up on praying for peace! We firmly believe God will make peace happen someday. We should pray for God to guide the leaders of Israel towards the proper path. This may take until the Messiah comes, but it will happen. For more on why we must never give up on our prayers, please see Chapter 24, "The Power of Prayer."

Notice the text of this prayer does not say, "Hear our prayer," but "Hear our voice." We may recite the same prayers as others, but we each have our own unique voice. This prayer is then asking, for each one who recites it, for God to listen to one's unique voice—one's unique personal meaning for each prayer. The Baal Haturim comments on Jacob's dream of a ladder extending to

Heaven, noting the *gematria,* the numeric value of *sulam* (ladder), is the same as *kol* (voice).[467] This teaches us if a person is righteous in his prayers—if he prays from the heart with sincerity—his voice becomes a ladder upon which his prayers ascend to Heaven.

"Be compassionate and have mercy upon us, and accept with mercy and favor our prayers." The word *chus,* which can be translated as "compassion," according to the Vilna Gaon,[468] is the feeling one has to protect something he has made with great care. "God," to again quote the cartoon character Snoopy, "doesn't make junk!" God created us with His loving energy with pride in what we can become. The word *Racheym* (mercy), comes from the word *rechem* (womb). It refers to an unqualified motherly love that endures forever. In this verse we implore our creator's compassion and unqualified love to accept our prayers.

"Do not allow us to go away empty-handed." It is after reciting this that we are encouraged to insert our own personal prayers, to entreat God's compassion to help us with our list of things and people we want to pray for. As mentioned earlier, do not rush through your list. Take your time and recite it in a pleading manner. Pour out your heart to God. It is at this point you can incorporate the exercise at the end of Chapter 4, "*Avoda,*" by asking God for help. Say, "Hashem help me!" again and again—even ten times. Say it with all your heart from the deepest recesses of your soul, and as you repeat, "Hashem help me," say it with increasing intensity.

"Blessed are You, Hashem, Who hears prayer." What a miracle it is that God, Who created and manages the world, takes the time and makes the effort to listen and consider each of our prayers. Not only do we not deserve what God has given us, we do not even deserve His attention. When we recite this signature blessing, we ought to try to feel the power of God's great love for us, and be grateful He desires such a relationship with us as we picture Him before us eagerly listening.

Thank God!

To be a Jew is to be a "thanking" being. This stems from Mother Leah in the Torah, who after giving birth to her fourth child said, *Hapa-am odeh et Hashem* (This time I will thank God), *al keyn kara sh'mo Yehuda* (therefore she called his name Judah).[469]

After the death of King Solomon, the Land of Israel was divided, with the kingdom of Israel in the north and Judea (mostly the Tribe of Judah) in the south. The northern kingdom of Israel, with its ten tribes, was destroyed by the Assyrians in the 8th century BCE and then lost—dispersed throughout the Empire and hence referred to as "the Lost Ten Tribes." Jews today are mostly descendants of the tribe of Judah that remained, and this is why they are called "Jews." The word "Jew" itself—in Hebrew, *Y'hudi*—actually means "one from the Tribe of Judah," but literally it means "one who gives thanks." So to be a Jew is to be a "thanking being."

As we learned in the *Amidah* Supplement, Part 1, "The *Amidah*: How It Works," the Talmud divides the *Amidah* into three discernible sections. The first section is referred to as *shevach* (praise), the second as *Bakasha* (Petition), and the third as *hoda-ah* (thanks). We have reviewed the first two sections, so let us now turn to the third and final section, the section of thanksgiving.

AVODA (WORSHIP)   The first blessing in this concluding section of the *Amidah* asks God to be pleased with our *avoda*. In the first few chapters I have referred to the term *avoda* as "worship—deep prayer and meditation." Actually, the word itself literally means "work." In our prayers this refers to holy work, and when the ancient Temple stood, it specifically referred to the formal worship in the Temple of old as prescribed by the Torah. We had previously learned that the *Amidah* can be seen as a substitute for the Temple *avoda*, and so as we end the *Amidah*, it is fitting to include a plea to restore this worship.

I know some people today are not comfortable with the whole concept of restoring the Temple worship that included animal sacrifices. We will deal with this soon, but before we do, I would like to ask you a personal question: What is your *avoda*, your holy work, the service of your heart? What do you do to regularly communicate with God and to do His work in this world as part of His people? For me this blessing is also a prayer for God to be pleased with and accept our personal *avoda*, the holy work we do to attach ourselves to Him.

רְצֵה יי אֱלֹהֵינוּ בְּעַמְּךָ יִשְׂרָאֵל וּבִתְפִלָּתָם וְהָשֵׁב אֶת הָעֲבוֹדָה
לִדְבִיר בֵּיתֶךָ. וְאִשֵּׁי יִשְׂרָאֵל וּתְפִלָּתָם. בְּאַהֲבָה תְקַבֵּל בְּרָצוֹן.
וּתְהִי לְרָצוֹן תָּמִיד עֲבוֹדַת יִשְׂרָאֵל עַמֶּךָ: וְתֶחֱזֶינָה עֵינֵינוּ בְּשׁוּבְךָ
לְצִיּוֹן בְּרַחֲמִים: בָּרוּךְ אַתָּה יי, הַמַּחֲזִיר שְׁכִינָתוֹ לְצִיּוֹן:

Grant favor, Hashem our God, to Israel Your people and to its prayers. Return the *avoda* worship to Your most Holy House. And the fire offerings and their prayers, in love accept with favor. And may the *avoda* worship of Israel Your people always find favor. And may our eyes witness Your return to Zion with mercy: Blessed are You, Hashem, Who returns His *Shechina* (Divine Presence) to Zion."

"Grant favor, Hashem our God, to Israel Your people and to its prayers." At first glance, this blessing seems to repeat the theme of the previous blessing, *Shema koleynu* (hear our voice), since this also asks God to accept our prayers. The difference is that the previous blessing is asking God to grant our personal petitions while in this blessing we do not ask to receive anything. It is mostly about how we as God's people should serve Him—how we can sanctify His Name in this world. What is implicit in this blessing is that if God is pleased with our *avoda*, He will restore the *Shechina*, His Presence, to Zion, to Israel, to Jerusalem, and with this we will be able to fulfill our destiny as His people.

"Return the *avoda* worship to Your most Holy House. And the fire offerings..." As we mentioned, there are some people today who are uncomfortable with the whole concept of restoring the Temple worship that includes animal sacrifices. How can we kill an animal to worship God? To them this seems barbaric.

We use animals for food, for shoes, for clothing, for the leather seats in our cars. Why not for a higher spiritual purpose? Furthermore, we are commanded by God in the Torah to offer animal sacrifices. How can we ignore God's command? In fact, it is a *mitzvah* to offer sacrifices, even if the Temple is not yet rebuilt.[470] And so the returning exiles, after the destruction of the first Temple, set up an altar for sacrifices even before building the second Temple.[471] Although Jewish law forbids such sacrifices to be done by Jews in our current impure state, an exception is made, according to some authorities,[472] for public sacrifices like the Passover sacrifice. This could be done with just an altar constructed on the Temple Mount—something we could do today if both Jewish and Middle East politics permitted.

As a young man I shared some of these ambivalent feelings about animal sacrifices, so much so that on Shabbat and holidays I had trouble reciting the Musaf *Amidah* which features some of these sacrifices. After years of Torah study, I came to understand the whole ritual of animal sacrifices as a holy barbecue. The *Kohanim* (Priests) and the Levites did not receive a portion of land like the other tribes and relied upon contributions from the offerings of their fellow Jews to feed their families. The Levites received certain tithes[473] and the Kohanim certain gifts like the first fruits[474] and a portion of most offerings.[475] The animals brought for sacrifice were ritually slaughtered, like any kosher animal slaughtered for meat, in the most humane way possible, and then specially roasted on the *mizbeyach* (the holy altar).

There was no cruelty to animals in these offerings. Cruelty to animals is specifically forbidden in the Torah and is one of the seven Noahide Laws. On the contrary, a sacrificed animal was elevated to a very special holy status.

Today, one cannot possibly imagine the pageantry, the pomp and ceremony that accompanied these Temple sacrifices with its special music, incense and song, and how this helped bring every participant closer to God. In fact, a sacrifice is called by the Torah *korban* from the Hebrew *karov* (close). Sacrifices thus became a major way of coming closer to God. Although we do not have "fire-offerings" now, until the Temple is rebuilt, the fire burning inside every person, that *pintele Yid* (the Jewish spark), the passion and energy for serving God can be our fire-offering.

"And may our eyes witness Your return to Zion with mercy: Blessed are You Hashem, Who returns His *Shechina* (Divine Presence) to Zion." In the Torah God directed us to build a Temple where we could feel His Presence—the *Shechina*—as intensely as possible: *V'asu li mikdash v'shachanti b'tocham* (And make for Me a sanctuary that I may dwell among them), commands the Torah.[476] The command to build a Temple is remarkable in that it signifies to us that God wants to live among us. He wants us to experience His Presence. It is also remarkable that for 2,000 years this prayer, calling for the return of Jews and God to Zion and Israel, has been recited faithfully by Jews three times every day. Just as God has never given up on the Jewish people, the Jewish people have never given up the hope of the return to Zion and the Land promised by God.

Maimonides teaches that the site of the Temples—i.e. the

Temple Mount in Jerusalem—will retain its holiness forever because the *Shechina* (God's Presence) cannot be removed.[477] However, the Talmud[478] teaches the *Shechina* departed from the Temple because of the sins of Israel. The contradiction can be resolved if we understand what the Talmud meant: the *Shechina* became more and more hidden as the people sinned and withdrew themselves from God. Note that this blessing is in the present tense, "Who returns His *Shechina* to Zion." It means the return of the *Shechina*, God's Indwelling Presence, is in process. The more the Jewish people return to God, the more His *Shechina* can be felt. When we recite this blessing, we should resolve to do all we can to make our personal *avoda*—the holy work we do—more effective in bringing God's Presence into this world.

MODIM   (Thanksgiving): As we learned in the first chapter, God created the world to have an opportunity to display His goodness. In order to do so He created a being as much like Him as possible. God's display of His goodness would then be revealed in the subsequent relationship with this being. God wants to shower His love upon us and what God wants from us more than anything is a relationship so He can be good to us! Remarkable!

Our task is to acknowledge, appreciate, and give thanks to God for all He has given us. However, gratitude is not the natural state of a human being. This is a learned behavior. A child does not think to thank others for the things they do for him unless he is taught this is good manners and that acknowledging and showing appreciation for even small favors will come back to his benefit. The recitation of this prayer of thanksgiving three times a day in the *Amidah* helps to train us to acknowledge, appreciate, and give thanks to each other as well. It cannot be stressed enough how important acknowledging, showing appreciation, and giving thanks are in our interpersonal relationships. If only we would show appreciation to those we love three times a day—as we do with God in the *Amidah*—or even once a day, how much better our relationships and our lives would be. It is not that hard. Just say, "I appreciate that you … ," and fill in the blanks.

So many of us, however, fall victim to what Dennis Prager calls, "The Missing Tile Syndrome."[479] He suggests if you look up at a tiled ceiling in which one tile is missing, you will most likely focus primarily on the missing tile. In fact, the more beautiful the ceiling, the more you are likely to see nothing but the missing tile and let it ruin your enjoyment of the rest of the ceiling. When it comes to ceilings, your clothes or your car, such obsession with the missing piece may be desirable, but what can be desirable or necessary in the physical world can be destructive to personal happiness. When people focus on what is missing, they make themselves chronically unhappy because while ceilings can be perfect, life can never be. There will always be missing tiles.

Therefore, when a bald man sees a crowd of people, he sees that everyone has hair, or a woman struggling to become pregnant sees pregnant women wherever she goes. An overweight man will see almost everyone else as thin, and a divorcee will see mostly happy couples. All of these people focus on what they do not have, and this robs them of being able to appreciate all they do have. The end result is that they are more miserable and less happy and more distanced from God.

> There was once an old man at the *Kotel*, the Western Wall, in Jerusalem, who always carried a bottle of *schnapps* and a bag of cookies. He would come up to people and say, "Today is a *simcha*—a happy occasion—for me. Please join me for a *l'chayim*, a toast." Suspicious tourists soon discovered he was no *schnorer*—he asked nothing from them—so they asked what kind of *simcha* is it? His answer? "Being alive! You see, I survived Auschwitz and since then every day is a *simcha!*"

This is why when a religious Jew rises in the morning he immediately recites a prayer, *Modeh Ani*, thanking God for reviving his soul within him and for a new day. Then, after taking care of his bodily functions, he recites a blessing, thanking God for giving him working organs and reminding himself that if any of these should malfunction, his continued life would be jeopardized.[480] Judaism wants us to start the day by reflecting on how our very lives are a gift, a miracle we live daily. Do we have to survive an Auschwitz, or a car crash, or cancer in order to appreciate the redeeming significance of the ordinary, daily stuff—the beating heart, a child's smile, the company of those whom we love or those with whom we work?

Let me suggest that when you recite this prayer of thanks in the *Amidah* you take a moment to think briefly about the things that might have happened—but did not. The yellow light you ran, for which you did not get a ticket; and the car you did not see behind the bush that did not jump the green light and smash into you; and the elevator that worked exactly as it was supposed to and let you off at the floor of your choice, instead of getting stuck somewhere between here and there; the phones and computers that worked; the ice storm that did not happen; and the potentially ugly confrontation stayed by a kind word or perceptive gesture. Many things might have happened, or possibly came close to happening, but did not. Thank God!

But mostly, when you recite this prayer, think about the good things that did happen and might not have. The parking place that stood empty, waiting for you, just a few doors from the store you had to visit; the open and easy trip on the highway you expected to be gridlocked; and all the daily, everyday things you could not do without: family, friends, food, water, air. There is so much we just take for granted. It is good to pause in our rapid and rushed routines to appreciate the basic good things in our lives—the pleasures of a good meal eaten in the company of others, shared memories, shared hopes.

The deeper truth is that God usually gives us what we need, rather than what we want—and we have so much!

One of the true weaknesses of our modern culture is the pervasive feeling of entitlement. "Everything we have—and a lot we do not yet have—is mine by right," many say. So they do not have to say, "Thank you" to God or to anyone else. But the grateful heart is a healthy heart. The grateful heart is a power plant for the light which lights our lives. Each day is, in some way, an occasion for celebration. Let us choose to be happy—to see more than the missing tiles of our lives—because there is so much in our lives worth rejoicing over. The psalmist teaches: *Zeh hayom asa Hashem, nagila v'nism'chah vo* (This is the day God has made, let us rejoice and be happy in it) ... *Hodu laHashem ki tov, ki l'olam Chasdo* (Give thanks unto God for He is good; His kindness endures forever).

מוֹדִים אֲנַחְנוּ לָךְ. שָׁאַתָּה הוּא יי אֱלֹהֵינוּ וֵאלֹהֵי אֲבוֹתֵינוּ לְעוֹלָם
וָעֶד. צוּר חַיֵּינוּ. מָגֵן יִשְׁעֵנוּ אַתָּה הוּא לְדוֹר וָדוֹר: נוֹדֶה לְךָ וּנְסַפֵּר
תְּהִלָּתֶךָ עַל חַיֵּינוּ הַמְּסוּרִים בְּיָדֶךָ. וְעַל נִשְׁמוֹתֵינוּ הַפְּקוּדוֹת לָךְ.
וְעַל נִסֶּיךָ שֶׁבְּכָל יוֹם עִמָּנוּ. וְעַל נִפְלְאוֹתֶיךָ וְטוֹבוֹתֶיךָ שֶׁבְּכָל עֵת.
עֶרֶב וָבֹקֶר וְצָהֳרָיִם: הַטּוֹב כִּי לֹא כָלוּ רַחֲמֶיךָ. וְהַמְרַחֵם כִּי לֹא
תַמּוּ חֲסָדֶיךָ. מֵעוֹלָם קִוִּינוּ לָךְ:

וְעַל כֻּלָּם יִתְבָּרַךְ וְיִתְרוֹמַם שִׁמְךָ מַלְכֵּנוּ תָּמִיד לְעוֹלָם וָעֶד: וְכֹל
הַחַיִּים יוֹדוּךָ סֶּלָה. וִיהַלְלוּ אֶת שִׁמְךָ בֶּאֱמֶת. הָאֵל יְשׁוּעָתֵנוּ
וְעֶזְרָתֵנוּ סֶלָה. בָּרוּךְ אַתָּה יי, הַטּוֹב שִׁמְךָ וּלְךָ נָאֶה לְהוֹדוֹת:

We give thanks to You for You are Hashem our God and the God of our fathers forever. You are the Rock of our lives, the Shield of our salvation. From generation to generation we will thank You and tell Your praises for our lives are in Your care and our souls in Your charge. And for Your miracles that are with us every day and for Your wonders and favors at all times—evenings, mornings and afternoons—You who are good, for Your mercies never cease, You who are the Merciful One whose kindness never fails, forever we have hoped in You.

For all these things may Your Name be blessed always and forever. And all the living will thank You. Selah! And praise Your Name truthfully. O God Who saves us and helps us. Blessed are you Hashem, The Good is Your Name and to You it is befitting to give thanks.

"We give thanks to You for You are Hashem our God and the God of our fathers forever." The *Modim* blessing is so crucial because it allows us to express one of the three key actions of prayer. As we have learned, prayer can express praise, petition or thanksgiving. The first section of the *Amidah* expresses God's praise; the second section has thirteen petitions; and now we have the third and final section that expresses thanksgiving and its core theme is manifest in this *Modim* blessing. It is interesting that if you count the number of words in the *Modim* prayer, you will find 86, which is the numerical value of *Elohim*, (God), teaching us that as we give thanks by reciting these 86 words, we come closer to God.

The sages placed such importance on this *Modim* blessing that they ruled one should bow at its beginning as well at its end.[481] We bow at no other blessing in the *Amidah* after the first introductory blessing. Bowing, as we have learned in Chapter 17, "The Posture of Prayer," can be an amazingly intimate experience—a prayer experience more powerful than any with words.

In the ancient world, bowing was a sign of respect or friendship. When one bowed before another, one put oneself in a very vulnerable position—and the deeper the bow, the more vulnerable one was. In the *Modim* blessing, we thank God for His mercies He extends to us "at all times, evening, morning and afternoon," without which we could not live. Bowing from the waist as we recite this blessing brings home to us in a powerful way—a way no words can convey—our ultimate vulnerability. So as you begin this blessing with a bow, before you straighten up, try to feel the reality of how truly vulnerable you are before God, how, as the prayer says, "Our lives are in Your hands and our souls are entrusted to You."

"You are the Rock of our lives, the Shield of our salvation." We thank God for being our "rock" because He is the foundation of everything—everything is God's energy and, therefore, everything comes from God. Sometimes God protects us as a high rock, lifting us out of harm's way. And sometimes He is our Rock acting like a *Mageyn,* a "Shield," as we learned in Chapter 15, "Four Words of Increasing Intimacy," a shield protecting us from danger in so many ways.

And so, "From generation to generation we will thank You and tell Your praises, for our lives are in Your care and our souls in Your charge." The word for "thank You" here, *nodeh,* also denotes "confession." In this prayer we confess, we admit we need God and are grateful for his mercies and we have no way of repaying Him. It is so difficult for many of us to admit we need anything from anyone. The truth is we need each other and the beginning of understanding comes from admitting we need God in our lives—without Him we are nothing. It is with this understanding that we thank God and sing His praises.

Our confession continues: "And for Your miracles that are with us every day and for Your wonders and favors at all times—evenings, mornings and afternoons." Life itself is a miracle, and one of our problems is that we, too, often fail to appreciate the miracle of the "ordinary."

Let me illustrate the miracle of the "ordinary" with one of my favorite legends[482] about the miraculous food, manna, the Jewish people ate in the desert for 40 years after leaving Egypt. The Torah does not say much about the manna other than it appeared every day. When the Jewish people came out to collect the manna on the first day as Moses instructed, they must have said, "This is amazing. Wow! We came into the desert and did not know how we were going to survive, and now this manna rains down from heaven. It's a miracle!"

The manna had a wonderful taste; it was nutritious;

it was not fattening; and there was enough for everyone. After they collected the manna on that day, they asked, "But what are we going to do tomorrow?" Moses reassured them there would be more manna tomorrow. On Friday a double portion fell so it would not have to be collected on Shabbat. From the double portion of manna we learn the custom of having two loaves of challah on Friday night.

After a while, the manna raining from heaven became a natural phenomenon for the Children of Israel. When the 40 years of wandering in the desert was over and a new generation appeared to enter the Promised Land, Moses had to break the news to them that once they entered the land there would be no more heavenly manna. One can imagine Moses saying something like this, "I've got good news and bad news. The good news is that you are going into the Land of Israel. The bad news is that the manna is going to stop."

The people then asked him, "But what are we going to eat?"

Moses responded, "This is what you should do. You should take seeds and throw them into the ground."

The people were astonished and said, "Are you crazy? Seeds in the ground are going to rot."

"Trust me on this," Moses, replied. "Yes, the seeds will rot, but then something will grow from it. You will then take the kernel within it, get rid of the chaff, and grind it into flour. Take the flour, mix it with water, let it rise and bake it. It will turn into bread."

They looked at Moses as if he was crazy. Moses pleaded with them to follow his advice and then they would see. So the people went into Israel. They planted strictly on faith because planting was not part of their experience. Lo and behold, they ground down the kernels and made flour and then bread. With this first bread from their land, they shouted out for the first time the following words—*Baruch*

Ata Hashem Eloheynu Melech Ha-olam, Hamotzi Lechem Min Haaretz (Blessed are You Hashem our God, King of the universe, who brings food from the earth).

"We have seen a miracle," they said, "because any fool knows that bread comes from the heavens and we saw it come from the ground."

What a great legend! The point is that something seems like a miracle only when we experience it infrequently. Why do we say blessings before eating food? To awaken within us a sense of the miraculous in what we would otherwise take for granted, so we can then express our gratitude to God.

"Your wonders and favors at all times—evenings, mornings and afternoons." Why does the prayer mention that God's miracles and kindness are here for us "evenings, mornings and afternoons"? The times of the day represent the emotional times of our lives as well.[483] One can be in an emotional state of "evening," where life seems so dark it is hard to see any light ahead. One can be in a "morning state" where light begins to enter one's life and one can then see things beginning to get better, and then there is the "afternoon" state where the light is the brightest and everything seems to go one's way. But no matter what state we are in, God is here for us and deserves our thanks and appreciation.

"You who are good, for Your mercies never cease, You who are the Merciful One whose kindness never fails." "Your mercies never ceases" and "whose kindness never fail" refers as well to those mercies, those miracles occurring every day which we are not even aware of.

One of the first anti-Semites in history was Balak. It was during the forty year trek to the Promised Land that Balak saw he could not defeat the Jews militarily, and so he decided to defeat them spiritually by hiring the heathen prophet Bilaam[484] to curse them. It is an elaborate story, the end of which has Bilaam's attempts at cursing the Jews turned into blessings—especially the famous blessing, *Ma tovu ohalecha Yaakov* (How good are your tents, O Jacob). The amazing thing about this story is that the Jewish people had absolutely no idea it was happening. The interaction between Balak and Bilam, and the building of altars and sacrifices and attempted curses that turn into blessings, took place on cliffs that overlooked the Jewish camp. At the time, the Jews had no idea that God was shielding them from harm, turning the curses into blessings. It is a great example of how God's mercies never fail us—a wonderful example of how God has our backs!

"And all the living will thank You." It is up to us who are living to thank God because, as King David notes, *Lo hameytim y'hal'lu ya* (The dead cannot praise God).[485] *V'chol hachayim* (And all the living) can also be translated as, "And all of life," including the good and the bad. Hence the blessing ends: "Blessed are You, Hashem, The Good is Your Name and to You it is befitting to give thanks."

It is always befitting to thank God, even when life is hard and bitter. We may not understand why life is so hard, but as the Talmud[486] teaches: "A person is obligated to bless God for the bad just as he blesses God for the good." Why? Because, as we have learned, each challenge we face in life is an opportunity for growth and the expansion of our souls. In this sense, each challenge is a good-not-yet-understood.

SHALOM (Peace): Peace is a core Jewish value. This is why King David, in Psalm 34, implores us to "seek peace and pursue it." The Midrash[487] goes even further by telling us peace is the purpose of Torah itself: "All that is written in the Torah was written for the sake of peace." What is this peace King David and the Midrash refer to? It must be more than the cessation of war.

The word for peace in Hebrew, *shalom*, is derived from the root word *shaleym*, meaning "complete" or "whole." The Midrash would then be saying living a Torah way of life brings us peace because it completes us, restores us to who we were meant to be—an image of God—making us whole. Another aspect of finding peace and feeling whole comes when one finds healing for one's emotional wounds. All of us experience emotional wounding of one sort or another throughout our lives and it is so hard, at times, to come to peace with this. One path to inner peace is to draw closer to God and accept what life has in store for us and grow from those experiences.

On a global level, peace comes when there is a state of "wholeness" among people—when nations are interconnected and fulfill each other's needs. When we pray for peace, we should be asking God to bring peace to the world, to help us find the spiritual peace that comes with becoming whole with God and His Torah, and to bring healing to our emotional wounds so we can find inner peace. If one does not have peace, all his other blessings are worthless.

How important is peace? Is it as important as truth? Both are important core values. But which is of higher value?

The Torah[488] commands us "Distance yourself from a false word." The essence of one of the Ten Commandments is truth—"You shalt not bear false witness against your neighbor." Thus truth is a supreme value. Peace, however, is not one of the Ten Commandments. Does that mean peace is of lesser value?

It is told that Reb Zalmeli, the brother of the Vilna Gaon (d. 1797), once came with another rabbi to visit a friend. The friend looked at these great rabbis and invited them to eat. Rabbi Zalmeli knew that the friend was a very poor man and could not afford much food, and so he immediately told the friend that his doctor had informed him that he was not allowed to eat these specific foods. When they left, his colleague asked him, "I didn't know that you are sick. Is it true?"

Reb Zalmeli answered, "No, not really."

And so he asked him with astonishment, "You of all

people are so careful not to involve yourself in any false-hood, how could such a falsehood leave your mouth?"

Rabbi Zalmeli responded, "Maimonides was a great doctor and he has written that it is forbidden to enjoy a meal from a man who does not have sufficient food." Apparently, some things are more important than truth.

In a *Peanuts* cartoon, Charlie Brown says to Linus, "We're supposed to write home to our parents and tell them what a great time we're having here at camp."

Linus answers, "Even if we're not? Isn't that a lie?"

Charlie Brown explains, "Well ... it's sort of a white lie."

To which Linus questions, "Lies come in colors?"[489]

The Talmud[490] tells us we should always tell a bride she is beautiful and graceful even if she is not—just as when a friend shows you something he has bought, you should express praise even if you do not like the item. Jewish law tells us one may, and even should, tell a white lie in certain circumstances to spare someone's feelings. Any parent holding his/her new-born child will tell you this baby is the most beautiful in the world. What do you say to that parent? "Of course!" What should we tell our children to say if they receive a gift they do not want? Certainly we should tell them to thank the giver and find some way to praise the gift—even if they have to exaggerate.

And so the Talmud[491] codifies: "One may modify a statement in the interest of peace." This is proven from the statement of Joseph's brothers in the Torah,[492] who told Joseph after their father Jacob's death that their father had commanded them to tell Joseph that he, Jacob, commands Joseph to forgive them—although the Torah never records that he actually said this.

Also in the Talmud[493] we find: "Hillel said, 'Be of the disciples of Aaron, loving peace and pursuing peace, loving thy fellow creatures and drawing them near to the Torah." Aaron was the great peacemaker in rabbinic legend.[494] When two people would argue, he would go to each one saying, "If you would only know how he with whom you quarreled regretted his harsh words to you." They would then forgive each other. Aaron teaches us that for the sake of peace we can, or even should, extend and exaggerate the truth in order to preserve peace among people.

In the *Uva l'Tziyon* prayer after the *Amidah* we say: *Titeyn emet l'Yaakov*[495] (Attribute truth to Jacob). Father Jacob, in other words, is the model for the virtue of truth. How can this be? Was it not Jacob who deceived his father Isaac and stole the blessing from his brother Esav? Yes, this is true. However, Jacob had previously purchased the birthright from Esav; and it was Jacob who merited receiving the blessing of Abraham through Isaac, not Esav. Sometimes, in order to preserve a higher truth, one must act in a way that appears untruthful. Yes, peace takes precedence over truth at times, but only because peace can be a higher truth!

שִׂים שָׁלוֹם טוֹבָה וּבְרָכָה. חֵן וָחֶסֶד וְרַחֲמִים עָלֵינוּ וְעַל כָּל יִשְׂרָאֵל עַמֶּךָ. בָּרְכֵנוּ אָבִינוּ כֻּלָּנוּ כְּאֶחָד בְּאוֹר פָּנֶיךָ. כִּי בְאוֹר פָּנֶיךָ נָתַתָּ לָנוּ יי אֱלֹהֵינוּ תּוֹרַת חַיִּים וְאַהֲבַת חֶסֶד. וּצְדָקָה וּבְרָכָה וְרַחֲמִים וְחַיִּים וְשָׁלוֹם. וְטוֹב בְּעֵינֶיךָ לְבָרֵךְ אֶת כָּל עַמְּךָ יִשְׂרָאֵל בְּכָל עֵת וּבְכָל שָׁעָה בִּשְׁלוֹמֶךָ: בָּרוּךְ אַתָּה יי, הַמְבָרֵךְ אֶת עַמּוֹ יִשְׂרָאֵל בַּשָּׁלוֹם:

Bring peace, goodness and blessing, grace, kindness and compassion upon us and upon all Israel Your people. Bless us, our Father, all of us as one with the light of Your face, because by the light of Your face you have given us, Hashem our God, a Torah of life and a love of kindness, righteousness and blessing, and compassion, and life and peace. And may it be good in Your eyes to bless Your people Israel at all times and at every hour with Your peace. Blessed are You, Hashem, Who blesses His people Israel with peace.

"Bring peace, goodness and blessing, grace, kindness and compassion upon us and upon all Israel Your people." The Talmud[496] tells us the word *Shalom* (peace) is also a name of God, and so today, rabbinic authorities have ruled that one is not permitted to have a doormat with "*Shalom*" written on it so one does not step on the name of God. If you think about this, it is remarkable. Peace is so important that it is a name of God. From this we can learn: Since all blessings flow from God, all blessings, therefore, flow from peace. When we pray for God to "bring peace upon us," we are, in effect, praying for all those blessings that are components of that peace, such as "goodness, blessing, grace, kindness and compassion."

"Bless us, our Father, all of us as one." What parents want most is for their children to get along. When we get along with each other, no doubt, God has a smiling face and will shower blessings upon us. The paradigm example of this is the Jewish people at Sinai. The Torah[497] tells us: *Vayichan sham Yisrael neged hahar* (And Israel encamped there opposite the mountain). The word, *Vayichan* (encamped), is in the singular, prompting Rashi to comment: "as one man with one heart." In no other encampment is this singular form used. This was a very special moment when the Jewish people were so united that they were like one heart. Thus they merited the blessing of God speaking directly to them as He began to give them the Ten Commandments and the Torah. There is nothing the Jewish people cannot accomplish; there is no threat they cannot repel if they are united as one.

"With the light of Your face." This blessing of peace is the final blessing of the *Amidah*. In the *Amidah* we seek an intimate connection with God. It is our opportunity to stand before Him and pour out our hearts asking for help in our lives. There can be no better way to facilitate this intimate connection with God than for Him to pour His light upon us. As it says twice in Psalm 80: *V'ha-eyr panecha v'nivasheya* (Shine Your face upon us and we will be saved). It was the light of God's loving energy that created us and connecting with this light will give us the strength to move forward and be a blessing to the world. So we pray, "Bless us, our Father, all of us as one, with the light of Your face."

"Because by the light of Your face you have given us, Hashem our God, a Torah of life and a love of kindness, righteousness and blessing, and compassion, and life and peace." What comes from the blessing of God's light? So many blessings: "a Torah of life and a love of kindness, righteousness and blessing, and compassion, and life." God gave us not just a Torah, but a living Torah—a Torah that will inform our lives as we grow because it continues to grow. Yes God's (Oral) Torah continues to grow as each generation encounters new circumstances and—using the principles of the Torah—finds new insight into what is right and wrong.

"A love of kindness." This is a special blessing in itself. Not only is God kind to us, but His light brings us the special blessing of the desire to do kindness. This is such a special blessing because doing acts of kindness, as we have learned, is one of the three paths to God and soul growth. The icing on the cake is that there is no better way to foster peace among people than for people to be kind to each other.

"And may it be good in Your eyes to bless Your people Israel at all times and at every hour with Your peace." We need peace at all times and at every hour—peace of body, peace of mind, peace with each other, and peace between nations. Without this, we cannot fulfill our individual and collective tasks and purpose in this world. In effect we are praying, "Dear God, bring us peace so we can be who we were meant to be."

"Blessed are You, Hashem, Who blesses His people Israel with peace." Our generation has been blessed to see the return of the Jewish people to their land after 2,000 years of exile and persecution. We ought to focus on, as we recite this blessing, asking God to protect His people Israel and bring peace to the Land of Israel.

One could ask, if the theme of the final section of the *Amidah* is thanksgiving, what place is there for this prayer for peace, and why make it the final blessing? The question is strengthened as the blessing asks, in addition to peace, for "goodness, blessing, grace, kindness and compassion." If we are to be thanking God, why do we make these requests? The answer is all these requests are really an acknowledgment of thanks to God because without God's blessings we are nothing and cannot accomplish anything.[498]

It is saying "Thank You" to God because we need Him. Peace is the final blessing because it is what we need above and beyond all else to do God's work and help bring God's light into this world.

ENDNOTES

PREFACE

1   God has both male and female aspects, but for the purpose of textual flow, I will usually refer to God using the common usage, "He."

2   Abbreviated from: Maurice Samuel, *Prince of the Ghetto: Isaac Loeb Peretz*, A. A. Knopf Press 1948, p. 199.

3   Jerusalem Talmud, *Brachot* 4:4.

CHAPTER 1

4   *Mishneh Torah, Hilchot Tefilah 1:1.*

5   Exodus 23:25.

6   Based on Numbers 10:9. See *commentary to Maimonides' Sefer Hamitzvot, Positive Commandment #5.*

7   Rabbi Ed Feinstein.

8   Mishnah Berachot 4:4, "He who makes his prayer a mechanical task—his prayer is not a prayer."

9   www.chabad.org

10   Literally, "The Name," used as a reference to the Tetragrammaton, God's holy four letter Name.

CHAPTER 2

11   Chaim Vital, *Shaar HaGilgulim, Hakdama* 31, 32.

12   Ari, *Shaar Ruach Hakodesh.*

13   Moshe Chayim Luzzatto, *The Knowing Heart*, Feldheim Publishers Ltd., Jerusalem, 1982, p.103. The Kotzker Rebbi in answering the question, "Why did God create human beings [note the plural]?" said God put us on earth to keep the heavens aloft—to help our fellow human beings and bring ho-liness to the world. The two approaches are not mutually exclusive, for in

the process of perfecting our souls we must reach out to our fellow human beings and bring holiness to the world.

14   *Life After Life,* by Raymond Moody, 1975, published by MBB.

15   If you want to see how this directly correlates to Kabbalah and Jewish tradition, see *Asey L'cha Rav,* by the late Chief Rabbi of Tel Aviv, Rabbi Chaim David Halevi, volume 2, where he discusses Moody's work.

16   pp. 65, 92-93.

17   Ramchal, *Derech Hashem* 2:1.

18   *Pesachim* 112a.

19   *Nefesh Hachayim* teaches that if God would withdraw His loving energy from the world even for a moment, the world would cease to exist.

20   Psalm 89:3, translation by Arye Kaplan, *The Arye Kaplan Reader,* Mesorah 1983, p. 150. See also Rabbi Shlomo Carlebach's translation found in, *Shlomo Carlebach: A Friend to Our Generation,* Zivi Ritchie, 1997, p. 221.

21   *Zohar, Raya Mehemna, Pinchas; Tikunim* 57.

22   Joseph B. Soloveitchik, *Family Redeemed: Essays on Family Relationships,* Ktav Publishing House, 2002, p. 38-39.

23   *Endless Light,* Rabbi David Aaron, Simon & Schuster, 1997, p. 20.

CHAPTER 3

24   *Pirkey Avot* 1:2.

25   *Berachot* 32b: Rabbi Eleazar said: "Prayer is greater than good deeds. No one had more good deeds than Moses, but still he was only answered after he prayed."

26   Genesis, chapter 18.

27   Teaching us the importance of *bikur cholim,* "visiting the sick".

28   Shevuot 35b; Shabbat 127a.

29   Proverbs 11:4.

CHAPTER 4

30   In fact, the verse from Psalm 51:17, "My God open my lips that my mouth may declare Your praise," which is recited before the *Amidah*, does just that.

31   *Berachot* 30b.

32   Jerusalem Talmud, *Berachot* 9:1.

33   Isaiah 30:15.

34   I'm grateful to Rabbi Jack Reimer for this thought.

35   Genesis 2:5.

36   Chullin 60b.

37   Exodus 25:8.

38   Exodus 29:46.

39   If it is philosophically too difficult to say that God has a need, then a divine desire.

40   Ibn Ezra Exodus 29:46.

41   Berachot 6b.

42   Jeremiah 29: 12-13.

43   *Mishnah Sotah* 7:1; *Berachot* 13a; *Shulchan Aruch, Orach Chayim* 101:4.

44   Art Scroll has completely transliterated *Siddurim: ArtScroll Transliterated Linear Siddur, Sabbath And Festival,* and there is a *Weekday* edition as well, both by Nosson Scherman.

45   *Keser Shem Tov* 44.

CHAPTER 5

46   Tosfot: *Bikshu, Brachot* 12b, cites the Jerusalem Talmud that teaches that these 3 passages were chosen because they contain within them allusions to the Ten Commandments (which were removed from the daily liturgy).

47   *Berachot* 13b.

48   The *Tzlach* in the 4th Chapter of *Pesachim* teaches the meaning of the *Shema* as presented in our chapter on the *Shema*.

49   Akiva Tatz, Shavuot lecture, *Seeing Sound,* http://www.simpletoremember. com.

50   I Samuel 15:4.

51   Akiva Tatz, Shavuot lecture, http://www.simpletoremember.com/authors/a/ rabbi-akiva-tatz/.

52   *Brachot 1:5;* Tosfot: *Bikshu, Brachot* 12b.

53   Deuteronomy 5:19-22. The change to the 3rd person in the 3rd Command- ment makes the point.

54   There are more interpretations of the meaning of *Yisrael.* See *Rashi* Genesis 32:29, for example, but in this chapter are the interpretations, from my ex- perience, that can help us climb the ladder to our higher selves, the *Yisrael* in each of us.

55   I prefer the Biblical "Esav" to the common English usage of Esau.

56   Genesis 32:29.

57   Bereshit Rabba 77:3.

58   Genesis: 12:2-3, 17:7-8, 22:17-18, 28:13-15, 35:11-13.

59   Ralbag (Rav Levy Ben Gershon also known as Gersonides, 14th century Jewish philosopher and scholar), *Peyrush Al HaTorah Al Derech Beyur,* Rabbi Jacob Shurkin, NY 1958, p. 41. Dr. J. H. Hertz, *Pentateuch and Haftorahs,* notes: "The name is clearly a title of victory; probably a 'champion of God.'"

60   *Kli Yakar,* Rabbi Shlomo Efraim of Luntchtitz , 16th century commentary on the Torah: Genesis 32:29.

61   *Tanna D'bey Eliyahu Rabba* 27, 107b.

62   Numbers 23:9.

63   Isaiah 45:7.

64   Exodus 14:31.

CHAPTER 6

65   Aryeh Kaplan, *Jewish Meditation,* Schocken Books Inc., 1985, p. 126.

66   As we see in Exodus 3:15.

67   Rabbi Benjamin Blech, *Understanding Judaism,* Jason Aronson Inc., 1991, p.95.

68   *Kiddushin* 71a; *Tur, Orech Chaim* 5.

69   Ibid.

70   *Sifre* on Deuteronomoy 3:24.

71   Each letter has a specific numerical value. The first 10 letters—*alef through yud*—are the numbers 1 through 10. The next letter, *caf,* is 20 and the next, *lamed,* is 30 and so on till the letter *kuf,* which is 100. The next letter, *reysh,* is 200, then *shin,* which is 300 and the last letter, *tav,* is 400.

72   Genesis 31:29.

73   See Ramban Genesis 1:3 for a slightly different approach that comes to virtually the same conclusion.

74   Ibn Ezra on Genesis 1:1 maintains that *Elohim* in the plural form is just an honorific terminology and does not refer to God as more than one. The proof, he shows, is that the verb *bara* (He created) for *Elohim* in the first verse of the Torah is written in the singular form. We see the exclusive use of singular verbs with the name *Elohim* throughout the Torah.

75   Exodus 21:6; 22:8.

76   God's Name is often abbreviated by using two *yud*'s because if you combine the special four-letter name of God, ה־ו־ה־י, and in between the letters you insert the letters of the permitted pronunciation of this name, א־ד־נ־י, meaning, "my Lord," then you will see that this special writing of God's Name both begins and ends with the letter *yud.*

77   Rabbi Benjamin Blech, *The Secrets of Hebrew Words,* Jason Aronson Inc., 1991, p. 23.

78   See, "A Caveat" at the end of chapter 22, "Is it Kosher to Pray?" for a more detailed discussion of when suffering seems to occur unjustly.

CHAPTER 7

79   Christians are not considered idolaters by most authorities even though there are idolatrous aspects to Christianity—i.e. icons, the Trinity.

80   *The Rebbe, An Appreciation,* 6/30/11, on the 70th anniversary of the Rebbe's arrival to the shores of the U.S., www.chabad.org.

81   *Tanya, Shaar HaYichud*: 6-7.

82   Neil deGrasse Tyson, Astrophysicist, American Museum of Natural History, on the History Channel program, "The Universe: Beyond/Big Bang," 3/8/09. Although deGrasse does not connect this with belief in God, and although he himself has not avowed such a belief, nevertheless, his point is compelling in helping us understand the Oneness of God.

83   Deuteronomy 6:5.

84   Isaiah 43:10.

85   *The Shema,* Rabbi Norman Lamm, Jewish Publication Society 2000, p. 17.

86   *The Pentateuch,* Rabbi Samson Raphael Hirsch, Vol. V, Deuteronomy 6:4.

87   Ibid; See Exodus 34:14 for the word *acheyr* written with a large *reysh.*

88   Genesis 4:1.

89   Berachot 13b.

90   *Sefer haYirah,* p.20.

91   Ibid.

92   Deuteronomy 6:7.

93   Brachot 33b warns that saying, "*Shema Shema,*" may indicate two gods that hear your prayers.

94   Victor Frankl, *Man's Search For Meaning,* Simon & Schuster 1959, p. 137.

CHAPTER 8

95   Berachot 21a; 12b.

96   Deuteronomy 6:7; 11:19.

97   Numbers 15:41.

98   Deuteronomy 16:3.

99   *Taanit* 16b.

100   *Pesachim* 56a.

101   Genesis 49:1.

102   *The Authorized Daily Prayer Book*, p. 117.

103   *Pesachim* 56a.

104   Midrash Rabba Devarim 2:36.

105   Deuteronomy 6:5-9.

106   *Mishneh Torah, Hilchot Yesodey HaTorah* 2:1-2; *Hilchot Teshuva* 10:3,6.

107   *Shlomo Carlebach, A Friend to Our Generation*, Zivi Ritchie, 1997, p. 94.

108   *The World of Prayer*, Rabbi Dr. Elie Munk, Feldheim Publisher, NY 1954, p. 113.

109   Rashi is an acronym for Rabbi Shlomo Yitzhak. He died in the year 1104 CE in France. He is renowned for his commentaries on the Torah, the rest of Tanach (the Bible) and on the Talmud. He is considered the father of Jewish commentators.

110   See Rashi on Deuteronomy 6:5.

111   *Mishnah Berachot* 9:5.

112   Brachot 61b.

113   Ibid.

114   Jerusalem Talmud *Sotah* 5:5.

115   Genesis 1:31.

116   *M'od* as "might" refers to one's additional strength—more than the normal. The Talmud Berachot 61b understands it as one's wealth; Schwab, *Iyun Tefilah*, on p. 242 adds one's talents that God has blessed one with.

117   Menachem Leibtag, *Parshat Va-etchanan & Ekev*, www.tanach.org , p. 3.

118   Schwab, *Iyun Tefilah*, p. 243.

119   Rashi, Deuteronomy 6:7.

120   Jerusalem Talmud, *Sotah* 7:1.

121   Exodus 13:1-10; Exodus 13:11-16; Deuteronomy 6:4-9; Deuteronomy 11:13-21.

122   See the preparatory prayer before donning tefilin, *ArtScroll Siddur*, p.6; see also *Sefer HaMitzvot HaGadol, Smag*, Positive commandments #3.

123 *The Aryeh Kaplan Anthology II*, Aryeh Kaplan, NCSY/ Mesorah Publications, 1974, p. 273.

124 *Journal of Chinese Medicine*, Number 70, October 2002, p.5. Also see "Tefillin and Acupuncture: The Magic Touch," *The Forward*, 12/16/02, p. 13.

125 *The Aryeh Kaplan Anthology II*, p. 263.

126 Menachot 73a.

127 Exodus 13:9.

128 Rabbi Mordechai Friedfertig, email Parshat Bo, 5762.

129 Exodus 13:9.

130 Menachot 33a.

131 In the Old City of Jerusalem, it was the custom—as can be seen in the Jewish Quarter as well as in formerly Jewish homes now occupied by Arabs in the Moslem Quarter—not to affix a box for the mezuzah scroll, but to make a slit in the stones of the doorposts and place the scroll there, covered with cement.

132 Jerusalem Talmud, *Peyah* 1:1, 15d; it is also found in the *Midrash Rabba*, Genesis 35:3.

133 More stories and copies of these actual mezuzot are available at http://www.campsci.com/mezuzah/.

CHAPTER 9

134 Brachot 13a.

135 Deuteronomy 11:13-21.

136 The Talmud, Taanit 2a, as opposed to Maimonides and Nachmanides that we spoke of previously, learns that this verse is the source of the *mitzvah* of prayer—the service of the heart.

137 Devarim Raba 2:7*.

138 Deuteronomy 11:11-12.

139 Genesis 2:5.

140 Bava Metzia 32b.

141   Deuteronomy 22:6-7; 25:4.

142   Brachot 40a.

143   Deuteronomy 31:17. Schwab, *Iyun Tefilah*, p. 258 expresses this idea as follows: "The understanding of the meaning of 'burning anger' is that God will display His attribute of justice without sweetening it with His attribute of mercy."

144   Exodus 20:12.

145   Sanhedrin 90b.

CHAPTER 10

146   Brachot 12b.

147   Numbers 15:37-41.

148   Deuteronomy 22:12.

149   According to Jewish law they can also be made from the same material as the garment itself. So if the garment is silk, the *tzitzit* can also be made of silk.

150   Menachot 44a.

151   Sotah 17a.

152   Ideally, the one blue strand should be half white so that when it is folded over there are seven white strands and one blue.

153   Taught to me by Rabbi Benjamin Blech.

154   Rashi, Numbers 15:38.

155   Menachot 43b.

156   Ibid.

157   Deuteronomy 6:13.

158   Ibn Ezra, Deuteronomy 15:38.

159   Menachot 44a.

160   Mishnah Brachot 1:5; this Talmudic passage is repeated in the Passover Haggadah.

161   Deuteronomy 16:3.

162   See Chapter 21: The Greatest Love of All: *Birkat Geula.*

CHAPTER 11

163   Rabbi Moshe of Trani, *Bet Elohim, Tefillah* 7: "One must stand while involved
       in both prayer and sacrifice. The reason for this is because one of the most
       visible differences between man and beast is the fact that man stands erect
       on two feet."

164   Berachot 33a.

165   Talmud *Megilah* 17b-18a, see Maimonides *Yad Chazakah, Tefilah* 1:3-4 for
       a historical rendering of how this came about.

166   *Jewish Meditation,* p. 101.

167   Rabbi Dov Baer (18th century), The Maggid of Mezrich, *Magid D'varav l'Yaa-
       kov* 269, p. 100a-b: "The Men of the Great Assembly knew the transmission
       of Godly force that is necessary at all times…They therefore composed an
       order of worship containing all the words and letters necessary to transmit
       this life force. God granted them the wisdom to do this…and everything
       in the worship service is thus calculated with great accur⸱cy." Translation:
       Aryeh Kaplan, *A Call To The Infinite,* Moznaim Publish⸱ng Corp. 1986, p.
       26.

168   Mishnah Berachot 4:4.

169   *Mishneh Torah, Hilchot Tefillah,* 4:15.

170   *Brachot* 30b.

171   *Brachot* 34b; *Shabbat* 118.

CHAPTER 12

172   As related to me by Rabbi Benjamin Blech.

173   Exodus 15:1-18.

174   Berachot 33b.

175   Psalms 65:2.

176   See also Maimonides, *Moreh Nevuchim* 1:59.

177 Rashi *Megilah* 18a.

178 Maimonides: *Guide To The Perplexed*: 1:58.

179 Deuteronomy 10:17.

CHAPTER 13

180 Abraham similarly "approached God." See Rashi on Genesis 18:23 for this and other examples.

181 Deuteronomy 4:11; see *Sefer Taamey HaMinhagim,* Shay Lamora Publishing, Jerusalem, 75; see also *HaRokeach*: 325.

182 At the end of the *Amidah*, we bow and take three steps back in taking leave of the King of kings, turning to the left, the right and forward like a servant before his master. *Shulchan Aruch Orach Chayim* 123:1.

183 Aryeh Kaplan, *A Call To The Infinite,* p. 212.

184 Psalm 51:17.

185 Deuteronomy 32:3.

186 Samuel I chapter 1.

187 *Meyam Loeyz*, Samuel I 1:3.

188 Samuel I 1:6.

189 Ibid 1:13.

190 *Berachot* 31a.

191 *Shulcan Aruch, Orach Chayim* 101:2.

192 The *Zohar,* on the words, *Vayiteyn et kolo bivchi vayishm'u Mitzrayim vayisha-ma beyt Paro* (And he [Joseph] raised his voice and wept and the Egyptians heard and the house of Pharaoh heard), Gen. 45:2, teaches that we should mouth the words of our prayers without making any actual sounds at all.

193 *Berachot* 30b.

194 ArtScroll translation.

195 *Berachot* 32b.

196 *Jewish Meditation,* p. 105.

197 *Berachot* 34b.

198 Deuteronomy 9:25.

199 Numbers 12:13.

200 *Midrash Tehillim* 61:2.

CHAPTER 14

201 *Berachot* 33b.

202 *Berachot* 7a.

203 Rabbi Samson Raphael Hirsch, Genesis 9:28.

204 *The Authorized Daily Prayer Book,* Joseph H. Hertz, p. 10.

205 Rabbi Yisrael of Koznitz, *Avodas Yisroel, Lech L'cha,* p. 6a.

206 *Shulchan Aruch, Orech Chaim* 5.

207 *Hakdamat Tikuney haZohar* 8a; Maharal, *Derech Chaim* 3:7; R. Chaim Vital *Shaarei Hakavanot, Inyan Kavanat HaAmidah, Cheilek alef shaar* 6; *Zohar, Eykev,* 1.

208 *Jewish Meditation,* p. 111.

209 *Mechilta,* Bo 13:3.

210 Exodus 3:15.

211 *Berachot* 26b.

212 Hosea 14:3. See Rashi and Yoma 86b.

213 The elaboration of the prayer experiences of the Patriarchs follows Rabbi Shlomo Riskin, *The Jewish Week, Tzav,* March 28, 1986.

214 A third opinion is found in Talmud *Yerushalmi, Brachot* 4:1. Rabbi Shmuel bar Nachmani said: They parallel the three times that the day changes for man.

215 Deuteronomy: 10:17.

216 Exodus 34:6.

217 Avot 4:1.

218   Genesis 28:17.

219   Avraham ben haGra.

220   Yoma 87a.

CHAPTER 15

221   *Zohar Chadash, Megilat Rut,* Reuven Margolios Edition, p. 80:4.

222   *Siach Yitzchak* in *Siddur HaGra,* p. 127: *Ozeyr hu b'tziruf histadlut haneh-ezar,* "The word *ozeyr* indicates that God will assist in the efforts of the one being helped."

223   *Makot* 10b.

224   As told to me by Gedalia Fleer.

225   Found in the classic story of Rebbe Nachman: *Chacham v' Tam,* "The Wise Man and the Simpleton."

226   Rabbi Yitzchak Benzecry, *Siach Yitzchak,* p. 127.

227   Exodus 14:10.

CHAPTER 16

228   *Siach Yitzchak,* p. 127.

229   An *amah* is a Biblical measurement that begins at the elbow and stretches to the middle finger tip. According to various opinions in Jewish law, it is between 18 inches (Rabbi Avrohom Chaim Na'eh) and 24 inches (*Chasam Sofer*) in length.

230   https://www.heartmath.org/research/science-of-the-heart/energetic-communication/.

231   *Berachot* 34a.

232   Genesis 15:1.

233   Genesis Rabah 44:4.

CHAPTER 17

234   Genesis 19:27.

235 Berachot 10b; Yerushalmi Brachot 1:1; Rashba (13th century), found in *Eyn Yaakov*, Berachot 54.

236 Ezekiel 1:7.

237 *Arba Turim, Orech Chaim, Hilchot Tefilah* 95:3-4.

238 Isaiah 45:23.

239 *Shulchan Aruch Orach Chayim I, Hilchot Tefilah* 95.

240 Ibid., "right hand over the left hand."

241 Yehuda Halevi, *The Kuzari*, 2:79-80.

242 Quoted in *Menorat Hamaor* 3:3:1:13.

243 *Zohar* 3:218b.

244 *Shulchan Aruch: Orach Chayim* 48.

245 Some examples: 1Kings 8:38; Psalm 63:5; Psalm 88:10.

246 Brachot 16b.

247 *Midrash Raba Vayeyra* 56:2.

248 *Berachot* 12a.

249 *Malachi* 2:5.

250 *Berachot* 34b.

251 *Berachot* 28b.

252 *Michtav mey-Eliyahu* vol. 4, p. 67.

253 *Berachot* 12b.

CHAPTER 19

254 From Numbers 10:9: "When you are at war in your own land against an aggressor who attacks you, you shall sound short blasts on the trumpets, that you may be remembered before the Lord your God and be delivered from your enemies."

255 From Exodus 23:25, "And you shall serve the Lord your God."

256 Berachot 4:4.

257 Rachel Sofer, "Struggle for Prayer," www.ou.org.

258 Ezriel Tauber, Shalheves, 1991, P.53.

259 Beginning with the Men of the Great Assembly, 5th century BCE, later refined again and again.

260 Berachot 1:4.

261 The recitation of the Shema is also considered Torah study, and according to the Talmud, Shabbat 127a, "the study of Torah is above all," and so it comes first.

262 Berachot 12a, this source deals specifically with the blessing of *Geula*, "Redemption," recited immediately after the Shema—*Emet v'emuna* or *Emet v'yatziv*.

263 *Shulchan Aruch, Orech Chaim, Hilchot Kriat Shema* 61:3.

264 *Midrash Tanchuma, Kedoshim* 6.

265 Deuteronomy 5:19-22. The change to the 3rd person in the 3rd commandment makes the point.

266 On Deuteronomy 6:4.

267 Zecharia 14:9; with thanks to Rabbi Benjamin Blech.

CHAPTER 20

268 Exodus, chapter 32.

269 Numbers, chapters 13 and 14.

270 A long blessing by definition begins and ends with the formula, *Baruch Ata Hashem. Mishnah Berachot* 1:4.

271 Maimonides, *Guide To The Perplexed*, Book 2, chapter 6.

272 Isaiah 6:3.

273 Ezekiel 3:12.

274 Kabbalah teaches that Ezekiel in his vision is standing in the *Olam Yetzira* (The Word of Formation), and looking up at what's going on in the *Olam B'riah* (The World of Creation). Therefore, Ezekiel has a more constricted view of what's happening. He sees it more secondhand. Isaiah is higher, and he sees his vision from the *Olam B'riah* (The World of Creation), where it is

actually taking place. This accounts for the phrases *Ayey m'kom k'vodo* and *maley olam*. See Aryeh Kaplan at the end of *Inner Space* for a more detailed explanation of the difference between the visions of Isaiah and Ezekiel.

275   With thanks to Rabbi Benjamin Blech who first introduced me to this story and the following story of the Chafetz Chaim and their deeper meaning.

276   Genesis 22:1.

277   See *Amida* Supplement, Part 3: Help My People, section, "Kibutz Galiyot, *Bring our people home.*"

278   Exodus 15:26.

CHAPTER 21

279   Berachot 11b.

280   *Shulchan Aruch, Orech Chaim, Hilchot Brachot* 47:7.

281   Deuteronomy 4:4.

282   *Arba Turim, Orech Chaim, Hilchot Tefilat Arvit* 236; *Shulchan Aruch, Orech Chaim, Hilchot Kriat Shema* 61:3.

283   Berachot 9b.

284   Berachot 4b.

285   Ibid

286   Quoted in the *Bet Yosef* in *Arba Turim, Orech Chaim, Hilchot Tefilat Arvit* 236.

287   Berachot 57b.

288   Translation using the word "impediment" from *The Complete ArtScroll Siddur*, p. 265.

289   Art Scroll translation, *The Art Scroll Siddur*, p. 263.

290   Likutey Halacha, Yoredeya, K'ley Hakeren 2:9.

291   Yaakov Emden.

CHAPTER 22

292   Deuteronomy Chapter 27.

293 Shabbat 119b.

294 Mishnah Sanhedrin 10:1; see The *Amidah* Supplement, Part 1: *Gevurot* section for how this Mishnah defines the three core Jewish beliefs and how it connects to the word *Amen*.

295 Rabbi David Kimchi, *Sefer Hashorashim, Amen*, 39.

296 Shabbat 119b.

297 Berachot 53b.

298 *Likutey Moharan*, vol. 1, 66.

299 Berachot 47a.

300 Shabbat 119b.

301 Berachot 47a.

302 Ibid.

303 Rabbi Bernard L. Berzon, *Sermons The Year Round,* Jonathon David Publishers, 1978, *Ki Tavo*, p. 318. I'm indebted to Rabbi Berzon for his thoughts on the three types of *Amen*.

CHAPTER 23

304 As related to me by Rabbi Benjamin Blech, who heard R. Soloveitchik say it, but this thought is not original with him. Many others have had the same thought. In the introduction to the *Hirsh Siddur* (Feldheim Publishers, NY 1978), for example, Dr. Joseph Breuer summarizes a teaching of Rabbi Samson Raphael Hirsch, analyzing the root word of תפלה (prayer) as פלל, which means, "to judge." The infinitive is a reflexive, and strangely enough, להתפלל (to pray), therefore indicates the idea that one prays "to stand in self-judgment" in order to change one's behavior and thus be worthy of a new decree.

305 Rabbi Meir Aldabi, *Sh'viley Emunah* 1, 6a-b. Also, Rabbi Abraham Ibn Ezra writes: "We know that the Blessed Creator is One and is not changed by His creatures, for they are all made in wisdom. But all change involves the recipient." (Translation by Kaplan, *A Call To The Infinite*, p. 26.)

306 *The Atlanta Journal-Constitution*, 3/6/10, Lorraine V. Murray, "Prayer is the easiest gift we can give," Section D p. 4.

307 As related to me by Rabbi Benjamin Blech.

308   Genesis 18:25.

309   Ibid.

310   Deuteronomy 32:4.

311   *Yevamot* 64a.

312   Numbers 3:4.

313   Rabbi David Feinstein, *Kol Dodi On The Torah,* Mesorah Publications Ltd. 1992, P. 212.

314   The Chassidic master, Elimelech of Lizensk (18th century) gives an answer on God changing His mind from a Kabbalistic perspective. "All that exists in this world existed in potential within God even before Creation. Therefore, when one's prayers are answered and one is healed—either through his prayers or that of another—it is because this healing already existed potentially within God. It is not a change in God's mind ... *Noam Elimelech, Vay'chi* 27a.

315   *Chagiga* 4b.

316   Proverbs 13:23.

317   *Zohar, Bo,* 36a: Noach.

318   Berachot 10a.

319   Baba Kama 93a.

320   Mishnah Berachot 9:3-4.

CHAPTER 24

321   It is interesting to note that the word *shira* (song) and also the words, *b'ka-vanat haleyv* (concentration of the heart), have the same numerical value as *tefilla* (prayer), 515.

322   Deuteronomy 3:26.

323   *Dudaei Reuven, parshat Va-etchanan.*

324   Brachot 10a.

325   *Tanchuma, Beshalach* 9.

326   Isaiah 41:14.

327   Story by Rabbi Earl A. Grollman found in *Eulogies,* edited by Morton A. Wallack, Jonathan David Publishers, NY, 1965, p. 87.

328   Saadia Gaon, *Emunot V'Deyot* 5:6.

329   Micah 3:3-4.

330   *Pirke Avot* 2:4.

331   *Brachot* 5a.

332   *Brachot* 32b.

333   *Bava Kama* 92a.

334   Job 42:10.

335   See Rashi on Genesis 21:1.

336   Heard from Rabbi Brian Glusman.

337   *Avoda Zara* 7b.

338   Psalm 145:16.

339   Psalm 55:23.

340   Genesis 12:2.

341   Genesis Raba 39:11.

342   When the groom puts the veil on the bride before the wedding ceremony.

343   *Brachot* 32b.

344   Ibid 10a.

345   Job 14:19.

346   Sichot HaRan 234, translation by Kaplan, *A Call to the Infinite,* p. 198.

347   http://www.aish.com/sp/pr/Insulting_God.html.

348   Exodus 4:10.

349   Sichot HaRan, p. 233.

350   *Maharal, N'tivot Olam, Avoda* 2.

351   *Sefer haIkkarim* 4:16; translation by Kaplan, *A Call to the Infinite,* p. 19.

352   Daniel 9:18.

353   *Mishhnah Brachot* 5:5; *Brachot* 34b.

CHAPTER 25

354   S. Y. Agnon, *Eylu Va-Eylu,* Schocken Publishing House Ltd., p. 289, first published in the newspaper *Haaretz* in 1937.

355   See Rabbi Jeffrey Cohen, *Blessed Are You,* Jason Aronson Inc., 1993, p. 40, for an alternative view for why there are nineteen blessings in the *Amidah.* In short, he claims it was of Babylonian origin and resulted from subdividing the blessings for Jerusalem and the Davidic Dynasty.

356   Berachot 28b.

357   *The Aryeh Kaplan Reader,* p. 188.

358   Berachot 34a.

359   See commentary of Rabbi Azariah Figo on Psalm 115:17: *Lo hameytim y'hal'luka* (The dead cannot praise you). It is cited in ArtScroll's *Tehillim,* in the *ArtScroll Tanach Series,* Mesorah Publications, Ltd., Vol II, 1977, on this verse.

360   I'm indebted to Rabbi Benjamin Blech for his insights in this *Mishnah.*

361   Genesis 3:19.

362   Genesis 2:7, the phrase, *nishmat chayim,* has often been translated as "the breath of life," as well.

363   Reincarnation is accepted by most Torah luminaries. There were notable exceptions like Saadia Gaon and Joseph Albo. Today research has uncovered thousands of stories of people who through hypnosis or other means recalled details of their past lives that were impossible for them to otherwise know.

364   Zohar Mishpatim.

365   *Etz Hayim,* by David Lieber & Jules Harlow, Jewish Publication Society of America, 2001: the Conservative movement's new *chumash,* see Introduction p. xxii.

366   *Sefer HaIkrim,* "The Book of Principles."

367   For a more detailed discussion, see Benjamin Blech, *If God is Good, Why is the World is so Bad?,* Simcha Press, 2003.

368   The *Yigdal* prayer, recited in the early morning and in some congregations, after the evening service on Friday nights, was written by Daniel ben Yehuda, Dayan of Rome, circa 1800, as a summary of Maimondies' 13 Principles. (Hertz p. 6).

369   Shabbat 119b.

370   Leviticus 19:2.

371   *Shabbat* 133b: "Just as He is compassionate and merciful, so must you be compassionate and merciful." Or as the Torah (Deut. 28:9) puts it, *v'halachta bidrachav* (You shall walk in His [God's] ways).

372   *Sotah* 14a.

AMIDAH SUPPLEMENT: PART 2

373   Tanchuma Vayera 1.

374   Ibid.

375   Psalm 145.

376   Shulchan Aruch Orach Chaim 119:1.

377   Avraham Weiss, *Holistic Prayer*, p. 3.

378   Genesis 4:1.

379   Isaiah 55:7; there are 15 words in this blessing of repentance corresponding to the 15 words of this verse. The number 15 in Hebrew is written with the letters *yud* and *hey* which spells one of God's names.

380   Ezekiel 33:11.

381   *Hilchot Tehuvot* 1:1; Maimonides lists three steps of repentance: recognizing that one has sinned: *Chatati, Aviti, Pashati l'fanecha*, admitting that we have sinned; regret: *v'harey nichamti uvoshti b'ma'asai*; and commitment not to sin again: *ul'olam eyni chozeyr l'davar zeh*.

382   *Cheeseburgers*, by Bob Green, Holiday House Inc., 1985, p. 102-105.

383   Mishnah Yoma 8:9.

384   *Avot* 2:18.

385   Berachot 32b.

386   As told to me by Rabbi Gedalia Fleer.

387   Chulin 7b.

388   Leviticus 23:27.

389   Megilah 17b; Sanhedrin 97a.

390   See Rashi, Megilah 17b.

391   Bereishit Rabba Toldot 65:9.

392   I urge you to read, Rabbi Benjamin Blech, *If God is Good, Why is the World so Bad*, Simcha Press, 2003, for a masterful presentation of the whole question of theodicy—i. e. why do the righteous suffer and the evil people prosper?

393   Berachot 5a.

394   Baba Kama 85a; Berachot 60a.

395   Exodus 21:19.

396   Berachot 60a. It is true that there were Torah giants who believed that truly righteous people did not need doctors. Knowing the state of medicine in those times, it is not hard to argue with the conclusions they made, but it is hard to find a great scholar of Torah today who will not go to the doctor when necessary.

397   Beytzah 16b.

398   Eruvim 54a.

399   Yoma 76a.

AMIDAH SUPPLEMENT: PART 3

400   Riva, cited in *Avudraham*, Warsaw, 5638 (1877), p. 60.

401   Shavuot 39a.

402   Isaiah 27:13.

403   Sanhedrin 110b.

404   Joseph Klausner, *From Jesus To Paul*, p. 33; Salo Wittmayer Baron, *A Social And Religious History Of The Jews*, vol. 1, pp. 170-171, see note #7 p. 370–372 for a more detailed explanation of estimating the Jewish population at the end of the second Temple; *Encyclopaedia Judaica*, vol. 13, p. 871.

405 Current World Jewish population for the beginning of 2014 is 14,212,800, according to the *American Jewish Year Book, 2014,* Chapter 19.

406 Pirke Avot 1:18.

407 Genesis 18:19.

408 Deuteronomy 16:20.

409 Deuteronomy 16:18.

410 Deuteronomy 32:35.

411 Leviticus 19:18.

412 Maharal on Sotah 14a, where *Halachta bidrachav* (You shall go in His ways) is discussed.

413 Much of the thought expressed here is based on R. Israel Reisman, *Pathways of the Prophets,* Yirmiyahu, Y67, "Judging People," 1/28/2006.

414 But only if it is beyond your reach to seek justice in the courts. Baba Kama 93a.

415 The *Nefesh HaChayim* is quoted in the *V'halachta bidrachav* commentary on *Tomer Devorah shaar 1,* note 29. Also in Rav Tzodik in *Takanas haShavim* 37.

416 Deuteronomy 10:17.

417 *Bamidbar Rabbah* 11:4.

418 *Beyt Halevi, Vayigash.*

419 Bereshit Rabba 22:8.

420 Genesis 4:8.

421 Berachot 10a, Soncino translation.

422 Psalm 104:35.

423 Isaiah 55:7.

424 Ezekiel 18:32.

425 Isaiah 60:21.

426 Nidah 30b.

427   Sanhedrin 97b.

428   Proverbs 10:25.

429   *Mishneh Torah, Talmud Torah* 5:5.

430   Leviticus 19:34; Deuteronomy 10:19.

431   Tanchuma Lech Lecha 6.

432   Jeremiah 17:7.

433   Psalm 137:5-6.

434   Kiddushin 49b.

435   Succah 51b.

436   Mount Zion is an essential part of Jerusalem containing the tomb of King David. Zion is often used to refer to Jerusalem or even the whole Land of Israel..

437   Isaiah 2:3.

438   Deuteronomy 16:16; 31:11.

439   *Die Entstehung der Kontinente und Ozeane,* 1915.

440   Genesis 1:9.

441   Psalm 122:3.

442   Yoma 9b.

443   Isaiah 1:27.

444   Midrash T'hilim, Shocher Tov: 20:4.

445   Sanhedrin 98b.

446   Ezekiel 36:33-34.

447   Isaiah 43:5-6.

448   Isaiah 65:20.

449   Malachi 3:23-24.

450   Ezekiel chapter 38.

451   Midrash Tehillim, Psalm 118; the 1st and 2nd are the subject of Ezekiel, chapter 38, and the 3rd is described in Zechariah chapter 14.

452   Zecharia 14:9.

453   *Hilchot M'lachim* 12:5.

454   Ari in Sefer Halikutim, R. Meir Paprish, Parshat Haazinu.

455   *Or Hachama, Zohar* II:7b; R. Chaim Vital, *Arba M'ot Shekel Kesef,* p. 241a-b.

456   Isaiah 11:1.

457   Zechariah 3:8; see also 6:12; Psalm 132:17; Jeremiah 23:5.

458   I Samuel 16:13.

459   Exodus 34:35.

460   Sanhedrin 98a.

461   Maimonides' Commentary to the Mishnah Sanhedrin 10:1.

462   Shabbat 31a.

463   Sanhedrin 98a.

464   Isaiah 60:22.

465   Jerusalem Talmud Ta-anit 1:1; Shabbat 118b has two Shabbatot.

466   Brachot 32b.

467   *Baal Haturim* on Genesis 28:12. Note that the *gematria* of *sulam* and *kol* are the same whether they are spelled *maley,* with the full speliing—136—or *chaseyr,* with the abbreviated spelling—130.

468   *Avney Eliyahu, B'sidur Ishey Yisrael,* Mentioned in *Iyun Tefilah*, Shimon Schwab, p. 374.

AMIDAH SUPPLEMENT: PART 4

469   Genesis 29:35.

470   Zevachim 62a.

471   Ezra 3:2.

472   See Mishna Eduyot 8:6, Maimonides, *Beit Hab'chira* 6:16. Rabbi Adin Steinsaltz has led a movement in our time to restore the Passover sacrifice.

473   Numbers 18:24.

474   Numbers 18:12-20.

475   Deuteronomy 18:3.

476   Exodus 25:8.

477   Hilchot Beyt Hab'chira 6:16.

478   Rosh Hashana 31a.

479   Dennis Prager, *Think A Second Time,* Harper Collins, 1995, p. 12-13.

480   ArtScroll Siddur, p. 14.

481   *Brachot* 34b.

482   As related by Benjamin Blech. It also appears in a story written by Rabbi Edward Garsek in, *Three Times Chai,* by Laney Katz Becker, Berman House, Inc., 2007.

483   *Iyun Tefilah,* Shimon Schwab, p. 388.

484   Numbers chapters 22-24.

485   Psalm 115: 17.

486   Brachot 54a.

487   *Tanchuma Shoftim* 18.

488   Exodus 23:7.

489   This cartoon first appeared in syndication in 1997. It was quoted in *The Ten Commandments,* by Dr. Laura Schlessinger & Rabbi Stewart Vogel, Harper Collins 1998, p. 285.

490   Ketubot 16b.

491   Yevamot 65b.

492   Genesis 50:17.

493   Pirke Avot 1:12.

494   Avot DeRebbe Natan chapter 12.

495   *The Artscroll Siddur,* p. 156.

496   Shabbat 10b.

497   Exodus 19:2.

498   Rav Yitzchak Hutner, *Pachad Yitzchak,* Chanukah 2:2.

INDEX

Rabbi Mark Hillel Kunis was ordained from Rabbi Isaac Elchanan Theological Seminary of Yeshiva University. He has dedicated his life to reaching out and touching Jewish souls. Rabbi Kunis possesses a passion for the mystical and a unique ability to inspire with the depths of Torah. His classes, articles and sermons are renowned in Atlanta where he has been a pulpit rabbi for the past 27 years. Previously, he served pulpits in New Jersey and New York. His essays have appeared in several books, and now, with the publication of *Dancing With God: How to Connect With God Every Time You Pray*, Rabbi Kunis introduces readers to a prayer experience they may never have imagined they were capable of.